The Genesis
of Liberation

The Genesis
of Liberation

*Biblical Interpretation
in the Antebellum Narratives
of the Enslaved*

Emerson B. Powery
Rodney S. Sadler Jr.

WESTMINSTER
JOHN KNOX PRESS
LOUISVILLE · KENTUCKY

© 2016 Emerson B. Powery and Rodney S. Sadler Jr.

First edition
Published by Westminster John Knox Press
Louisville, Kentucky

16 17 18 19 20 21 22 23 24 25—10 9 8 7 6 5 4 3 2 1

Scripture quotations from the New Revised Standard Version of the Bible are copyright © 1989 by the Division of Christian Education of the National Council of the Churches of Christ in the U.S.A. and are used by permission.

Scripture quotations marked NIV are from The Holy Bible, New International Version. Copyright © 1973, 1978, 1984, 2011 by Biblica, Inc.® Used by permission. All rights reserved worldwide.

Scripture quotations marked KJV are from the King James Version of the Bible.

Book design by Drew Stevens
Cover design by Lisa Buckley Design
Cover art: Budding Scholar *by Harry Herman Roseland (1866–1950) /*
Private Collection / Photo © Christie's Images / Bridgeman Images

Library of Congress Cataloging-in-Publication Data

Names: Powery, Emerson B.
Title: The genesis of liberation : biblical interpretation in the antebellum
  narratives of the enslaved / Emerson Powery, Rodney S. Sadler Jr.
Description: Louisville, KY : Westminster John Knox Press, 2016. | Includes
  index.
Identifiers: LCCN 2015035313 | ISBN 9780664230531 (alk. paper)
Subjects: LCSH: Bible—Black interpretations—History. | African
  Americans—Religion—History. | Liberty—Biblical teaching.
Classification: LCC BS521.2 .P69 2016 | DDC 220.6086/250973—dc23 LC
record available at http://lccn.loc.gov/2015035313

♾ The paper used in this publication meets the minimum requirements of the American National Standard for Information Sciences—Permanence of Paper for Printed Library Materials, ANSI Z39.48-1992.

Most Westminster John Knox Press books are available at special quantity discounts when purchased in bulk by corporations, organizations, and special-interest groups. For more information, please e-mail SpecialSales@wjkbooks.com.

For
Stephanie Egnotovich

Contents

Foreword

Readers will welcome this book as a long-sought-after treasure, because it provides a compelling answer to a question people have asked for generations: "Why did enslaved Africans embrace the religion of their captors, who had used the Bible to justify the brutal trans-Atlantic slave trade?" The authors answer that question and many similar ones by discussing the work of several prominent pre-Civil War black abolitionists whose freedom narratives reveal an astonishingly creative approach to the Bible. Contrary to the biblical arguments advanced by countless slaveholding preachers to justify slavery, black leaders like Frederick Douglass, Peter Randolph, William J. Anderson, Henry Highland Garnett, and Harriet Jacobs eventually discovered alternative biblical support for their cause that both contradicted and trumped the claims of the former. And even at an earlier time, persons like Maria Stewart and Sojourner Truth recognized the symbolic power of the Bible as containing something good for blacks, since otherwise their slave owners would not have expended so much time and energy preventing them from learning to read.

Fully aware of the preeminent place of the Bible in antebellum American culture, especially its significance as an uncontested moral guide on all matters pertaining to both personal and social issues, the authors praise the wisdom of the freedom narrators in their development of a counterbiblical argument supportive of their cause. Clearly, the curse of Ham (Gen. 9:18–27) constituted the archetypal basis for the slave owners' preachers' justification for the enslavement of African peoples. That so-called Hamitic myth, along with the Pauline teaching in Ephesians 6:5 admonishing slaves to be obedient to their earthly masters, added fuel to their moral arsenal. Thus armed with such a spiritual and moral foundation, they could not have imagined the emergence of an effective counteragency.

The authors of this book rightly claim that enslaved Africans never affirmed the biblical teaching about slavery as delivered by the slave owners' preachers. Rather, they wholly rejected Christianity throughout their first century in slavery. Accordingly, the freedom narrators viewed their Christian slave owners as hypocrites because of their abuse of the gospel of love that they knew Jesus embodied and practiced. Even illiterate slaves like theologian Howard Thurman's grandmother, Nancy Ambrose, who refused to have any of Paul's letters read to her because of his charge to slaves to obey their masters, did consent to listen occasionally to his great song of love in 1 Corinthians 13. Similarly, enslaved Africans fully embraced the Paul they encountered in Acts 17:26, which they made the basis of the "one blood doctrine," which the freedom narrators cherished, because they viewed it as trumping Paul's doctrine of "obedience to earthly masters."

Intrigued by the frequent mention of the Bible in many of the pre–Civil War freedom narratives composed by former slaves who became leaders in the abolitionist movement, and discerning that usage of the Bible to be different from earlier autobiographical narratives, in which it was not mentioned, the aim of the authors of this book is to analyze how the Bible functioned in those antebellum speeches and writings. In doing so, they uncover a reservoir of creative biblical exegesis undertaken by men and women, literate and illiterate, who were bent on discovering how the creator of the universe related to them and their enslaved condition. The result was indeed amazing, not only to those who were still in slavery, but also to the abolitionist cause both then and thereafter. As a matter of fact, these rhetoricians and writers gave birth to a new biblical hermeneutic.

Because the slave owners' preachers had used the Bible regularly to support their enterprise, formerly enslaved Africans used that same Bible to support their cause, even if it meant occasionally tweaking certain texts to bring them into alignment with their desired goal of freedom. Contrary to the thought of Abraham Lincoln, those on opposing sides of the Civil War did not read the same Bible and pray to the same God. Rather, with respect to slavery, their respective interpretations of both God and the Bible were diametrically opposite.

I am confident that many will read this book with great enthusiasm. Moreover, they will be amazed by the ways in which the agents of the freedom narratives generated and employed biblical criticism, not in the twentieth-century academic sense of "historical criticism," but in the sense of discerning the implications of the text for ordinary people like themselves and its application to their daily struggles. Such an orientation enabled black leaders and others to discern God's liberating spirit confronting all forces bent on destroying or hindering the healthy development of God's creation, including "the least of them." In fact, readers will discover that enslaved Africans found solace in many parts of the Bible and especially in the lesson of the last judgment, where the Lord says, "Inasmuch as ye have done it unto one of the least of these my brethren, ye have done it unto me" (Matt. 25:40 KJV). Identifying themselves with "the least of these" implied their affinity with the Lord's salvific message. One cannot overestimate the impact of that passage and similar ones on these oppressed people.

The readers of this book will encounter some surprises, however, among which two are worthy of mention: (a) the interpretation of Psalm 68:31, the basic text of most black nationalist movements, is based on a faulty understanding of the context in which it occurs; (b) William J. Anderson's focus on 2 Kings 5 to account for the origins of whiteness as the curse, instead of that of blackness. never took root among blacks. Nevertheless, many biblical texts reveal a piety in the Bible that enslaved Africans were able to adopt as helpful to them both in their self-understanding and their quest for freedom.

Finally, readers will be pleased with the new knowledge this book provides concerning the agency of enslaved Africans in constructing a creative and effective hermeneutic that nurtured their hopes, inspired their souls, trumped the biblical teaching of their enslavers, and strengthened their resolve to be free from the trauma of slavery. Most important, their diligence in searching the Scriptures as evidenced in the freedom narratives eventually resulted around 1820 in making Christianity their own. The emergence of the spirituals at that time provides a lasting testimony to that collective conversion experience. Discovering texts that trumped those used by the slave owners to justify their cruel enterprise marked the beginning of their newly found dignity. Not only did they make Christianity their own, but inspired by this newfound dignity, they could move forward toward the goal of making the nation their own as well.

Peter J. Paris
Professor Emeritus
Princeton Theological Seminary

Preface

Good ideas often originate in conversations with friends. As graduate students at Duke University in the 1990s, we were each engaged in our course work and examinations on separate Testaments. During this time, Dr. William Turner invited us to precept for his "Introduction to African American Religion(s)" course. As students of the Bible, we immediately began to notice the use and appropriation of a wide array of biblical passages in the literature we were reading for the course. These conversations forced us to grapple with these citations within their respective contexts, especially in light of the history of biblical interpretation within African American history. Among so many intriguing reading selections, we also read a few short selections of the so-called "slave narratives," which became a fortuitous opportunity. This opened up a world of enriching possibilities for thinking about the function of Scripture, African American identity, and the history of the developing US democracy.

In the aftermath of participating in this course, we began meeting to read through several key texts on African American biblical interpretation, beginning with *Stony the Road We Trod*. We soon moved on to *The Recovery of Black Presence*. While we were affirmed by the perspectives presented and the hermeneutical strategies employed in these texts, we noted a significant gap in the learning that we were doing in our graduate programs. The voices of African American thinkers were absent in this context, as were the particular ways of reading that sustained African Americans in their struggles for freedom and equality in the United States. What was particularly compelling was that not only were contemporary African American authors invisible in the academy, but so were those early authors whose genius transformed the Bible, from a weapon of a supremacist status quo used against them into a tool that they could use for their own work of liberation. Once we saw this, our conversations evolved to consider how we could reclaim these texts as an object of our own inquiry and foster a greater understanding of the emerging field of African American biblical hermeneutics based in the work of these early liberation writers.

Initially, these conversations, albeit enriching and life-sustaining ones in the middle of challenging graduate work, remained conversations. We had dissertations to research, families to support, and professional employment to secure. Finally, in 2004, a number of years after departing Durham, we decided to present an introductory essay on how formerly enslaved African Americans interpreted the biblical Sabbath law, especially its impact on the conditions of the institution in their everyday lives. Serendipitously, Stephanie Egnotovich—executive editor of Westminster John Knox Press—heard the regional presentation in Atlanta and, equally important, overheard the conversation Emerson had with historian Prof. Sandy Martin of the University of Georgia, who provided reassurance that the initial stages of the research were moving in the right direction. Stephanie immediately instigated a lunch conversation to encourage the project and from that point until her passing in 2009 was one primary reason we continued to think through these issues formally.

Together with Stephanie we envisioned a book that would explore the origins of distinctive African American readings of the Bible in the narratives of formerly enslaved authors. From readings that we had already done, we knew that there were interesting interpretive strategies being employed by these writers, seeking to sway American public opinion to oppose slavery. The Bible was not just a religious book. It was a tool that promised not only to serve as an effective commonplace resource in which both whites and blacks sought to find meaning, but a grounding text for the development of a narrative that placed God on the side of the enslaved. We were convinced that lodged in this genre of nascent African American Christianity were the roots of the tree of contemporary African American biblical appropriation. That became the focal concern of this project, tracing the origins of current reading strategies in these antebellum texts.

Although we continued to pursue our own individual writing endeavors, the *Genesis* project remained a central theme of our conversations with one another. Stephanie combined her encouragement with patience, until we could determine the right time to pursue the research related to this project with more purposeful intentions. Three of the chapters are coauthored (chapters 1, 3, and the excursus), one of them a thoroughly revised chapter of our initial work on the Sabbath. The other chapters (chapters 2, 4, 5, 6) Emerson wrote, presented, and rewrote, in hopes that these essays would fit the parameters of this small volume. More formally, Rodney shares ideas in chapter 1 that stem from his previously published essay "African Americans and the King James Version of the Bible," in *The King James Version at 400: Assessing Its Genius as Bible Translation and Its Literary Influence*, ed. David G. Burge, John F. Kutsko, and Philip H. Towner (Atlanta: Society of Biblical Literature, 2013), 455–74. In addition to presenting several early drafts at the Society of Biblical Literature, we are grateful for invitations to give talks on this topic at the following institutions: Greensboro College, Princeton Theological Seminary, Indiana University-Purdue University Indianapolis Conference on "The Bible and American Life," and the University of Detroit Mercy. We will always cherish the people who extended those invitations: Rhonda Burnett-Bletsch, Teddy Reeves, and J. Todd Hibbard. Also, Emerson could not have made necessary progress in the research without a generous early sabbatical from Messiah College. Emerson is grateful to administrators—Dean Peter Powers, Provost Randy Basinger, and President Kim Phipps—who understand the commitment to balance research and teaching as a professional calling.

We have had so many wonderful persons who encouraged us in the work on this project. The lively reception of each audience reminded us of the need to carve out time, despite other commitments and research. There are more specific people who deserve mention, if only briefly. Jean Corey, Cheryl Kirk-Duggan, Luke Powery, and Beth Ritter (Emerson's former graduate assistant) either heard ideas or read portions of the manuscript in its earliest stages and provided helpful advice along the way. William Andrews also met with us at an early stage of this project, and we are grateful to him both for his encouragement and for his online collection of liberation narratives (housed at the University of North Carolina) that served as the basis of our work. The members of SBL's Slavery, Resistance, and Freedom section heard drafts of several chapters and have continued to express a deep interest in the direction of the project. Peter Paris, Yolanda Pierce, and Ross Wagner provided helpful listening ears during Emerson's time at Princeton Theological Seminary. We are so honored that Peter decided to write the foreword!

Michael Fuller offered the kind of attention to detail that a colleague always hopes to secure from friends and does so with carefulness to the authors' own writing styles and rhetoric. We will, forever, be in his debt for taking time away from other more pressing duties to attend to *Genesis*. The project reads much more smoothly because of his time and consideration.

Bridgett Green inherited a difficult project (as many coauthored ones are) but with kindness and wisdom shepherded the manuscript to its completion. Without Bridgett, we would have written this book without "Jesus" (see appendix). The book has been dedicated to Bridgett's predecessor—Stephanie Egnotovich—a person she never met but in whose footsteps she admirably walks. Without Stephanie's initial "discovery," we would have never dreamed that there might be others who would want to hear about this incredible story in the way in which we would tell it. Daniel Braden (managing editor at WJK) and Hermann Weinlick (copyeditor) have helped us to tell the story with more clarity. The authors are responsible for any errors that remain.

We save our final words of appreciation for each other. I (Emerson) am grateful for the level of commitment Rodney was able to devote to this project, despite the many other significant duties that warranted so much of his attention and energy over the last few years—activities, in the long run, that will have a far greater effect on society than this book. The regular conversations we shared over the last few years helped inspire and shape the direction of this study. I am thankful for his friendship and the "fruit" of our labor together. His awareness of the primary sources, attention to the sensibilities of the enslaved, and gift for the rhetorical flare greatly enhanced the project and assisted in the completion of this work. I will miss our late afternoon conversations and intense work meetings in Richmond!

And I (Rodney) want to thank Emerson for his partnership on this project and for his tireless efforts to bring this work to completion. In part I am grateful for his friendship/brotherhood over these past two decades. He has been a wonderful dialogue partner, not just in this work, but also in my other work on nineteenth-century racial politics and the intersection of race and biblical interpretation. As I have been inspired by these liberation texts increasingly to engage in work in the public square, I am grateful to Emerson for keeping me rooted in the work of the academy and for pressing on with this project, so that it too may play a role at the intersection of biblical interpretation and justice bringing. I have been pleased to share in this work, to explore the roots of African American interpretive traditions, and to consider the continuing role of Scripture in movements fostering social change with him.

Emerson Powery
Messiah College

Rodney S. Sadler Jr.
Union Presbyterian Seminary

August 2015

1

The Genesis of Liberation

The Function of the Bible in the Freedom Narratives[*]

AUTHORITY OF SCRIPTURE
FOR EARLY AFRICAN AMERICANS

African Americans' respect for the authority of the Christian Scriptures is a miracle in itself. Their introduction to the Bible frequently came by way of sermons from Colossians 3:22–25, Ephesians 6:5–8, and 1 Peter 2:18–20, directed at ensuring their obedience to their masters. The God they met in these sermons was firmly on the side of their tormentors, opposing their freedom, reifying the status quo. The religion they were offered did not emphasize the love of Christ in response to their choice of will, but the subjugation of their wills as a divine duty to other humans who laid claim to their bodies. In spite of this cultural introduction to the Bible, many African Americans have greatly revered the Christian Scriptures throughout their acquaintance with them. But why did African Americans attribute authority to the Bible?

Of course the simple answer is that they fell in love with the God of Scripture. In Christ they found salvation from their sins and reconciliation with the Creator of the universe. Their experience of Christianity resonated with aspects of the religions of their African forebears. They

---

[*]These narratives are generally labeled "slave narratives" in contemporary scholarship. We prefer the phrase "freedom narratives," since the authors wrote these stories—either with their own pens or voices—*after* slavery. Throughout the book, we will also use the syntactically awkward, yet precise, phrase "narratives of the formerly enslaved." Asterisks after page numbers indicate freedom narratives, which are accessible online.

were even able to incorporate cultural particularities into Christianity without compromising their expression of the faith. The Christian God was a source of strength and sustenance to them in the midst of the persistent turmoil that defined their lives. When they were weak, they could be assured that their God was strong and that they were not left to suffer the indignities of slavery alone; no matter what, Scripture testified that God was with them. This was certainly enough to lend authority to these texts. However, there may be additional contributing factors as well.

The authority of Scripture for African Americans, at its root, has the authority granted to these texts by their ancestors; so it is reasonable to begin this inquiry by reflecting on the works of some notable early authors. Often their introduction to Scripture was not a neutral spiritual experience but a hostile activity whereby Holy Writ was used to pacify them (Exod. 20, 21; Eph. 6:4–9) and justify their subjugation (Gen. 9:18–27; Gen. 10). But in these texts they found not just an otherworldly God offering spiritual blessings, but a here-and-now God who cared principally for the oppressed, acting historically and eschatologically to deliver the downtrodden from their abusers. They also found Jesus, a suffering Savior whose life and struggles paralleled their own struggles. In the biblical narratives that describe these characters they found reasons to believe not only in the liberating power of the God of Scripture, but in the liberating emphasis of Scripture itself.

Because they learned that the Bible did not denigrate African identity, they were able to use it to ground their humanity, subversively to rebut biblically based supremacist readings, to validate their right to be free and function as equals in this nation. For them Scripture generally had both spiritual and political implications;[1] in fact, it could not have one without the other. Scripture also addressed many dimensions of the lives of African Americans. In addition to its role as a religious document offering spiritual blessing, it was also consulted as the primary record for ethnographic information, a source of myth making for a people with a stolen history, a tool for political empowerment, and a guide for establishing social order. The Bible had become an indispensable part of their lives.

---

1. C. Eric Lincoln notes that there was "no division between sacred and secular, especially between religion and politics" in African American communities (*The Black Church in the African American Experience* [Durham, NC: Duke University Press, 1990], 199–200). Aspects of this integration of sacred and secular persist in African American Christian contexts determining that the religious character of the black church is necessarily political. For a larger discussion of politics and African American religion, see Lincoln, *Black Church*, 199–204.

As they became familiar with the Bible, it soon became apparent that the same book that was used to justify their oppression also provided hope for American African liberation. Further, recognizing that this collection of ancient texts was a seminal commonplace grounding for the development of Western civilization, they hoped that by employing the narratives found in the Bible they could find a means to argue for their full equality in terms their adversaries would have to respect. After all, even their adversaries, steeped in the Christian faith and committed to arguments based on Scripture, would have to heed the Word of God or be exposed to have failed hypocritically to adhere to the precepts of the ground of their faith. Frankly, it would have been counterproductive for this oppressed group to ignore such a valuable resource.

Below we will explore several practical reasons why many African Americans became faithful adherents of Scripture, developing their own distinctive hermeneutical traditions for reading it. Early African Americans found that they could benefit from employing the Bible as it:

1. gave them hope that God would act without human (political) intervention to provide justice for enslaved Africans;
2. grounded subversive arguments against the type of Christianity practiced by Southern slaveholders;
3. provided a mythic system that could explain their plight and a symbolic world that resonated with their own[2] while demonstrating God's fidelity to those similarly situated (slaves, exiles, sufferers);
4. allowed them the latitude to emphasize or exclude portions of Scripture based upon their needs without compromising the core of the Christian message;
5. envisioned human origins in a manner that allowed them to discern a glorious past for African peoples and discern positive dimensions of African identity;

---

2. Consider the following quotation, wherein Olaudah Equiano reflected on his preenslavement existence among his own people and the similarity between their customs and those of the Jews in Scripture: "Such is the imperfect sketch my memory has furnished me with of the manners and customs of a people among whom I first drew my breath. And here I cannot forbear suggesting what has long struck me very forcibly, namely, the strong analogy which even by this sketch, imperfect as it is, appears to prevail in the manners and customs of my countrymen and those of the Jews, before they reached the Land of Promise, and particularly the patriarchs while they were yet in that pastoral state which is described in Genesis—an analogy, which alone would induce me to think that the one people had sprung from the other" (*The Interesting Narrative of the Life of Olaudah Equiano, or Gustavus Vassa, the African. Written by Himself*, vol. 1 [London: Author, 1789], 37–38*).

6. continued to be flexible enough to address their evolving plight in America (slavery, segregation, persistent inequality, etc.).

These six points do not exhaust the fullness of African American engagements with Scripture, but they do describe key interpretive advantages that the biblical narratives provided to early African American literati. Below we will briefly discuss both apolitical spiritual and subversive political appropriations of Scripture, in order to illustrate two key dimensions of their scriptural engagements.

FREEDOM IN GOD'S HANDS: APOLITICAL SPIRITUAL READINGS

Before we consider texts written by African Americans with a discernable political agenda, it is important to establish that Scripture was from the earliest times understood as the ground of ultimate trust in the Christian God. In this regard, some of the earliest African American readers found solace in the Bible as a source of spiritual transformation, even if it meant that the body would remain enslaved. We would identify such readings as "fundamentalist" readings today. Containing an evangelical zeal for Christ, such readers eschewed this-worldly politics for total reliance on the God of Scripture to rescue them from the evils of slavery and dehumanized status.

Examples of this type of reading can be seen in the work of Jupiter Hammon. One of the first African American authors, Hammon was a devout Christian. One might expect him, as an early enslaved author, to use his literacy to critique his life situation. However, though his writing addressed the contemporary crisis of North American slavery, it failed to provide a thoroughgoing critique of that institution, as would the work of later authors. Hammon instead presented a decidedly mainstream moralistic view of the Christian faith, employing the Bible as a life guide for purposes of self-improvement. Though he subtly argued against slavery, he reserved this-worldly freedom for younger people, not for himself. To him God's Word provided all the freedom that he required, as it facilitated access to heaven. Only there could humans find liberation from all that ails them.[3]

---

3. Jupiter Hammon, "Address to the Negroes in the State of New York," in *African American Religious History: A Documentary Witness*, ed. Milton C. Sernett (Durham, NC: Duke University Press, 1999), 34–43.

In his 1786 "Address to Negroes in the State of New York," Hammon's apolitical sentiments were evident: "Let me beg of you my dear African brethren, to think very little of your bondage in this life, for your thinking of it will do you no good. If God designs to set us free, he will do it in his own time and way; but think of your bondage to sin and Satan, and do not rest until you are delivered from it."[4] Here bondage of the flesh is deemed unimportant when compared to spiritual bondage, and the potential for earthly freedom pales in light of the promises of Christ.

A similar all-encompassing reliance on God was echoed in the work of political activist Maria Stewart. Though she had spent much of her life seeking the abolition of slavery, she had come to the opinion that her efforts were for naught. In her 1832 farewell to her friends in Boston, her theological reasons were evident: "It is high time for us to drop political discussions, and when our day of deliverance comes, God will provide a way for escape, and fight his own battles."[5] Like Hammon, she concluded that morality and godliness were to be her goals and that abolitionist political strivings were incompatible with the radical trust in "pure religion." It was up to God alone to determine the time of freedom; Hammon and Stewart viewed political activity seeking social change as vain. As these two authors illustrate, early African American authors were capable of apolitical hermeneutics expressing reliance on God alone to provide liberation, even during the antebellum period.

SUBVERSIVE POLITICAL READINGS OF BIBLICAL FAITH

Subsequent texts more thoroughly critiqued slavery. Writers like Peter Randolph and Frederick Douglass exemplify the use of the Bible to achieve other ends. Though their faith was apparent, it was not expressed with Hammon's fundamentalist zeal. Instead, their faith could not abide a separation of the spiritual and social dimensions of life; valid faith must attend to liberation and freedom in order to realize God's promise.

In his autobiography published in 1893, Peter Randolph demonstrated why initially it would have been difficult for African Americans to believe the Bible, particularly inasmuch as they received it from the

---

4. Hammon, "Address," 42.
5. Maria Stewart, "Mrs. Stewart's Farewell Address to Her Friends in the City of Boston," in *African American Religious History*, 208.

hands of less-than-reliable sources. Randolph critiqued slaveholders who ironically preached against theft to those they held enslaved, deeming them like Ananias and Sapphira, who "betrayed the trust committed to them, or refused to bear true testimony in regard to that trust."[6] For him "[t]he Gospel was so mixed with slavery, that the people could see no beauty in it, and feel no reverence for it."[7] From this statement we could almost conclude that he would reject the Christian God and Scripture.

As he attests, it was not the faith with which he had a problem, however, but preachers who got caught up in the spirit in worship on Sunday morning and then would whip an enslaved woman on Monday morning. He declared that "[s]uch preachers ought to be forbidden by the laws of the land ever to mock again the blessed religion of Jesus, which was sent as a light to the world."[8] For Randolph, the "religion of Jesus" was distinct from the expressions of white, slaveholding religion he was forced to endure. He could thus level a critique against slavery in Christian terms, demonstrating the failure of his ideological opponents to surmise properly the true scriptural message.

The hypocrisy of white Christianity was also a major theme for Frederick Douglass. In essence he determined that slaveholding religion was different altogether from the Christianity of Christ: "I assert most unhesitatingly, that the religion of the south is a mere covering for the most horrid crimes,—a justifier of the most appalling barbarity,—a sanctifier of the most hateful frauds,—and a dark shelter under which the darkest, foulest, grossest, and most infernal deeds of slaveholders find the strongest protection."[9]

On the surface, this statement may appear to be a rejection of Christianity, but Douglass clearly emphasized that it was not Christianity with which he had problems, but a bastardized version of American religion. He continued: "What I have said respecting and against religion, I mean strictly to apply to the *slaveholding religion* of this land, and with no possible reference to Christianity proper; for, between the Christianity of this land, and the Christianity of Christ, I recognize the widest possible difference. . . . I can see no reason, but the most deceitful one, for calling the religion of this land Christianity."[10]

---

6. Peter Randolph, "Plantation Churches: Visible and Invisible," in *African American Religious History*, 64.

7. Randolph, "Plantation Churches," 64.

8. Randolph, "Plantation Churches," 65.

9. Frederick Douglass, *Narrative of the Life of Frederick Douglass, an American Slave. Written by Himself* (Boston: Anti-Slavery Office, 1845), 77*.

10. Douglass, *Narrative*, 118*. Some question Douglass's commitment to Christianity later in life (see *By These Hands: A Documentary History of African American Humanism*, ed. Anthony B. Pinn [New York: New York University Press, 2001], 75–100).

Raised with the hypocrisy of slaveholding Christianity, Douglass had ample reason to dismiss the Bible or to conclude that it was nothing more than a tool used to control blacks. Rather than rejecting Scripture, he used it to hold accountable those who abused it. Likening Southern slaveholding Christians to biblical scribes and Pharisees, he declared that they "attend with Pharisaical strictness to the outward forms of religion, and at the same time neglect the weightier matters of the law, judgment, mercy, and faith . . . professing to love God whom they have not seen, whilst they hate their brother whom they have seen."[11]

By finding biblical examples of pious people who were portrayed negatively in the Bible, Douglass was able to redeem a faith in Scripture despite the failings of Southern Christianity. Slaveholders, though pious, were not faithful Christians, but similar to central religious hierarchy during Jesus' times; like scribes and Pharisees, they misconstrued the essence of religion. In this way the Bible's authority could be upheld in spite of the rampant abuses by many Christian proslavery advocates.

AFRICAN AMERICANS AND THE KING JAMES VERSION OF THE BIBLE

It is not by happenstance that the first African American orators were eloquent speakers who wrote in lofty, regal English prose, a language far removed from the common verbiage of their African American enslaved and impoverished freed colleagues. The stammering slave tongue reflected in the conversations recorded in their own narratives was quite distinct from the elegant and astute rhetoric of these formerly enslaved authors. It is almost as if they were speaking an alien tongue, a language of refinement and contemplation that transcended the mundane experiences of the enslaved. It is almost as though they were speaking with the "Master's tongue," and to a certain extent, perhaps they were—but just not the masters of whom we might be thinking.

They were speaking the "Master's" language as they understood it to be reflected in the pages of the King James Version of the Bible (KJV). It was a sacred tongue, a respected tongue, a tongue that if mastered could both serve to assert the full humanity of the enslaved by demonstrating their intellectual acumen and serve as a commonplace cultural

---

11. Douglass, *Narrative*, 122*.

connection to the largely white audience (for their "narratives"), whom they sought to persuade through careful use of pathos and ethos to become abolitionists.

The King James Version of the Bible has been a prominent document consulted to frame theological discourse around key political movements throughout the development of life in the Americas.[12] This has been evidenced in many distinctive ways in the African American community, beginning with the first black encounters with this text in the Western world. As a people, African Americans were not easy converts to Christianity. In fact, it took more than a century, two Great Awakenings, and the typically more egalitarian evangelistic tactics of the Baptists and Methodists for Christianity to begin to make significant inroads into African American communities. But just as important as the sociological factors involved, it took the stories from the pages of the Bible to open up the hearts and souls of enslaved Africans to the Christian faith.

In "Re-reading *Their* Scriptures: An Analysis of the Authority of Scripture among Early African Americans," Sadler argues that African American readers discovered within the pages of the Bible the stories of God's interaction with key biblical figures, where the Lord provides liberation, redemption, and deliverance.[13] These stories served as the mythopoeic, or "myth making" basis for African American visions of freedom and self-determination and thus gave Christianity a certain appeal to enslaved Africans. As historian Albert Raboteau discusses in his now-classic text *Slave Religion*,

> [s]laves prayed for the future day of deliverance to come, and they kept hope alive by incorporating as part of *their* mythic past the Old Testament exodus of Israel out of slavery. The appropriation of the Exodus story was for the slaves a way of articulating their sense of historical identity as a people. That identity was also based, of course, upon their common heritage of enslavement. The Christian slaves applied the Exodus story, whose end they knew, to their own experience of slavery, which had not ended. In identifying with the Exodus story, they created meaning out of the chaotic and senseless

12. For a fuller version of this discussion, see Rodney Sadler, "African Americans and the King James Version of the Bible," in *The King James Version at 400: Assessing Its Genius as Bible Translation and Its Literary Influence*, ed. David G. Burge, John F. Kutsko, and Philip H. Towner (Atlanta: Society of Biblical Literature, 2013), 455–74.

13. Rodney Sadler, "Re-reading *Their* Scriptures: An Analysis of the Authority of Scripture among Early African Americans," *Ex Auditu: An International Journal of Theological Interpretation of Scripture* 19 (2003): 153–65.

experience of slavery. Exodus functioned as an archetypal event for the slaves.[14]

Scripture and the stories of a God who rescued the oppressed and redeemed the abused served as the entrée into the Christian faith. As John Saillant reflects, "In the second half of the eighteenth century, therefore, African American hermeneutics was born. . . . The Bible provided a context in which the sufferings of slaves could be understood and the misdeeds of the slavers judged, even if blacks could not at the moment free themselves. . . . The Bible provided an anti-slavery interpretation of history."[15]

Thus began the romance between some African Americans and the Bible. And when they were converted by the God of this book, it was the great eloquence and the archaic voice of the King James Version that evoked divinity in the text by its poetry and its royal grandeur. These stories are told in "God's language," and because of that, the King James Version quickly captured African Americans' hearts and minds. This phenomenon did not end in the nineteenth century either. African Americans retain an affinity for the King James Version, as if it were an inheritance from their formerly enslaved ancestors.[16] Alice Ogden Bellis notes in her article "The Bible in African American Perspectives" that even today

[t]he translation of choice for African Americans is usually the King James Version. Blacks revere the KJV for the same reason many Roman Catholics still are fond of the Latin/Vulgate Bible: the poetry and antiquitous tone associated with a spirituality of earlier times, even another world. That some of the text is "mysterious,'" i.e., not fully understood, is what makes it special, instantly beckoning one to prayer and active dialogue with God. Modern translations, in

14. Albert J. Raboteau, *Slave Religion: The Invisible Institution in the Antebellum South* (New York: Oxford University Press, 1978), 311. While the exodus theme may have been present in the spirituals (which are more difficult to date), the biblical theme was less popular in the narratives of the formerly enslaved before 1860. According to Sylvester Johnson, the exodus story became prominent among African Americans *after* emancipation, not before (*The Myth of Ham in Nineteenth-Century American Christianity: Race, Heathens, and the People of God* [New York: Palgrave MacMillan, 2004], 53).

15. John Saillant, "Origins of African American Biblical Hermeneutics in Eighteenth-Century Black Opposition to the Slave Trade and Slavery," in *African Americans and the Bible: Sacred Texts and Social Textures*, ed. Vincent Wimbush (New York: Continuum, 2000), 236–37.

16. In one recent national study, completed in March 2014, it was determined that preference for the King James Version remains significantly more prominent (more than 20 percent higher) among African American readers than among their white counterparts ("The Bible in American Life: A National Study by the Center for the Study of Religion and American Culture," 13), accessed January 19, 2015, http://www.raac.iupui.edu/files/2713/9413/8354/Bible_in_American_Life_Report_March_6_2014.pdf.

making the text idiomatic in a contemporary way, cause the Bible to become suspect as a dubious translation of modernisms.[17]

The King James Version is to African American preaching, oration, and literature what Alexander Pushkin was to Russian literature. Without the Shakespearean poetry and prose of this text, born during the life of this great Old English–speaking literary genius, the black bards would not have had the platform from which to soar to the remarkable heights that they reached with such memorable offerings as Frederick Douglass's "What to the Slave Is the Fourth of July?" or Maria Stewart's "Farewell Address to Her Friends in the City of Boston," or Martin King's "A Letter from a Birmingham Jail," or even James Weldon Johnson's "The Creation."

A fair treatment of this subject is not possible in the brief space of this introductory chapter. For the sake of introduction, in this chapter we will explore the role of the King James Version in early black literacy then divide the historical African American appropriation of the King James Version into two basic types, "functional quotations" and "literalist interpretations," and talk about the implications of both of these hermeneutical moves on formerly enslaved African American autobiographers.

KING JAMES VERSION AS THE BASIS OF LITERACY

Stephen B. Reid notes in his book *Experience and Tradition*: "It was from the Bible that many black slaves learned to read and it was to the Bible that so many of them went to find guidance, comfort, a word of hope, and the promise of their deliverance from sin and slavery. The Bible has been the source of inspiration for poetry and song, as well as the inspiration for drama and sermon."[18]

These few words from Reid ably sum up the significance of the Bible for early African Americans. Though thought by most in contemporary society to be a religious book and a source of spiritual wisdom, for the first African Americans who encountered Scripture when enslaved, the Bible was far more important than that. It was a God book, a "talking

---

17. Alice Ogden Bellis, "The Bible in African American Perspectives," in *Teaching Theology and Religion* 1.3 (1998): 161–65 (162).
18. Stephen Breck Reid, *Experience and Tradition: A Primer in Black Biblical Hermeneutics* (Nashville: Abingdon Press, 1990), 11.

book,"[19] a book that controlled life and death. Because of this, the Bible inspired African Americans to learn to read and write. Harriet Jacobs illustrates this as she recounts her experiences tutoring an older enslaved man:

> As soon as he could spell in two syllables he wanted to spell out words in the Bible. The happy smile that illuminated his face put joy into my heart. After spelling out a few words, he paused, and said, "Honey, it 'pears when I can read dis good book I shall be nearer to God. White man is got all de sense. He can larn easy. It ain't easy for ole black man like me. I only wants to read dis book, dat I may know how to live, den I hab no fear 'bout dying."[20]

Jacobs's account demonstrates a common theme in the narratives of formerly enslaved African Americans: the Bible inspired them to want to learn to read. This same sentiment was expressed by Frederick Douglass as he recounted his initial quest for literacy in the 1895 Frederic Holland authored biography, *Colored Orator:*

> I remember the first time I ever heard the Bible read, and from that time I trace my first desire to learn to read. I was over seven years old; my master had gone out one Sunday night, the children had gone to bed. I had crawled under the center table and had fallen asleep, when my mistress commenced to read the Bible aloud, so loud that she waked me. She waked me to sleep no more. I have found since that the chapter she then read was the first of Job. I remember my sympathy for the good old man, and my anxiety to learn more about him led me to ask my mistress to teach me to read.[21]

Frederick Douglass's recollection of this pivotal event in his life exemplified the importance of the Bible to enslaved African Americans. It was Scripture that emboldened them to engage in the act of resistance that is reading; they knew that they were taking their lives into their hands[22] but deemed it to be worth the risk. It was Scripture

---

19. "I had often seen my master and Dick employed in reading; and I had a great curiosity to talk to the books, as I thought they did; and so to learn how all things had a beginning: for that purpose I have often taken up a book, and have talked to it, and then put my ears to it, when alone, in hopes it would answer me; and I have been very much concerned when I found it remained silent" (Equiano, *Interesting Narrative*, 106–7*). For a fuller analysis of this trope, see chap. 2.

20. Harriet Jacobs, *Incidents in the Life of a Slave Girl. Written by Herself* (Boston: Published for the Author, 1861), 112*.

21. Frederic May Holland, *Frederick Douglass: The Colored Orator* (New York: Funk & Wagnalls, 1895), 14*.

22. "Very soon after I went to live with Mr. and Mrs. Auld, she very kindly commenced to teach me the A, B, C. After I had learned this, she assisted me in learning to spell words of three or four letters. Just at this point of my progress, Mr. Auld found out what was going on, and at once forbade Mrs. Auld to instruct me further, telling her,

that captured the imagination of enslaved blacks, who had been legally prohibited from learning to read or write, because their enslavers feared what would happen if they developed their full intellectual capacity. In response to his stated desire to read, Douglass's enslaver noted that "if this one should ever be taught to read the bible, there would be no keeping him a slave."[23] But, as Douglass's legend states, having heard his enslaver prohibiting him from learning to read, "at once he made up his mind to get all he could."[24]

So began the rise of one of the most important intellectuals and social activists in the history of the United States. Through cunning he learned to read, often manipulating the free white youngsters in the neighborhood to share their school lessons with him. But it was always the King James Version that was his primary pedagogue.[25] Later in life, he recalled learning to read by picking up stray pages of the Bible from the gutter, cleaning and drying them, and then stealing away to study them in secret.[26] His scriptural studies would often occupy him until long into the night.[27]

Of course Douglass lived (1818–1895) during a period when the King James Version of the Bible was the dominant English version of the Bible. Not only might we suspect this because of the eloquent prose that he employed in his writing and oration; we can also recognize this from the quotations of Scripture that he used in his own writings. While we will address his use of Scripture more below, the King James Version was likely the first piece of literature that early African American literati encountered, desired to learn, and eventually mastered. This alone makes it a significant artifact for African American history and should pique our curiosity about the influence this version had on the intellectual development of black Americans. But the use of this text was not as straightforward as we might expect; instead of simply appropriating the text as it was given, they adapted this version

---

among other things, that it was unlawful, as well as unsafe, to teach a slave to read. To use his own words, further, he said, 'If you give a nigger an inch, he will take an ell. A nigger should know nothing but to obey his master—to do as he is told to do. Learning would *spoil* the best nigger in the world. Now,' said he, 'if you teach that nigger (speaking of myself) how to read, there would be no keeping him. It would forever unfit him to be a slave'" (Douglass, *Narrative*, 33*).

23. Holland, *Frederick Douglass*, 15*.

24. Holland, *Frederick Douglass*, 15*.

25. Another key book for Douglass was "The Columbian Orator," which helped Douglass improve his oratory skills and gain perspective on the master/slave relationship; see Frederick Douglass, *My Bondage and My Freedom* (New York: Miller, Orton & Mulligan, 1855), 157–58, 264, 275, 343.

26. Douglass, *Life and Times of Frederick Douglass: His Early Life as a Slave, His Escape from Bondage, and His Complete History to the Present Time* (Hartford, CT: Park Publishing Co., 1881), 83*.

27. Holland, *Frederick Douglass*, 48–49*.

of the text in several ways to address the concerns of African American rhetors.

FUNCTIONAL QUOTATIONS: USE OF
THE BIBLE IN FREEDOM NARRATIVES

One of the interesting trends with early African American appropriations of the King James Version in liberationist-oriented literature was the use of this translation as the basis of "functional quotations." By functional quotation we mean that they employed the King James Version as their base text and then playfully modified the text typologically, often replacing the biblical heroes with the African American community and the biblical villains with their enslavers or oppressors. They preserved the gist of the text as well as the poetic and archaic dimensions of its language, yet the exact words and word order were less important and often modified slightly to fit the authors' own narrative contexts.

In the appendix to Douglass's first autobiography, published in 1845, he offers an extensive citation from the King James Version of Matthew 23:

> The Christianity of America is a Christianity, of whose votaries it may be as truly said, as it was of the ancient scribes and Pharisees, "They bind heavy burdens, and grievous to be borne, and lay them on men's shoulders, but they themselves will not move them with one of their fingers. All their works they do for to be seen of men.— They love the uppermost rooms at feasts, and the chief seats in the synagogues, . . . and to be called of men, Rabbi, Rabbi.—But woe unto you, scribes and Pharisees, hypocrites! for ye shut up the kingdom of heaven against men; for ye neither go in yourselves, neither suffer ye them that are entering to go in. Ye devour widows' houses, and for a pretence make long prayers; therefore ye shall receive the greater damnation. Ye compass sea and land to make one proselyte, and when he is made, ye make him twofold more the child of hell than yourselves.—Woe unto you, scribes and Pharisees, hypocrites! for ye pay tithe of mint, and anise, and cumin, and have omitted the weightier matters of the law, judgment, mercy, and faith; these ought ye to have done, and not to leave the other undone. Ye blind guides! which strain at a gnat, and swallow a camel. Woe unto you, scribes and Pharisees, hypocrites! for ye make clean the outside of the cup and of the platter; but within, they are full of extortion and

excess.—Woe unto you, scribes and Pharisees, hypocrites! for ye are like unto whited sepulchres, which indeed appear beautiful outward, but are within full of dead men's bones, and of all uncleanness. Even so ye also outwardly appear righteous unto men, but within ye are full of hypocrisy and iniquity."[28]

In this instance he reproduced the passages that deal with the "woes" against the scribes and Pharisees and used these to critique the "religion of the South," the strange Southern perversion of the Christian faith that not only existed amid the dehumanizing conditions of the Southern slavocracy, but that was ultimately just "a mere covering for the most horrid crimes."[29]

As he reproduced the text, he began with the King James Version, but he deliberately altered his quotation at points relevant to his rhetorical aims to deal more precisely with his focal concerns and to avoid passages that adhered less to his interests. Douglass's quotation demonstrated that early African Americans made use of the King James Version, but that they appropriated the text in a manner that best suited their arguments for freedom and social transformation. Hence, instead of an actual quotation, Douglass employed a functional quotation, a quotation that achieved the author's rhetorical ends by altering the text in purposeful ways.

We see this strategy at work in the writings of another formerly enslaved person, William Anderson. Anderson also utilized the King James Version as the base text for his functional quotations. Consider the following quotation, wherein Anderson generally followed the King James Version but modified some terms, verb tenses, and word orders and even added material from other psalms almost as though he was reciting them himself, typologically assuming the identity of the psalmist:

Anderson's Text	KJV Psalm 23 w/ addition
"The Lord is my Shepherd, I shall not want; He maketh me to lie down in green pastures; He leadeth me beside the still waters.	**Psalm 23:1** The LORD *is* my shepherd; I shall not want. [2] He maketh me to lie down in green pastures: he leadeth me beside the still waters.

28. Douglass, *Narrative*, 120–21*.
29. Douglass, *Narrative*, 77*.

Anderson's Text	KJV Psalm 23 w/ addition
Yes, He restoreth my soul; He leadeth me in the paths of righteousness, for His **own** name's sake. Yea, though I walk through the valley of the shadow of death, I **shall** fear no evil, for thou art with me; thy rod and thy staff they comfort me.	[3] He restoreth my soul: he leadeth me in the paths of righteousness for his name's sake. [4] Yea, though I walk through the valley of the shadow of death, I will fear no evil: for thou *art* with me; thy rod and thy staff they comfort me.
Yes, thou anointeth my head with oil; thou spreadeth a table before me, in the presence of mine enemies.	[5] Thou preparest a table before me in the presence of mine enemies: thou anointest my head with oil; my cup runneth over.
Surely goodness and mercy **have followed me** all the days of my life, and I will dwell in the house of the Lord forever.	[6] Surely goodness and mercy shall follow me all the days of my life: and I will dwell in the house of the LORD forever.
I once was young, but now I am old, and I never have seen the righteous forsaken nor his seed begging bread.	**Psalm 37:25** I have been young, and *now* am old; yet have I not seen the righteous forsaken, nor his seed begging bread.
The earth is the Lord's and the fullness thereof."[30]	**Psalm 24:1** The earth *is* the LORD's, and the fulness thereof;

Anderson used this functional quotation almost as a triumphant crescendo in his narrative to affirm his faith in God despite the many "dangers, toils, and snares" that he had endured at the hands of those who sought to imprison or reenslave him. If we look carefully at his appropriation of this passage, we will note subtle purposeful changes in his appropriation of the King James Version:

1. the addition of the word "yes" to verses 3 and 5 to confirm that God has acted in his own life,
2. the addition of the word "own" in verse 3 to express the intimate relationship he has with God,

30. William J. Anderson, *The Life and Narrative of William J. Anderson, Twenty-Four Years a Slave* (Chicago: Daily Tribune Book and Job Printing Office, 1857), 44*.

3. the substitution of the term "shall" for "will" in verse 4 to demonstrate that he was kept from fearing evil,
4. the substitution of the past tense "have followed me" for "shall follow me" in verse 6 to demonstrate the faithfulness of the Lord throughout the various crises in his life.

This functional quotation of the King James Version personalized the passage and served as a powerful theological summation of his life experiences and a potent rhetorical tool to convince his readers of both the hardships he endured and the fidelity of God. Subsequent to this quotation of Scripture, he began to riff, if you will, off of several biblical and religious themes to describe his jubilation that the Lord had rescued him from his countless perils.[31]

LITERALIST INTERPRETATIONS: KING JAMES VERSION AS BASE TEXT FOR PARTICULAR MOVEMENTS

The King James Version of the Bible has also proven useful for certain Africana movements that, based upon particular translational choices made in this version, were able to frame their theologies. These groups developed particularized interpretations of Scripture that make them distinctive and that distinguish them from typical mainstream Africana Christian interpretive traditions.

One African American movement that has based fundamental details of its interpretive tradition on the King James Version is a group called the Ethiopianists. Growing from the seeds of mid-nineteenth-century ideas of David Walker and Henry Highland Garnet, this group blossomed in the latter half of the nineteenth and early part of the twentieth centuries in the work of religious leaders like missionary intellectuals Alexander Crummel and Edward Blyden and institutional leaders Bishop Henry M. Turner and Marcus Garvey. The thrust of their movement was based upon the understanding of one passage in

---

31. "Therefore I will trust in Him, as did Job, Peter, Paul and all the Apostles of old. O, like Jonah, I can almost say 'I have cried to God out of the belly of hell,' for some of these jails resemble a hell, and I have been in many of them in the United States; for where the slaveholders did not put me in, these mean Northerners or Free State men, both black and white, would concoct plans to imprison me. But, bless the Lord, the old man Anderson still lives, while many of them are falling to rise no more. Yes, glory to God, I expect to shout Victory when the world is on fire" (Anderson, *Life*, 44–45*).

the Psalter (Ps. 68:31 KJV): "Princes shall come out of Egypt; Ethiopia shall soon stretch out her hands unto God."

Over the years, this text has posed considerable problems for English translators who have understood it to mean very different things. For example: "Envoys will come from Egypt; Cush will submit herself to God" (NIV); "Let bronze be brought from Egypt; let Ethiopia hasten to stretch out its hands to God" (NRSV).

Attempts to make sense of this verse—which George Knight has deemed the "most notorious in the whole Bible"[32]—have led to some difficult and somewhat unsatisfactory text critical choices to arrive at translations that resemble the NIV's verse 31a "Envoys will come from Egypt" and the NRSV's verse 31b "Let Cush hasten to stretch out its hands to God." In essence, the passage seems to suggest a future moment when people of the great southern empires of Egypt and Cush will hasten to Jerusalem to worship YHWH. This verse is thus an attempt, as these translations suggest, to elevate the Judeans' self-estimation by predicting a moment when mightier nations, under which Judah has served as vassal, will prostrate themselves before Judah's God.[33]

From this obscure text grew an elaborate ideological movement that sought to make sense of African Americans' plight in the aftermath of the abolishment of systemic chattel slavery. It was a complex and internally conflicted ideology. It celebrated the sovereignty of God as the one who allowed the enslavement of Africans in order for them to become "civilized" and Christianized by the Europeans who oppressed them. It also hailed the providence of God, who would soon deliver Africans and give them an opportunity to exercise their superior genius in the reordering of the world. At the same time it both provided a theological legitimization for the horrors of slavery and it decried slavery as a crime against a once-and-soon-again-to-be-great people. As presented in the distinctive rendering of the King James Version, this text served as a prophecy of God's impending activity in the very near future; it was an eschatological foretelling of a return to prominence and purpose of a debased and humiliated people.

Based on the King James Version's translation of this single verse, members of the Ethiopianist movement were able to find biblically based theological support for their particular nationalist ideology. They took the text and exploited it, using the notion of "princes" to reflect

32. George A. F. Knight, *Psalms* (Philadelphia: Westminster Press, 1982), 1:315.

33. Rodney S. Sadler Jr., *Can a Cushite Change His Skin? An Examination of Race, Ethnicity, and Othering in the Hebrew Bible* (New York: T. & T. Clark, 2005), 135–37.

the former greatness of their ancestors and "Ethiopia" to refer to the entire continent of Africa poised on the brink of a revival.[34] Thus a historically significant faction that continues to impact contemporary life in Africana communities was born of a dubious translation of a difficult verse.

Consequently, we see that the King James Version served a distinctive purpose in shaping the aesthetic and the form of early African American rhetoric, and this aspect continues to influence everything from black preaching to black thought. The lyrical nature of the text, the archaic form of high English prose, and the descriptive literary elegance are evident in the writings of the previously enslaved.

For early African American writers, the King James Version was their pedagogue and primer to the literary world. It formed and shaped black thought in ways that are undeniable even today. Perhaps the intimacy of the African American romance with the King James Version is behind the contemporary African American aversion to recent translations built on more reliable and older witnesses to the original form of the biblical text. Perhaps the history of African Americans with this text has kept them beholden to it in a way that not only gives it primacy, but locates divine authority in its pages not easily transferred to other versions. The history of African American biblical interpretation begins with an engagement with one particular translation, the King James Version. And this translation floods the pages of the narratives of the formerly enslaved, who believed foremost in the God of liberation.

PURPOSE OF THIS PROJECT

To analyze the function of the Bible within the "Freedom Narrative" tradition. This project is an attempt to analyze the function of the Bible within the nineteenth-century narratives of the formerly enslaved prior to the Civil War. What role did the Bible play in the controversy surrounding slavery? How did various interpreters utilize its authority in maintaining their position, whether for or against the peculiar institution? Our primary focus is to explore the perspective of African Americans who had escaped bondage, since we have no written record from enslaved persons during their enslavement. At the time of their writings, the authors of the narratives were free—at least

---

34. George M. Fredrickson, *Black Liberation: A Comparative History of Black Ideologies in the United States and South Africa* (New York: Oxford University Press, 1995), 57–93.

in terms of their physical bodies. In their stories, they were attempting to free their minds and, they hoped, the bodies of others. Based on a firsthand experience of the peculiar institution, many of the African Americans who escaped became abolitionists, so the logic of liberation was the hermeneutical wedge they utilized to crack open the Bible. As scholars of the Bible, we are drawn to their use of the Bible—a collection of books that was frequently used ideologically to keep blacks enslaved—and how they negotiated the interpretations associated with this ancient collection. We want to narrate the interaction between their context and their Bible. And we want to recount this story through their voices.[35]

To reclaim early black interpreters. While it is important to state what this study is, it is equally important to be clear about what this project is not. It is not an analysis of how the formerly enslaved interpreted biblical texts in order to contribute to an understanding of the religious documents in their ancient settings.[36] They were not historical biblical critics. Rather, we want to narrate the stories of African American interpreters in the nineteenth century so that our readers are able to grapple with the significance of the reception and use of the Bible within the antebellum struggle of enslavement. So this study is secondarily a story about the Bible and its history and a story about nineteenth-century slavery. More significantly, this is primarily a study of African American identity and how nineteenth-century black Americans—all formerly enslaved—engaged the greatest theological conundrum of their day by challenging the appropriation of the Christian Bible to enforce their enslaved condition.[37] With W. E. B. DuBois, we assume what he asserted over a century ago: "The things evidently borrowed from the surrounding world undergo characteristic change when they enter the mouth of the slave. Especially is this true of Bible phrases."[38]

35. For this study, we utilize narratives "written by herself/himself" and those dictated to (usually white) editors. We are aware of the influence of some of these *white* abolitionist editors. See Frances Smith Foster, *Witnessing Slavery: The Development of Ante-bellum Slave Narratives* (Westport, CT: Greenwood Press, 1979), 144–45. If we were to make use only of narratives written by the formerly enslaved, we could not speak of *female* perspectives until 1861, when Harriet Jacobs penned her narrative.

36. Attention to the meaning of biblical passages within their ancient settings, from the perspective of nineteenth-century African American interpreters, would also be a fruitful project.

37. Of course, outside of the freedom-narrative tradition, African Americans read and appropriated the Bible for various reasons not limited to political and confrontational purposes. In most circumstances, they did not have white audiences in mind when they read their Bibles.

38. W. E. B. DuBois had the spirituals in mind specifically in *Souls of Black Folk* (orig. 1903; New York: Barnes & Noble Classics, 2003), 185.

Literacy rates among enslaved African Americans in the nineteenth century are difficult to determine.[39] Formal educational opportunities were generally illegal, so literacy was relatively low. Yet for various reasons, many slaveholders taught members of the enslaved to read.[40] Our narratives are filled with examples of these opportunities of learning. Furthermore, several of these authors—including Frederick Douglass, Sojourner Truth, James W. C. Pennington, and William Wells Brown—eventually became recognized public figures in nineteenth-century abolitionist circles.[41] Nonetheless, because of their direct experience of enslavement, they spoke on behalf of their fellow sisters and brothers in bondage, some of whom were their blood relatives.

To explore critical readers from the "underside." The Bible's role in religious and political debates leading up to the Civil War has received recent attention among historians and scholars of religion alike.[42] Mark Noll has presented the nineteenth-century debate over the Bible as the theological crisis of the century.[43] Most frequently, this "history" has been told from the perspective of white interpretation on both sides, with occasional references to a few major black voices (e.g., Frederick Douglass).[44] Our goal is to explore this area of history through the lens of one of the most significant primary sources available to studies on slavery, that is, from the perspectives of those recently held in bondage. What did those persons most directly affected by the enslavement system think about the perpetuation of religious ideologies that kept them in bondage? Did these persons on the margins of US society take opportunities to reflect on and respond to the cultural "logic" guiding the political and economic forces of the day, despite their condition?

The narratives of the formerly enslaved allow us an unprecedented opportunity to hear their contributions to the debates of their day, especially on the religious arguments behind this vast network of forces

39. The historian Eugene Genovese thought that W. E. B. DuBois's numbers—approximately 5 percent of the enslaved had learned to read by 1860—may "be too low" (*Roll, Jordan, Roll: The World the Slaves Made* [New York: Vintage Books, 1974], 563).

40. John Hope Franklin and Alfred A. Moss Jr., *From Slavery to Freedom: A History of African Americans*, 8th ed. (New York: Alfred A. Knopf, 2006), 155.

41. Sojourner Truth dictated her story to Olive Gilbert, who served as editor of *Narrative of Sojourner Truth, a Northern Slave, Emancipated from Bodily Servitude by the State of New York, in 1828* (Boston: The Author, 1850). Truth's contemporary biographer, Nell Irvin Painter, discusses the challenges encountered between the abolitionist editor and Truth's desire to relay her own story, in *Sojourner Truth: A Life, A Symbol* (New York: W. W. Norton & Co., 1996), 103–10.

42. Cf. Elizabeth Fox-Genovese and Eugene D. Genovese, *The Mind of the Master Class: History and Faith in the Southern Slaveholders' Worldview* (Cambridge: Cambridge University Press, 2005).

43. Mark Noll, *The Civil War as a Theological Crisis* (Chapel Hill: University of North Carolina Press, 2006).

44. To Noll's credit, he provides a brief section on "African Americans, the Bible, and Slavery" (*Civil War as a Theological Crisis*, 64–72). See Johnson, *Myth of Ham*.

maintaining the institution of enslavement. Of course, our consideration of the biblical texts within the freedom narratives is far more general than this. Many of the texts are not utilized as a critique of their white counterparts but simply for exploring their own concerns, celebrating freedom with a psalm, mourning death with a lamentation, as well as declaring their own theological justification of their freedom from their own Scriptures. We want to tell the story of their engagement with the Bible in light of that context.

To recover the early history of a black biblical hermeneutic. Many scholars frequently relay the story of black "critical" interpretation of the Bible as if it began *after* the Black Theology movement of the 1960s.[45] This is technically an appropriate way to report the history of African American interpretation, if "critical" is defined as awareness and use of the *historical critical* method. If we define "critical," however, as an engagement with the biblical text that accepts literal interpretations of the ancient text but rejects a simple contemporary application of that interpretation, then we should look further back into African American history.

To put it another way, frequently, the formerly enslaved were critical interpreters of the biblical text, not because they questioned the literal interpretation of a passage, but because they challenged the dominant cultural (and popular) paradigm of appropriation associated with the interpretive tradition of a biblical reading. Vincent Wimbush has recognized this kind of critical engagement with the Bible in African American interpretive circles long before the civil rights movement of the twentieth century.[46] He focused his attention, among other things, on the antebellum spirituals as one form of biblical interpretation, at least with respect to their critical reinterpretation of the Christian tradition.[47]

More recently, Wimbush has turned his attention to one of the earliest accounts in the freedom narrative tradition, one written by Olaudah Equiano, as a way of fully exploring the "first reading" contact of Africans with the Bible that he outlined in his 1991 "interpretive

45. See Michael Brown, *Blackening of the Bible: The Aims of African American Biblical Scholarship* (Harrisburg, PA: Trinity Press Int., 2004).

46. "The Bible and African Americans: An Outline of an Interpretive History," in *Stony the Road We Trod*, ed. Cain Hope Felder (Minneapolis: Fortress Press, 1991), 81–97. Also, Vincent Wimbush, "'Rescue the Perishing': The Importance of Biblical Scholarship in Black Christianity," in *Black Theology: A Documentary History, vol. 2, 1980–1992*, ed. James H. Cone and Gayraud S. Wilmore (Maryknoll, NY: Orbis Books, 1993), 210–15.

47. Wimbush, "The Bible and African Americans," 87–89.

history."[48] We too have tried to engage these early semibiographical narratives as significant, early examples of black critical readings of the Bible.[49] Part of our goal in this project is to recover and narrate some of this early engagement with the Bible as a way of tracing the origins of a black biblical hermeneutic. Generally, we are narrowly focused on the narratives of the formerly enslaved, primarily because these primary sources have been overlooked in this regard. A fuller investigation into African American hermeneutics would move beyond the narratives to include also the spirituals, sermons, ecclesial publications, and public speeches.[50]

To show the extensive role of black agency. All in all, our interest lies in relating part of the history of black agency.[51] African Americans were engaged in the processes of their day, despite the social, political, and ideological barriers challenging their involvement. The narratives give us one significant window into that period and allow us to hear, even if only partially, the words of those on the borderlines of bondage and freedom. In a country that considered itself to be a "Christian Nation,"[52] these Americans, without the rights of full citizenship, wrestled too with their Bible and discovered interpretations, whether in community or on their own, that allowed for potential liberating possibilities for their cause and for their own lives. These formerly enslaved individuals lifted up the pen to write and raised the voice to speak about an experience of enslavement that included a religious setting in which the Bible was frequently interpreted to enforce and maintain their status and condition. For the most part, they sifted through these theological constructions to reclaim the Bible for themselves and placed it on the side of the oppressed. In light of the conditions of the day, this took an unimaginable ingenuity.

---

48. Vincent Wimbush, *White Men's Magic: Scripturalization as Slavery* (Oxford: Oxford University Press, 2012). See also Willie Jennings's utilization of Equiano's story to explore the intersections of race and theology, in *The Christian Imagination: Theology and the Origins of Race* (New Haven, CT: Yale University Press, 2011), 169–203.

49. See Rodney Sadler and Emerson Powery, "Reading against Jesus: Nineteenth-Century African Americans' View of Sabbath Law," *SBL Forum* 3.5 (2004), www.sbl-site.org. Also, see Powery, "'Rise Up Ye Women': Harriet Jacobs and the Bible," *Postscripts: The Journal of Sacred Texts and Contemporary Worlds* 5.2 (2009): 171–84.

50. See Allen Callahan, *The Talking Book: African Americans and the Bible* (New Haven, CT: Yale University Press, 2006).

51. Walter Johnson explores the complex nature of discerning human "agency" among enslaved people within the North American context, in "Agency: A Ghost Story," in Richard Follett, Eric Foner, and Walter Johnson, *The Problem of Freedom in the Age of Emancipation* (Baltimore: Johns Hopkins University Press, 2012), 8–30.

52. See, among others, John Fea's *Was America Founded as a Christian Nation? A Historical Introduction* (Louisville, KY: Westminster John Knox Press, 2011); also Richard Hughes, *Myths America Lives By,* especially his chapter on the "Christian nation" (Urbana: University of Illinois Press, 2004). Sylvester Johnson tackles this popular assumption from the nineteenth-century black perspective (*Myth of Ham*).

They took a text—used against them—and made it their own, often reversing the implications of normative mainline interpretive patterns. Furthermore, many of them told their stories publicly. Countless others relayed them privately. As Yolanda Pierce recognizes, our authors operated out of a liminal space, neither enslaved nor free, that effected their hermeneutical decisions: "Because a liminal space is one of possibility, its occupant is free to determine his or her direction and identity."[53] In the public narratives, they left behind a legacy of their commitment, a snapshot of their lives, a challenge to the system of bondage, and a critical engagement with the sacred texts of the cultural religious tradition.

THE NARRATIVES: AN INTRODUCTION

As Albert Raboteau concluded in *Slave Religion*, "The missionary's ideal picture of a Christianized master-slave relationship contributed to the Southern myth of the benevolent, planter-patriarch presiding benignly over his happy black folks. In reality it was realized no more frequently than most religious ideals."[54] Among other things, the unsuccessful nature of this "Southern myth" was visible in the presence of the individuals who had escaped bondage and lived to tell a different story. When a few of the formerly enslaved picked up their pens, they responded directly to this myth in order to (re)shape Northern perspectives on the Southern institution; as persons tenuously free, their new interstitial existence belied the reality of the myth.

In this project, our primary interest lies in the dozens of narratives published before the Civil War (1861–1865). A large number of formerly enslaved persons wrote their accounts themselves; others dictated their stories to white abolitionist editors, who occasionally rearranged the story lines for a public hearing. In most of these political stories prior to the war, emancipation was the driving theme within the accounts and, for our purposes, one of the significant (if not the most significant) hermeneutical lenses for engaging biblical passages of relevance to their times.

These nineteenth-century African American autobiographical narratives are part of a specific genre, generally following prescribed themes

---

53. Pierce, *Hell without Fires: Slavery, Christianity, and the Antebellum Spiritual Narrative* (Gainesville: University Press of Florida, 2005), 67.
54. Raboteau, *Slave Religion*, 165.

laid out by the abolitionist community.[55] The majority of these individuals began their lives in bondage in the American South and gained their freedom after spending many years enslaved. These texts describe the nature of slavery, its effects on the subject, the institutions that governed enslaved lives, and significant events in the subjects' lives that led to their freedom. They were not simply dispassionate rehearsals of these events but were usually (though not exclusively) composed as public political documents, used to further the abolitionist cause by demonstrating that slavery was an inhumane institution that robbed human beings not only of their liberty, but of their very lives. As Harriet Jacobs wisely put it, "There are wrongs which even the grave does not bury."[56]

Our interest in this collection of material from the nineteenth century is of a *religious* nature; more specifically, the role of biblical interpretation within these narratives.[57] For many of the formerly enslaved (though not all), their stories reflect on their past circumstances of bondage and their present desires of freedom for others, with attention to the relationship between God and slavery. In the words of one of these authors, "There is not a solitary decree of the immaculate God that has been concerned in the ordination of slavery, nor does any possible development of [God's] holy will sanctify it."[58] These words come from the Rev. James Pennington, who was formerly enslaved and eventually became a leading African American abolitionist after gleaning his formal theological education sitting outside of classrooms at Yale Divinity School.[59]

In chapter 2, we discuss how the Bible functioned as a symbol within these narratives, marking title pages (occasionally) and appearing symbolically throughout their stories, even when no direct quotation was in mind. It is important, however, not to overstate the case. Many narratives of the formerly enslaved do not include references to the Bible, exegetically or figuratively. Several African American narratives were not influenced positively by any Christian ideas or rhetoric.

---

55. See Theodore Weld, *American Slavery as It Is: Testimony of a Thousand Witnesses* (New York: American Anti-Slavery Society, 1839). Benjamin Quarles calls Weld "the driving spirit behind the organized abolitionist movement" before 1840, in *Lincoln and the Negro* (New York: Oxford University Press, 1962), 46.

56. Jacobs, *Incidents*, 294*.

57. Charles Long, *Significations: Signs, Symbols, and Images in the Interpretation of Religion* (Minneapolis: Augsburg/Fortress Press, 1986), 179. See Abraham Smith, "Putting 'Paul' Back Together Again: William Wells Brown's *Clotel* and Black Abolitionist Approaches to Paul," *Semeia* 83/84 (1998): 251–62; R. S. Sugirtharajah, *The Bible and the Third World: Precolonial, Colonial, and Postcolonial Encounters* (Cambridge: Cambridge University Press, 2001), 74–109; Margaret Aymer, who focuses more on Douglass's letters than his narratives, in *First Pure, Then Peaceable: Frederick Douglass Reads James* (New York: T. & T. Clark, 2008); and Callahan, *Talking Book*.

58. James Pennington, *The Fugitive Blacksmith* (London: Charles Gilpin, 1849), 76*.

59. Pennington was a minister who succeeded Theodore Sedgwick Wright at Shiloh Presbyterian Church in New York City. In 1849, he received an honorary doctorate from the University of Heidelberg.

But most were! Many of these accounts engage the Bible, directly and indirectly, in order to place these sacred texts on the side of the cause of emancipation.

Furthermore, the *symbolic function* of the Bible expressed larger cultural expectations about its apparent usefulness to mark the significance of one's life, especially in ways that influence the conversation about slavery. As one (white?) anonymous author wrote, "Aaron has a great knowledge of the Bible but cannot read a word." In the nineteenth century, the Bible held an unmatched cultural position as a tool that speaks to peoples' lives—spiritually, religiously, and politically—and, accordingly, it held high cultural value within the African American oral community, even without African Americans ever reading it for themselves. (African American spirituals provide excellent examples of this oral cultural impact.)

On the other hand, once the formerly enslaved began to read and write *critically* (and these narratives were representative of this process), an engagement with the texts of the Bible (and the literacy needed to interpret it) began to produce some popular *but critical* assessment of the words in the Bible's pages. These stories, then, enlighten an immediate generation of the need to talk back to the "talking book" for purposes of individual survival and community uplift.[60]

THE SABBATH, BIBLE READING, AND LITERACY

Antebellum Sabbath gatherings among the enslaved were closely monitored and frequently disrupted. Nat Turner's insurrection (1831) forced many independent African American churches to join their white counterparts formally.[61]

From the religion of their oppressors, African Americans inherited a belief in the Sabbath that encompassed rest from labor, worship of God, and a time for social engagement. For some of them, this was an opportunity for subversive activity as well. Not only was it a time when God guaranteed them one day each week for respite and spiritual and intellectual nurture; a few of them could plan opportunities for escape.

---

60. The metaphor originates with James Gronniosaw, in the first published freedom narrative, *A Narrative of the Most Remarkable Particulars in the Life of James Albert Ukawsaw Gronniosaw, An African Prince, As Related by Himself* (orig. published in 1772). See Henry Louis Gates, *Signifying Monkey: A Theory of African American Literary Criticism* (New York: Oxford University Press, 1988), 132. Gronniosaw published seven editions and sold thousands of copies up through 1811.

61. Raboteau, *Slave Religion*, 178.

Yet many of the enslaved were not allowed to attend to this biblical Sabbath mandate, due to state literacy laws in some instances and
to local white religious biases in others. Much of the discussion in
the narratives of the formerly enslaved emphasized this point, that
is, how slave laws obstructed the observation and practice of Sabbath law.[62] In the narratives of the 1840s in particular, many discuss the unevenness of the practice of Sabbath law in their respective
enslaved communities, in order to inform Northern audiences of the
general failure of this biblical practice in Southern polite "Christian"
society.[63]

Two motifs predominate the discussions of the Sabbath day in the
slave narrative tradition, which we explore in chapter 3. First, on this
day, the establishment of Sabbath-day schools was a viable option,
which would allow for opportunities for securing literacy *and* developing community. The *second* major motif that emerges from the narratives of the formerly enslaved is that the Sabbath day was potentially
an occasion for the enslaved to make a literal, physical escape. Both
motifs can be viewed under the larger umbrella of "freedom"—spiritually, emotionally, intellectually, *and* literally—the theme that drove
these antebellum stories.

For authors of the autobiographical slave narratives, the Sabbath,
if practiced correctly, was a symbol for freedom in all of its manifestations. The freedom narratives call for a significant reorientation of
the belief in the Sabbath law. In an attempt to raise the ire of white
(Christian) abolitionists, African Americans endeavored to convince
their audiences of the inconsistent practice surrounding this biblical
commandment within the slaveholding communities of the South.
Whatever else the Sabbath day may have meant to nineteenth-century
African Americans in the antebellum period, it was also intended to
be a time for community and a time for liberation. In fact, Sabbath
ideology helped to facilitate the development of the early black church
movement and corporate autonomy.[64]

---

62. Mary Prince provides an excellent example in *The History of Mary Prince, A West Indian Slave. Related by
Herself. With a Supplement by the Editor* (London: Published by F. Westley and A. H. Davis, 1831), 23*. Almost a
decade later, in 1839, Theodore Weld published *American Slavery*, in which he requested more testimonies from
those who had escaped the immoral institution.

63. Prior to 1820, most of the enslaved had not yet been convinced of Christianity's value (Raboteau, *Slave Religion*, 149), so this may partially explain the rise of the freedom narratives during the 1840s and 1850s.

64. Without reference to Sabbath law, Raboteau makes a related point: "In some areas of the South, the 'rise of
the black church' was not a post- but a pre-emancipation phenomenon" (*Slave Religion*, 196). This seems to have
been true even among non-free African Americans.

THE CONSTRUCTION OF "RACE" AND THE BIBLE

It is not hard to imagine that one popular topic in Sabbath schools would have been the biblical origins of race. These issues inhabited the air of the decades leading up to the Civil War, and the Bible played a primary role in discussions on the origins of racial groups. A thorough biblical investigation of "race" was less popular, however, than interest in the scriptural passages supporting slavery. Indeed, in most circles the two were commonly conflated. Yet, as Mark Noll succinctly put it, "[o]n slavery, exegetes stood for a commonsense reading of the Bible. On race, exegetes forsook the Bible and relied on common sense."[65]

Of course, the so-called "curse of Ham" account provided wide popular support for the dominant racial myth of the nineteenth century, even though Genesis 9 was not closely examined by most.[66] Even among black interpreters, it was common to accept the *blackness* of Ham's (and, Canaan's) skin color, despite the lack of exegetical evidence within the biblical narrative itself. Many African Americans innocently shared the larger cultural assumption that Genesis 9 was a statement on racial origins.[67]

But independent African American thinkers discovered other biblical passages more suitable for their purposes. In chapter 4, we center our attention on William Anderson's interpretation of 2 Kings 5, which was examined to explain skin origins. Anderson discovered an alternative biblical story to confront the dominant popular myth and turned his attention to the story's conclusion: "And [Gehazi] went out from [Elisha's] presence," in the King James Version, "a leper as white as snow." For Anderson, *whiteness*, not blackness, was the curse![68]

THE "MASTER'S MINISTER" AND THE (PAULINE) BIBLE

In chapter 5, we give consideration to how Paul and his writings were reread in order to locate emancipation *from* the "master's minister."[69]

---

65. Noll, *America's God: From Jonathan Edwards to Abraham Lincoln* (New York: Oxford University Press, 2005), 418.

66. See Thomas Virgil Peterson, *Ham and Japheth: The Mythic World of Whites in the Antebellum South*, ATLA Monograph Series 12 (Lanham, MD: Scarecrow Press, 1978). As Stephen Haynes suggests, it is difficult to determine at what point slavery and race became conflated with Genesis 9 in Western interpretations (*Noah's Curse: The Biblical Justification of American Slavery* [New York: Oxford University Press, 2002], 6–8).

67. According to Sylvester Johnson, it was impossible to do otherwise, but William Andrews will be an example of one who did.

68. Toni Morrison's question seems apropos: "What happens to the writerly imagination of a black author who is at some level *always* conscious of representing one's own race to, or in spite of, a race of readers that understands itself to be 'universal' or race-free?" (*Playing in the Dark: Whiteness and the Literary Imagination* [New York: Vintage, 1993], xii).

69. The term "master's minister" derives from Nancy Ambrose, as told by her grandson, Howard Thurman, in *Jesus and the Disinherited* (Boston: Beacon Press, 1949), 30.

The "master's minister," as we learn from Nancy Ambrose (Howard Thurman's grandmother) and many other formerly enslaved persons, loved to pontificate on Paul. Sabbath schools, among the darker races, would have provided opportunities to compare notes on the sermons they heard. Was "Brother Saul" really in favor of their bondage and mistreatment? They could then wrestle, exegetically and critically, with the Pauline passages utilized in these speeches. Henry Bibb acknowledges as much in 1849, writing about the absence of *black* Sabbath schools in Kentucky.[70] The enslaved, "with but few exceptions," did *not* trust in this type of (white) utilization of the Bible. Despite the lack of religious education, the enslaved would not accept their condition as divinely ordained. Intuitively, black Christians developed a distinctive hermeneutical approach to these passages, while others walked away from such a Pauline-dominated religion.

Addressing the Paul of the "master's minister" was not the only focus within these African American sources. There were other active agents of interpretation who circumvented the Pauline obedience passages altogether and discovered a Paul they could embrace. Many of them—including Solomon Bayley (1825) and Richard Allen (1833)—found a cosufferer who could relate to their present circumstances of abuse, neglect, and impoverishment while they journeyed through life.[71] They discovered a biblical Paul (in the letters *and* the Acts of the Apostles) who spoke to their condition.

If the freedom narratives are representative of black interpretation, many of the enslaved discovered that the Pauline letters could be read in alternative ways. "Servants, obey your masters" would not be the final word. Rather, a theological commitment to God's love would preempt their hermeneutical approach. They knew it intuitively and believed it theologically. As many contemporary scholars recognize, however, the New Testament presented a critical challenge for the abolitionist position.[72] Yet these early black biblical interpreters developed a

---

70. "This is where they have no Sabbath Schools; no one to read the Bible to them; no one to preach the gospel who is competent to expound the Scriptures, except slaveholders. And the slaves, with but few exceptions, have no confidence at all in their preaching because they preach a pro-slavery doctrine" (Henry Bibb, *Narrative of the Life and Adventures of Henry Bibb, An American Slave, Written by Himself* [New York: Author, 1849], 23–24*).

71. The cosufferer motif is most clearly present in Solomon Bayley's and William Anderson's narratives (see chap. 5). See Raquel St. Clair's recent critique of womanist's emphases on Jesus as "co-sufferer," in *Call and Consequences: A Womanist Reading of Mark* (Minneapolis: Fortress Press, 2008).

72. See Caroline Shanks, "The Biblical Antislavery Argument of the Decade, 1830–1840," *Journal of Negro History* 16 (1931): 151; also J. Albert Harrill: "Most embarrassing for today's readers of the Bible, the proslavery spokesmen were defending the more defensible position from the perspective of historical criticism" ("The Use of the New Testament in the American Slave Controversy: A Case History in the Hermeneutical Tension between Biblical Criticism and Christian Moral Debate," *Religion and American Culture* 10 [2000]: 174).

hermeneutics of survival that allowed the biblical Paul—who believed in a God who "hath made of one blood all nations"—to remain within their canon.

SIGNIFICANCE OF THE NARRATIVE FOR AFRICAN AMERICAN BIBLICAL HERMENEUTICS

Raboteau wisely comments about the engagement between Christianity and African Americans in the early decades of the nineteenth century: "The slaves did not simply become Christians; they creatively fashioned a Christian tradition to fit their own peculiar experience of enslavement in America."[73] This "peculiar experience" was shaped—positively and negatively—by a sporadic and highly creative engagement with the Christian Bible. For the formerly enslaved who penned their own narratives, literacy meant the beginning of basic freedom. *Biblical* literacy allowed these black interpreters to "talk back" to the "talking book" and thereby to engage in a critical hermeneutical challenge to the widespread oppressive use of Scripture on the side of the peculiar institution.

Their God and their Bible would not allow for the dehumanization of those on the underside of life. Their God and their Bible were more inclusive than that. It was also, as Vincent Wimbush suggests, an attempt "to enter the mainstream of American society."[74] As interpreters of the sacred text, they too could engage in the religious practices informed by an interpretive tradition. And they would push back when they needed to do so. Critical interrogation of the Bible was as crucial, in American society, as a careful understanding of the United States Constitution. Therefore, as demonstrated by their reading of biblical texts—well before President Lincoln's Emancipation Proclamation[75]—there existed at the core of their religious beliefs a firm conviction in the God of freedom and a hermeneutical strategy that claimed the Bible as the *genesis of liberation*.

73. Raboteau, *Slave Religion*, 209.
74. Wimbush, "The Bible and African Americans," 93.
75. The proclamation to free the enslaved within Southern territories was a central political strategy to increase the success of Lincoln's primary goal to restore the Union. Also, the proclamation, at least, opened up the opportunity for the formerly enslaved to join the Union army (George M. Fredrickson, "A Man but Not a Brother: Abraham Lincoln and Racial Equality," *The Journal of Southern History* 41/1 [Feb. 1975]). Less well-known in the national memory surrounding the Emancipation Proclamation was Lincoln's desire to recolonize African Americans (i.e., "Negro deportation"). Yet, as Benjamin Quarles points out, the public document was well received, and Lincoln himself too became a positively mythic figure in the black imagination (*Lincoln and the Negro* (New York: Oxford University Press, 1962), 131).

2

The Bible and the Freedom Narrative

"Survival in fact is about the connections between things."
(Edward Said)

"Aaron has a great knowledge of the Bible but cannot read a word."
(Anonymous)

INTRODUCTION

President Abraham Lincoln's public announcement of the Emancipation Proclamation in 1863 was a formal declaration of liberation for enslaved individuals held in bondage in Confederate-held states.[1] Although this political pronouncement created anxious excitement throughout the land, emancipatory activities had been in motion for a period before 1863. Prior to Lincoln's proclamation, many African Americans had begun seizing opportunities for their own individual (and, at times, collective) "emancipations."[2] In the earliest stages of the Civil War, some Southern enslaved African Americans escaped from bondage, infiltrated the camps of the Union armies, and assumed (despite Lincoln's public political rhetoric) that they would be welcome, since this war was for their emancipation.[3] At the same time, many Northern African Americans, months *before* the proclamation,

---

1. This political proclamation applied only to slave states in rebellion against the Union, not border slave states (e.g., Delaware, Kentucky, Maryland, and Missouri).

2. Following the research in Wilbur H. Siebert, *The Underground Railroad from Slavery to Freedom* (New York: The MacMillan Co., 1898), Franklin and Moss, *From Slavery to Freedom: A History of African Americans*, 8th ed. (New York: Alfred A. Knopf, 2006), places the number at approximately 100,000 escapees between 1810 and 1850.

3. See Benjamin Quarles, *Lincoln and the Negro* (New York: Oxford University Press, 1962); Fredrickson, "A Man but Not a Brother: Abraham Lincoln and Racial Equality," *The Journal of Southern History* 41/1 (Feb. 1975), 39–58.

organized troops in order to enlist, although they were firmly turned away from Lincoln's army.

More directly related to this project, emancipation was signified most clearly in the stories of escape, both oral and written narratives, of the formerly enslaved—what we prefer to call the "freedom narratives." These nineteenth-century African American autobiographical freedom narratives describe the nature of slavery, its effects on the subject, the institutions that governed enslaved lives, and significant events in the subject's life that led to their freedom. Among other things, they were abolitionist documents utilized to rally Northern sympathizers for the cause of emancipation. Charles Long drew our attention to these literary sites long ago, as one way to gain understanding of the "experience of the holy" among nineteenth-century African Americans.[4] Our interest in this collection of material from the nineteenth century is of a *religious* nature, more specifically, the role of biblical interpretation within these narratives.

Approximately two years *after* the formal announcement of the Emancipation Proclamation, President Lincoln gave the Second Inaugural Address, a sober address, as the Civil War was near its end. In it, he exclaimed, "Both read the same Bible, and pray to the same God; and each invokes His aid against the other."[5] In this address on March 4, 1865, the most theological of its kind, Lincoln wrestled with the political and theological conclusions of the devastating Civil War.[6] "The prayers of both," he continued, "could not be answered; that of neither has been answered fully." Despite what many historians debate today, Lincoln stated unequivocally the purpose of the war in this address: "These slaves constituted a peculiar and powerful interest. All knew that this interest was, somehow, the cause of the war." Yet Lincoln still recognized the sovereignty of the Divine: "The Almighty has His own purposes." At the same time, he also implied that the time for the end of the peculiar institution had come, as (apparently) one of God's objectives.[7] As Richard Hughes assesses this speech, "Within this con-

---

4. Charles Long, *Significations: Signs, Symbols, and Images in the Interpretation of Religion* (Minneapolis: Augsburg/Fortress Press, 1986), 179. See recently the theological attention to these sources, e.g., Willie Jennings, *Christian Imagination: Theology and the Origins of Race* (New Haven, CT: Yale University Press, 2011). See Vincent Wimbush, "The Bible and African Americans: An Outline of an Interpretive History," in *Stony the Road We Trod*, ed. Cain Hope Felder (Minneapolis: Fortress Press, 1991), 88–89.

5. Abraham Lincoln, "Second Inaugural Address," Washington, DC, March 4, 1865.

6. See Ronald C. White Jr., *Lincoln's Greatest Speech: The Second Inaugural* (New York: Simon & Schuster Lincoln Library, 2006).

7. "If we shall suppose that American Slavery is one of those offences, which, in the providence of God, must needs come, but which, having continued through His appointed time, He now wills to remove, and that He gives to both North and South, this terrible war, as the woe due to those by whom the offence came, shall we discern

text, Lincoln understood the war as a judgment from a righteous God on a sinful people on both sides of the Mason-Dixon Line."[8]

The sixteenth president's theological reflection—"Both read the same Bible, and pray to the same God"—is central to our book's objective. But did they *really* read the same book?[9] To some extent they did, in that abolitionists and proslavery sympathizers used the same physical object, in the form of the King James Version. But did white Northerners and white Southerners—the interpreters Lincoln had in mind—make the same hermeneutical decisions? More directly related to our project is to give attention to specific members of the abolitionist wing who are often overlooked by contemporary historians and are not implied either in President Lincoln's remarks: *How did the formerly enslaved read the Bible?*

As a way of exploring the hermeneutical decisions of the enslaved that helped foster an African American hermeneutic of emancipation, this chapter will take up themes from within the tradition of the freedom narratives: (1) the slaveholder's Bible, to establish a broad context; (2) the trope of the "talking book"; (3) the enslaved's encounter with the Bible, symbolically (e.g., on title pages, etc.) and interpretively. We wish to show how formerly enslaved African Americans were active agents in the eventual liberation of all, rather than passive objects waiting for rescue. One way in which they did this was by carefully managing a religious interpretive tradition (especially as it related to the Bible) that was formidably stacked against them.[10]

THE SLAVEHOLDER'S BIBLE AND SLAVERY

Southern Christians—and many in the North—considered the Bible to be a supportive resource for a slaveholding society. Many biblical passages acknowledged the durable practice of enslavement in ancient Near Eastern contexts: Leviticus 25:44–46; Exodus 21:2–11; Ephesians 6:5; 1 Timothy 6:1–2. There is no reason to rehearse here the interpretation of these passages or the worldview surrounding the ancient texts

therein any departure from those divine attributes which the believers in a Living God always ascribe to Him?" (paragraph 3).

8. Richard Hughes, *Myths America Lives By* (Urbana: University of Illinois Press, 2004), 42.

9. Recently, much attention has been given to various interpretive approaches among abolitionists, on the one hand, and proslavery advocates, on the other hand (e.g., Noll, *The Civil War as a Theological Crisis* [Chapel Hill: University of North Carolina Press, 2006]).

10. Our larger objective is to investigate the origins of a *black* biblical hermeneutic, available to us in the narrative tradition of the formerly enslaved.

of the Bible in support of this critical sociopolitical and economic issue. The biblical injunction "Slaves, obey your masters" was part of the regular homiletical rhetoric of pre–Civil War society. With so much religious support for the institution, as Allen Callahan aptly put it in his study on African American interpretation, "The Talking Book was also a poison book."[11] What is not as clear within biblical literature itself was general support for the *racialist* tendencies of the slave institution within the United States. On this matter, ambiguity abounded in nineteenth-century interpretation. The racialist dimension of so-called "New World" slavery was a post-Enlightenment development that involved many members of the intelligentsia in philosophy, science, and the broader humanities. Our most immediate concern is with the standard belief in the antebellum period of the 1830s through the 1850s. What did slaveholding religion promote about the Bible's position on its support for slave labor?

More than forty years ago, H. Shelton Smith argued that antebellum Protestant ministers and Catholic priests alike (with key reinforcements in the North) considered African American people to be inferior *and* the enslaved to be "property."[12] In conjunction with this ideological perspective on basic humanity, the Bible provided a supportive theological resource for a slaveholding institution. A leading example of the influence of this position can be found in the words of the formidable statesman and senator from South Carolina who had earlier served as vice president of the United States, 1825–1832, John C. Calhoun, called by Herbert Aptheker, "the most profound and most influential of the officeholders and ideologists of the slaveholding class."[13]

In their "natural" position, the enslaved were, according to Senator Calhoun, in Aptheker's words, "indispensable to a viable social order, to the safety of the Republic, to a sane view of religion."[14] Here are Calhoun's own words, in a speech on the Senate floor in 1836: "The war which the abolitionists wage against us . . . is a war of religion and political favoritism . . . waged, not against our lives, but our character. . . . We cannot remain here in an endless struggle in defense of our character, our property, and institutions."[15]

11. Allen D. Callahan, *The Talking Book: African Americans and the Bible* (New Haven, CT: Yale University Press, 2006), 25.

12. H. Shelton Smith, *In His Image but . . . Racism in Southern Religion, 1780–1910* (Durham, NC: Duke University Press, 1972).

13. Herbert Aptheker, *Abolitionism: A Revolutionary Movement* (Boston: G. K. Hall & Co., 1989), 19.

14. Aptheker, *Abolitionism*, 20.

15. John C. Calhoun, Senate speech, March 9, 1836; cited in Aptheker, *Abolitionism*, 21.

In the same year, in the president's "Annual Message to Congress," President Andrew Jackson "decried the abolitionists' postal campaign and urged Congress to ban antislavery literature from the United States mail."[16] Generally, the political machine enforced the peculiar institution. But the mood was shifting. In the 1840s, there was a growing hesitation to enforce the Fugitive Slave Law of 1793.[17] As another sign of the political shift, the production of the freedom narratives increased significantly.

In 1849, in a literary review of the publication of Henry Bibb's *Narrative*, an anonymous reviewer concluded his favorable evaluation (e.g., "narratives of slaves go right to the hearts of [humanity]," he wrote) with a challenge to Calhoun: "If Mr. Calhoun really means to uphold slavery, he *must* . . . abolish Christianity, printing, art, science, and take his patriarchs back to the standard of Central Africa, or the days of Shem, Ham and Japhet [*sic*]."[18] According to this reviewer, slavery was directly opposed to Christianity and modern civilization, a direct challenge to Calhoun's arguments that "civilization" advances through the accumulation of wealth, even if human bondage was one of the necessary outcomes of this economic progress.[19]

These narratives—autobiographical as they may be with concise political objectives—tackled the difficult task of biblical interpretation within a nineteenth-century North American landscape in which the Bible supported many competing alliances.[20] Recall James Pennington's theological claim offered above that God had no hand in slavery. Pennington was not alone. The objective of all former slaves was well defined. In light of the Bible's dominant ideological function within

16. James B. Stewart, *Holy Warriors: The Abolitionists and American Society*, rev. ed. (New York: Hill & Wang, 1997), 71. According to Finkelman, from 1801 to 1861, only one president forcefully opposed slavery: John Quincy Adams ("Introduction: Defending Slavery," in *Defending Slavery: Proslavery Thought in the Old South: A Brief History with Documents* [Boston/New York: Bedford/St. Martin's, 2003; 2]). Although President Van Buren was apparently opposed to the institution, he did not actively develop policies to hinder it. On one occasion, Van Buren "asked for an amendment of the [slave trade] law" in 1839 so that the United States would keep its commitments, because the legal abolishment of the African slave trade in 1808 was not halting the process of the trade in human flesh (Franklin and Moss, *From Slavery to Freedom*, 136).

17. Stewart, *Holy Warriors*, 107. One primary difference in the 1850 version of the fugitive slave law was the severe penalty citizens and officials could receive for failure to return escapees to the slave states.

18. *The Anti-Slavery Bugle*, vol. 5, no. 85 (Nov. 3, 1849): 1; reprinted in *The Slave's Narrative*, ed. Charles T. Davis and Henry Louis Gates Jr. (New York: Oxford University Press, 1985), 28–29 (29).

19. Aptheker, *Abolitionism*, 19.

20. To be fair, because of the growing popularity of these accounts, a few penned their narratives for reasons besides their public, political value: Leonard Black wrote to receive financial support to secure ministerial education (*The Life and Sufferings of Leonard Black, a Fugitive from Slavery. Written by Himself* [New Bedford: Benjamin Lindsey, 1847], 3*); Noah Davis wrote to purchase the freedom of two of his children (*A Narrative of the Life of Rev. Noah Davis, a Colored Man. Written by Himself, at the Age of Fifty-Four* [Baltimore: J. F. Weishampel, Jr., 1859], 3*).

this developing "evangelical" environment,[21] the sacred text must be carefully interpreted in order to support the cause for emancipation.

But to claim some overarching general direction of all freedom narratives, with regard to the function of the Bible, is *only* a first step to analyzing the critical function of biblical themes, images, and passages within these (foremost) sources of nineteenth-century African American thought. First, we need to take a brief look at the encounter between African Americans and the Bible, as represented in the earliest narratives of the formerly enslaved.

THE TROPE OF THE "TALKING BOOK" IN THE EARLIEST FREEDOM NARRATIVES

[My master] used to read prayers in public to the ship's crew every Sabbath day; and when first I saw him read, I was never so surprised in my whole life as when I saw the book talk to my master; for I thought it did, as I observed him to look upon it, and move his lips. I wished it would do so with me. As soon as my master had done reading, I follow'd him to the place where he put the book, being mightily delighted with it, and when nobody saw me, I open'd it, and put my ear down close upon it, in great hope that it wou'd say something to me; but was very sorry and greatly disappointed when I found it wou'd not speak, this thought immediately presented itself to me, that every body and every thing despis'd me because I was black.[22]

Starting with this passage, published in the first "slave narrative" of its kind, Henry Louis Gates Jr. has argued for the existence of a trope present in the earliest narratives of the formerly enslaved, beginning with James Gronniosaw's *A Narrative of the Most Remarkable Particulars in the Life of James Albert Ukawsaw Gronniosaw, An African Prince, As Related by Himself* (orig. published in 1772).[23]

Gronniosaw offered no further reflection on his assessment of what was, in his mind, the *racist* "talking book": "every body and every

21. *The Bible in America: Essays in Cultural History*, ed. Nathan Hatch and Mark Noll (New York: Oxford University Press, 1982); Callahan, *Talking Book*.

22. *A Narrative of the Most Remarkable Particulars in the Life of James Albert Ukawsaw Gronniosaw, An African Prince, As Related by Himself* (orig. published in 1772), 10*.

23. Henry Gates Jr., *Signifying Monkey: A Theory of African American Literary Criticism* (New York: Oxford University Press, 1988), 132.

thing despised me because I was black."[24] According to Gates, the trope "of the (non-)Talking book becomes the central scene of instruction against which this black African's entire autobiography must be read."[25] Gates's assessment is worth repeating in full:

> [T]he book had no voice for Gronniosaw; it simply refused to speak to him, or with him. For Gronniosaw, the book—or . . . the very concept of "book"—constituted a silent primary text, a text, however, in which the black (person) found no echo of his own voice. The silent book did not reflect or acknowledge the black presence before it. The book's rather deafening silence renames the received tradition in European letters that the mask of blackness worn by Gronniosaw and his countrymen was a trope of absence.[26]

Gronniosaw was compelled to tell his own story and speak "his face into existence among the authors and texts of the Western tradition."[27]

Gates helpfully traces this trope throughout some of the earliest narratives of the African autobiographical tradition, including John Murrant's *The Narrative of the Lord's Wonderful Dealings with John Murrant, A Black* (1785),[28] Ottobah Cugoano's *Thoughts and Sentiments* (1787),[29] Olaudah Equiano's *The Interesting Narrative of the Life of Olaudah Equiano* (1789)—which become the prototype for the nineteenth-century freedom narrative[30]—and, finally, John Jea's *The Life, History, and Unparalleled Sufferings of John Jea* (1811).[31]

Gates argues that the presence of this trope in these narratives proves that these authors were reading one another's works.[32] Their familiarity and revision of the trope provides evidence of its prominence within the black literary tradition and its popularity among black people. Yet the trope ended with John Jea's 1811 publication. Gates shows that

24. Gates acknowledges that the book in Gronniosaw's account may have been *either* the Bible or a prayer book (*Signifying*, 137). See Callahan, *Talking Book*, 13.

25. Gates, *Signifying*, 137.

26. Gates, *Signifying*, 136–37.

27. Gates, *Signifying*, 137.

28. Murrant's "narrative" is not usually classified formally as a freedom narrative (Gates, *Signifying*, 142).

29. This book "is an impassioned and extended argument for the abolition of slavery, not primarily an autobiography" (Gates, *Signifying*, 147).

30. Gates, *Signifying*, 153. Wimbush assumes that the book that predominates Equiano's story was the Bible, even if other books may have been part of the original historical context (*White Men's Magic: Scripturalization as Slavery* [New York: Oxford University Press, 2012], 65).

31. "Jea's is the last of the great black 'sacred' slave autobiographies. After his text, slave narrators generally relegate the sacred to a tacit presence, while the secular concern with abolition becomes predominant" (Gates, *Signifying* 159). See Yolanda Pierce, *Hell without Fires: Slavery, Christianity, and the Antebellum Spiritual Narrative* (Gainesville: University Press of Florida, 2005). While arguments for abolition become more central in later narratives, the sophisticated rhetorical appropriation of conversion stories and the careful attention to the hermeneutical complexities of the Bible's role in the cultural debates still attest to a deep-seated sensitivity to the sacred.

32. Cugoano and Equiano were friends (Gates, *Signifying*, 152).

Jea's major revisions to ("or erasure" of) the trope caused "the trope of the Talking Book" to disappear from later narratives.[33] Indeed, as Gates recognizes (and as we wish to show further), "the post-Jea narrators refigure the trope of the Talking Book by the secular equation of the mastery of slavery through the 'simple' mastery of letters." Literacy became a prominent objective, even as liberation was the overarching goal. For many of the enslaved authors in the two decades leading up to the Civil War, in their liminal states of freedom, they expressed themselves in both public and written forums, and the emphasis on texts *written by him or herself* in particular displaced the earlier trope of the Talking Book.[34] They were now, in mass (as representatives of the larger race), writing themselves into existence.

The authors of the nineteenth-century freedom narratives had to express themselves to a largely white audience, committed (generally?) to the cause of abolition. These narratives functioned as both "public transcripts" and "hidden transcripts" (to use James C. Scott's and Toni Morrison's categories) for these audiences.[35] On the one hand, atrocities unimaginable needed to be told. On the other hand, the manner in which one told these personal stories was often constrained by the Victorian sensibilities of the wider culture. As William Andrews suggests, "white acceptance of a slave narrative as truth depended on how judiciously the slave had censored the facts of his life into something other than the whole truth," providing a story that was, on the surface, "consistent with white cultural ideals of justice."[36] The authors had serious objectives to accomplish (i.e., the abolition of slavery) and did not want to hinder these broader, desired goals by offending their audience.

It is true, on the one hand, that the specific trope of the "talking book" is absent in the antebellum narratives of the 1830–1861 period. Yet the encounter with the book still resonated with elements of the earlier African (American) tradition. Earlier eighteenth-century authors reflected a period in which they could only "voice" their anxiety over this powerful, symbolical presence of the book: "when nobody saw me, I opened it, and put my ear down close upon it, in great hopes that it

---

33. Gates describes this further as "Signif[lying] upon it by reducing it to the absurd," which did not allow future writers to revise it constructively (Gates, *Signifying*, 166).

34. Gates, *Signifying*, 167.

35. James C. Scott, *Domination and the Arts of Resistance: Hidden Transcripts* (New Haven, CT: Yale University Press, 1992); see Morrison, *Playing in the Dark: Whiteness and the Literary Imagination* (New York: Vintage, 1993).

36. William Andrews, *To Tell a Free Story: The First Century of Afro-American Autobiography, 1760–1865* (Urbana: University of Illinois Press, 1988), 26, 29.

would say something to me; but I was very sorry, and greatly disappointed, when I found that it would not speak."

For later writers, however, literacy was interconnected with notions of "freedom," so their ability to interpret (or reinterpret, reinscribe) meaning to the biblical tradition became central to their justice efforts. Frederick Douglass represented many within the formerly enslaved community when he emphasized in an 1855 speech, "Shall we, therefore, fling the Bible away as a pro-slavery book? It would be as reasonable to do so as it would be to fling away the Constitution."[37] The freedom narratives detailed encounters of literacy and the sacred text, including accounts about the opening of Sabbath schools (see chap. 3). Even those who could not read held the Bible in high regard and understood their spirituality and God's actions among them in relationship to it. For example, in an 1845 dictated narrative, Aaron's narrator claimed, "Aaron has a great knowledge of the Bible but cannot read a word."[38]

Take also, for example, James Pennington—a prominent pastor, thinker, and abolitionist in the 1840–1850s—who published his narrative in 1849. As historian David Swift notes, one of Reverend Pennington's sermons wrestled with the ideological challenge of the Bible:

> "Is the word of God silent on this . . . greatest of . . . curses?" he [Pennington] asked. "I, for one, desire to know. My repentance, my faith, my hope, my love, and my perseverance all . . . turn upon this point. . . . If the word of God does sanction slavery, I want another book, another repentance, another faith, and another hope!" Pennington left no ambiguity about his position on the matter, insisting that "slavery is condemned by the general tenor and scope of the New Testament," which did not sanction cruelty or the imprisonment, starvation, or torture of other human beings.[39]

As Vincent Wimbush has noted, nineteenth-century African Americans offered a "critical, polemical, and race- and culture-conscious reading of the Bible [that] reflected the desire to enter the mainstream of American society. The Bible itself had apparently come to represent American society. So a critical reading of it was a critical reading of

---

37. Frederick Douglass, speech in Boston, Feb. 8, 1855; cited in Harrill, "Use of the New Testament in the American Slave Controversy: A Case History in the Hermeneutical Tension between Biblical Criticism and Christian Moral Debate," *Religion and American Culture* 10 (2000): 160.

38. From the title page, *The Light and Truth of Slavery: Aaron's History* (Worcester, MA: The Author, 1845).

39. David Swift, *Black Prophets of Justice: Activist Clergy before the Civil War* (Baton Rouge: Louisiana State University Press, 1989), 236.

American society."[40] The critical reading of the Bible/society, in light of the condition in which they found themselves, was one of the primary objectives of the narratives of the enslaved. These freedom narratives provide an initial entry point into a critical black hermeneutic. A reconceived and reinterpreted Scripture functioned as an invaluable resource for the liberation of African Americans, serving as a common ground of meaning that facilitated the dialogue between them and their ideological opponents.[41] Before providing specific examples of biblical interpretation within the narratives, we turn our attention to the symbolic presence of the Bible on the cover and title pages of these African American autobiographies.

THE ENCOUNTER WITH THE BIBLE:
THE NARRATIVES' TITLE PAGES AND THE BIBLE

Several narratives offer a biblical verse as part of the title page to their "autobiographical" productions.[42] These verses provide insight into the authors' intentions with their stories, as literary forces for change, and into their understanding of how their objective was (in)directly connected to the Bible.[43] Most of these examples, however, derive from the earlier narratives within the tradition. During the heyday of the popularity of these narratives (1840s–1850s) up until the beginning of the Civil War,[44] few authors would complement their titles with a biblical

---

40. Wimbush, "The Bible and African Americans," 90. He continues: "The clamor from African Americans was for the realization of the principles of inclusion, equality, and kinship that they understood the Bible to mandate."

41. One excellent example is Dwight N. Hopkins and George C. L. Cummings, eds., *Cut Loose Your Stammering Tongue: Black Theology in the Slave Narrative*, 2nd ed. (Louisville, KY: Westminster John Knox Press, 2003). What is missing, even from this fine collection of essays, is any detailed and sustained analysis of the interpretation of biblical texts within the narratives of the formerly enslaved. It is increasingly clear that the genesis of the hermeneutical tradition that has nurtured contemporary African American biblical scholarship can be found in narratives of the enslaved. These black authors employed the Bible in their personal stories told for political reasons established paradigms and principles, and fostered distinctive readings that continue to influence interpretation by their ideological descendants today. Yet there has been little work validating this hypothesis. Despite the increasing activity of African American church historians and theologians examining this genre of literature, their interests lie elsewhere beside the nature of the use of Scripture and the discernment of interpretive strategies.

42. See Andrews, *To Tell a Free Story*. Indeed, the first *novel* by an African American female author, Hannah Craft's *The Bondwoman's Narrative* (b. 1853–1861), includes biblical verses at the beginning of fifteen of eighteen chapters. We are grateful to Jean Corey, a colleague at Messiah College, for bringing this observation to our attention.

43. This is less common than one might expect, even though, as Frances Smith Foster has noted, "[t]hey often prefaced their narratives with verses from the Bible" (Frances Smith Foster, *Witnessing Slavery: The Development of Ante-bellum Slave Narratives* [Westport, CT: Greenwood Press, 1979], 83).

44. Marion Wilson Starling, *The Slave Narrative: Its Place in American History* (Washington, DC: Howard University Press, 1988), 106–220.

verse. They were just as likely to include poetry from an antislavery writer of the previous generation, such as William Cowper.[45]

In the earliest examples of this phenomenon, the biblical citation generally alluded to the spiritual nature of the individual, rather than pointed to the larger political and communal concerns of the day. On his cover, Olaudah Equiano (1789) cited Isaiah 12:2, 4, which highlighted repetitive language of "salvation." George White (1810) included 1 Corinthians 1:27, a statement on God's choice of "the foolish things of the world to confound the wise."[46] Solomon Bayley (1825) also chose words from Paul: "Persecuted, but not forsaken; cast down, but not destroyed" (2 Cor. 5:16). Finally, in 1833, Richard Allen selected Psalm 37:37 to signify his intentions: "Mark the perfect man, and behold the upright; for the end of that man is peace." The latter three—White, Bayley, and Allen—were ministers, and their narratives wrestle as much with their spiritual callings as they do with the peculiar institution from which they were freed. Though few later narratives included a scriptural passage, the phenomenon changes in the decades leading up to the Civil War.

Many white editors of these volumes also included biblical verses on the covers. Abigail Mott (1826) underscored Acts 10:34–35, which provided a widely utilized theological presupposition among abolitionists, both black and white, that God was "no respecter of persons." Rebecca Warren Brown (1832) combined two biblical texts—from Ephesians 1:6 and the Gospel of John—on the cover of her narrative about Mrs. Chloe Spear, even though only the Gospel passage seemed to allude to liberation: "If the Son shall make you free, you shall be free indeed" (John 8:36). While Elizabeth's *Memoir of Old Elizabeth* (1863) and Peter Wheeler's *Chains and Freedom* (1839) were accounts taken from their "own lips," it was more likely that the white editors supplied biblical passages for the title pages, using Galatians 3:28 and Romans 12:16 respectively. Despite the apparent relevance of Galatians 3 ("there is neither bond nor free"), this passage was not commonly cited in black-authored narratives among the formerly enslaved.[47]

Among black-authored accounts, we find two examples of this phenomenon. On the 1849 title page of James Pennington's *The Fugitive*

---

45. E.g., William Craft, *Running a Thousand Miles for Freedom: Or, The Escape of William and Helen Craft from Slavery* (London: William Tweedie, 1860).

46. Yolanda Pierce recognizes the critical role a "conversion" played in George White's story, allowing him, "to create a new identity for himself," one "not assigned . . . by others" (*Hell without Fires*, 17).

47. As one of the early African American female ministers, it is at least possible that Gal. 3:28 also proceeded from Elizabeth's "own lips."

Blacksmith, in addition to mentioning his pastorate of the prominent African American congregation of Shiloh Presbyterian Church in New York City,[48] he cited a verse from the book of Isaiah: "Let thine outcasts dwell with thee, Moab; be thou a covert to them from the face of the spoiler" (Isa. 16:4).

Pennington's narrative provided a story about, as Yuval Taylor explains, "a lie as resourceful and inventive as any in the trickster-slave tradition,"[49] a lie necessary to overcome the impoverished and inhumane situation. Since America's laws classified the enslaved as human chattel, Pennington identified "truths" or "lies," in his own words, as "private property."[50] At first glance, the Isaiah citation could be interpreted to emphasize the covert nature of Pennington's undertaking, an escape from bondage in Maryland. But God, through the prophet Isaiah, requested for Moab, Israel's neighbor, to be the "covert."[51] In the Old-English discourse of the King James Version, "covert" was a noun for a "covering, shelter, or hiding place." The verses surrounding the prophet's specific citation, Isaiah 16:3–5, provide a fitting context and may indicate Pennington's interest more clearly:

> Take counsel, execute judgment; make thy shadow as the night in the midst of the noonday; hide the outcasts; betray not him that wandereth. *Let mine outcasts dwell with thee, Moab; be thou a covert to them from the face of the spoiler:* for the extortioner is at an end, the spoiler ceaseth, the oppressors are consumed out of the land. And in mercy shall the throne be established: and he shall sit upon it in truth in the tabernacle of David, judging, and seeking judgment, and hasting righteousness.[52]

With this verse, Pennington signified a God who, he believed, prepared a "covert" (KJV) or a "refuge" (NRSV) for those escaping from the crucial Southern institution and, in his case, did not betray the "fugitive blacksmith."[53]

A late contemporary of Pennington, William Craft, also appropriated this passage from Isaiah in his freedom narrative, *Running a*

---

48. A congregation Theodore S. Wright, a free black (who died in 1847), founded. Wright's protégé, Henry Highland Garnet, succeeded Pennington in 1856. See Timothy Smith, "Slavery and Theology: The Emergence of Black Christian Consciousness in Nineteenth-Century America," *Church History* 41 (1972): 497–512 (511).

49. *I Was Born a Slave: An Anthology of Classic Slave Narratives, Volume One, 1772–1849*, ed. Yuval Taylor (Chicago: Lawrence Hill Books, 1999), 104.

50. James Pennington, *Fugitive Blacksmith* (London: Charles Gilpin, 1849), 22.

51. "Covert" (KJV) is translated as "refuge" in the NRSV.

52. Pennington cited the italicized segment.

53. Pennington's language of the "fugitive" for the title of his narrative may derive from Isaiah as well, "betray not him that wandereth."

Thousand Miles for Freedom (1860), although not on the title page. Craft cited Isaiah 16:3, which Pennington only alluded to: "Hide not the outcast. Betray not him that wandereth." Craft did so in the context of his challenge to the Fugitive Slave Law of 1850 and the active involvement of some Northerners in tracking down and returning so-called fugitives in the 1850s. After the passing of the Fugitive Slave Law, between 9,000 and 15,000 African Americans escaped to Canada.[54] Along with Deuteronomy 23:15–16,[55] Isaiah 16:3–4 was a passage that had been "overlooked," according to Craft, to prove that "it is unscriptural for anyone to send them back."[56] Apparently, this was also Pennington's intention, though writing before the act of 1850 (which renewed the act of 1793), when he placed Isaiah 16:4 on his title page.

When the *Fugitive Blacksmith* was published in 1849, Pennington had been in formal ministry for over a decade and had maintained the secrecy of his status (even from his closest friends); so he too desired a covert for his mission once his secret was revealed publicly. The words of Isaiah provided Pennington with biblical justification for his action, a defense this abolitionist minister sorely needed to maintain his theological positions about God and justice, freedom and human agency. God would "hide the outcasts," even if a covert operation was necessary to the cause. Pennington's hermeneutical strategy allowed him to turn repeatedly to Isaiah's words to find comfort and divine direction.[57]

Our final example comes from Harriet Jacobs's 1861 *Incidents in the Life of a Slave Girl*, the first female narrative "written by herself."[58] For the first time in the tradition, the public would hear a firsthand female perspective—largely unrevised—on the degradations women (and young girls!) suffered under enslavement. On her title page, Jacobs summoned Isaiah 32:9 to give voice to her ensuing narrative cry: "Rise

---

54. Stewart puts the number at 9,000 (*Holy Warriors*, 143–44). Quarles places the number between 15,000 and 20,000 (*Lincoln and the Negro*, 49).

55. "Thou shalt not deliver unto his master the servant which is escaped from his master unto thee: He shall dwell with thee, even among you, in that place which he shall choose in one of thy gates, where it liketh him best: thou shalt not oppress him."

56. Craft, *Running a Thousand Miles*, 98.

57. Pennington would find the words of Isaiah (14:3) useful again, as he prepared *A Narrative of Events of the Life of J. H. Banks, an Escaped Slave* for a British audience (Liverpool: M. Rourke, 1861). The context of Isaiah 14 seems to suggest a reversal motif, when the defeated make "captives of their captors," which would have caused great alarm among slaveholders (see Isa. 14:2–6). Also of interest, in the introduction to this narrative, Pennington riffs on Micah 6:8: "Let the American people then do justice, love mercy, and *let my oppressed people go free*" [a replacement for the KJV "walk humbly with God"] (6–7*; emphasis added).

58. She omits, however, her name on the title page and uses a pseudonym, Linda Brent, in the preface. A few years earlier Josephine Brown penned *Biography of an American Bondman* (Boston: R. F. Wallcut, 1856) about her father, William Wells Brown, partly based on his own narrative, *Narrative of William W. Brown, A Fugitive Slave* (Boston: The Anti-Slavery Office, 1947).

up, ye women that are at ease! Hear my voice, ye careless daughters! Give ear unto my speech."

Like Pennington, Jacobs appealed to the prophet Isaiah. Unlike Pennington, Jacobs petitioned the *unnamed* women and daughters, in the words of the prophet, in conjunction with (also on her title page) an *unnamed* "woman of North Carolina" who offered the following charge: "Northerners know nothing at all about Slavery. They think it is perpetual bondage only. They have no conception of the depth of *degradation* involved in that word, Slavery; if they had, they would never cease their efforts until so horrible a system was overthrown."[59]

In the book of Isaiah, this verse falls within a lament—"in little more than a year you will shudder, you complacent ones"—as a reference to the Assyrian conflict Israel has undergone (Isa. 32:10). Jacobs's forewarning to the "women at ease" was a clear challenge to the white women of the North, among whom was Lydia Maria Child, whose name appeared as editor on the title page of *Incidents*. The gender-specific nature of Jacobs's "incidents," most clearly signified on her title page, was most likely due to the fact that her narrative provided an extraordinary example of the subversion of "sexual roles she has been given, politicizes her sexuality, and uses it as a weapon"[60] in her literary and political battle against the "degradation" of slavery.[61] Taking on the taboo of public speech about female sexuality and, even more seriously, "sexual exploitation" lay at the heart of this story and marked what Jean Fagan Yellin calls a "special moment in the history of women's literature in America."[62]

While some of the earlier authors appealed more to God than human partners as active agents of change,[63] James Pennington and Harriet Jacobs recognized more human involvement in their narratives of freedom. They discovered biblical allusions that supported their theological

59. Jacobs was apparently citing Angelina Grimké's 1838 essay, "An Appeal to the Christian Women of the South," in *Against Slavery: An Abolitionist Reader*, ed. and with intro. by Mason Lowance (New York: Penguin Books, 2000), 200.

60. Taylor, ed., *I Was Born a Slave*, 536. This emphasis on sexuality did not attract a wide audience during Jacobs's lifetime.

61. Frances Smith Foster added a chapter on the depiction of females in the slave narrative tradition in her second edition: "most slave narratives stereotyped slave women as sexually exploited beings" (*Witnessing Slavery*, xxx); the male authors, according to Smith Foster, "shared nineteenth century's predilection for defining women in terms of manners, morals, and motherhood" (xxx).

62. Jean Fagan Yellin, "Texts and Contexts of Harriet Jacobs' *Incidents in the Life of a Slave Girl: Written by Herself*," in *The Slave's Narrative*, ed. Davis and Gates, 276 (262–82). On issues of agency within these female-authored *and* -dictated narratives, see Xiomara Santamarina, "Black Womanhood in North American Women's Slave Narratives," in *The Cambridge Companion to the African American Slave Narrative*, ed. Audrey Fisch (Cambridge: Cambridge University Press, 2007), 232–45.

63. E.g., Equiano's citation of Isa. 12:2–4: "Surely God is my salvation; I will trust, and will not be afraid, for the LORD God is my strength and my might; he has become my salvation."

understanding that God prepared the abolitionist community to assist in the liberation of individuals even in "the face of the spoiler."

Despite the significant symbolic presence a biblical passage would mark on the cover of one of the freedom narratives, it was not as widespread as some might expect. It was not a mandatory or expected feature in the narrative tradition, and many of the more popular narratives did not include one. The feature was absent from all four of Douglass's narratives (1845, 1855, 1881, 1892) and William Wells Brown's narrative (1847). Among those popularly sold, only Pennington's *Fugitive Blacksmith* included such a reference on his title page.[64] Even William Anderson—not widely popular—did not incorporate a citation, even though his title encompassed the following topic: "Containing Scriptural Views of the Origins of the Black and of the White Man." In the heyday of the popularity of these accounts, only the occasional freedom narrative would contain a biblical reference. Infrequent examples of this phenomenon may stem from the ongoing debate, in African American circles, about the positive role the Bible could play in the liberatory actions related to the peculiar institution.

THE DOUGLASS-GARNET DEBATE OF 1849

In African American abolitionist circles, sincere and passionate debates ensued about the function of the Bible in inducing slave insurrections. Nat Turner's rebellion was fresh on the minds of most. One such debate, famously known as the Douglass-Garnet Debate of 1849 (i.e., Frederick Douglass vs. Henry Highland Garnet),[65] occurred over a series of evenings in May of 1849. The issue at stake was the organization of special economic efforts to purchase Bibles to send covertly to the enslaved.

Douglass respected Garnet's intellectual ability.[66] According to the account of *The Liberator*, Frederick Douglass was successful in his opposition to the measure to transport Bibles to the South, a position

64. See Starling for the most popular narratives, among which were the stories of William Wells Brown, Frederick Douglass (1845 and 1855), Josiah Henson, James Pennington, Moses Roper, Austin Steward, William Craft, and Samuel Ward (Starling, *The Slave Narrative*, 36).

65. This account was originally published in *The Liberator*, June 1, 1849; it was reprinted as "A Douglass-Garnet Debate, 1849," in *A Documentary History of the Negro People in the United States*, ed. Herbert Aptheker (orig. 1951; New York: Citadel Press, 1968), 289. The editor of *The Liberator*, William Lloyd Garrison, strongly opposed sending Bibles into the Southern states. In 1849, both Douglass and Charles Remond were vocal supporters of the Garrisonian camp.

66. Sterling Stuckey, "'My Burden Lightened': Frederick Douglass, the Bible, and Slave Culture," in *African Americans and the Bible: Sacred Texts and Social Textures*, ed. Vincent Wimbush (New York: Continuum, 2000), 262.

forcefully defended by Henry Highland Garnet and Henry Bibb.[67]
Douglass "exhort[ed] the vast audience not to give one cent towards
this doubtful scheme." The evening was late and Douglass, according to *The Liberator*'s description, "was in the act of retiring from the
house, when Mr. Garnet rose to reply to his remarks, and called on
Mr. Douglass to stop and answer a question. . . . Mr. Garnet asked
Mr. Douglass if he did not, on Tuesday evening, say that the Bible
made slaves unhappy." The newspaper article, then, continues with
this dialogue:

> Mr. Douglass (says): Yes, but I—
>
> Mr. Garnet (responds): That will do. I have the floor.
>
> Mr. Douglass (replies): I wish to state the connection in which I
> said it.
>
> Mr. Garnet (says): I have the floor, and will not yield it.

Great confusion (was present) in all parts of the house; some calling
for Douglass to explain, others for Garnet to go on, Douglass and
his friends insisting upon it that he should be permitted to answer,
as he had been called up for that purpose, Garnet and his friends
refused permission; and thus the confusion continued for an hour
and a half. Neither gentleman could be heard, but both kept their
feet until the lights were blown out, and it was not known which
left the stand first.

The Liberator ended its account here. We may wish for more information on the debate, since the details of their arguments were scarce
in this report. The issue of the debate was stated; the sides were clearly
drawn. But the arguments for or against the usefulness of sending
"contraband"[68] Bibles into Southern slave territories were missing. We
are left with this historical gap.[69] The historian Sterling Stuckey concludes that Garnet regarded religion as a "greater weapon" against slavery than Douglass assumed.[70]

---

67. On the previous night, Charles Remond supported Douglass's position; Samuel Ward supported Garnet's and Bibb's.

68. Callahan's term, in *Talking Book*, 21. See his extensive discussion of this debate (21–26).

69. It is interesting that the refrain of "No Bibles, No Tracts, etc." was a common complaint among some of the formerly enslaved, e.g., Henry Bibb and James Pennington, both of whom published in 1849.

70. Stuckey, "'My Burden Lightened,'" 262.

Allen Callahan agrees with this assessment and adds: "Garnet saw the liberating power of the Bible as self-evident. It was so for him: he assumed it would be so for slaves in the South who might manage to read or have read to them a contraband copy of the holy scriptures that he knew so well."[71] Perhaps, in the spirit of Denmark Vesey and Nat Turner, Garnet also "conjured apocalypse" (in J. Albert Harrill's words); that is, he imagined that the enslaved would interpret the biblical text in a way that would incite "holy war against slavery."[72] But Douglass's more recent escape from the peculiar institution gave him an experiential advantage over his colleague and intellectual equal.

Illiteracy was predominant on plantations throughout Southern territories. Douglass's own failed efforts to organize Sabbath schools attested to the slaveholding strategies to minimize any educational development. As for Douglass, Stuckey surmises, "[t]he slave masters' admission of the potential explosiveness of slaves' exposure to the Bible is consistent with their clever yet sorry efforts to focus mainly on slaves obeying their masters when the Bible was used in directly addressing them."[73] (We will take up a fuller discussion of this brand of slaveholding "biblical" teaching in a later chapter.) Among other things, the dissolution of Douglass's own efforts to organize a weekly gathering for the purposes of literacy, community, and spirituality led to a more realistic view of the physical dangers associated with Garnet's strategy of widespread Bible distribution. Plus, as Callahan recognizes, "Douglass knew intimately what Garnet's limited experience with slavery could not teach: that the justice of the Bible was not self-evident."[74] Hermeneutical guidance, for Douglass, was essential, because a haphazard approach to biblical instruction would do more damage than good.

ENCOUNTERING THE BIBLE AS SYMBOL

For many of the enslaved, the Bible could be experienced only as a symbol, because of the lack of access to its pages. A number of these authors bemoan the fact that most of the enslaved had "no Bibles, no Tracts,

---

71. Callahan, *Talking Book*, 22.

72. J. Albert Harrill, *Slaves in the New Testament: Literary, Social, and Moral Dimensions* (Minneapolis: Augsburg Fortress Press, 2006), 180. Harrill's insight is a good one, but—if the slave narratives are representative—more African Americans were on the side of Douglass than on the side of the "holy war" advocates. Eventually, by 1850, Douglass would swing to Garnet's side on the necessity of arms, one of the issues that divided Douglass from Garrison (see Stewart, *Holy Warriors*, 143).

73. Stuckey, "'My Burden Lightened,'" 263.

74. Callahan, *Talking Book*, 23–24.

or religious books of any kind."[75] It was common for these authors to share stories about the leaders of the "invisible institution" (i.e., the brush-arbor religion of the enslaved community), kindhearted persons without (literate) knowledge of the biblical text, except as it came to them through the spirituals and the images of the "biblical heroes" passed along through oral tradition. Of course, many of the enslaved would hear preaching from the Bible in white settings, remembering some of the lead characters from these stories, and then develop their own interpretive possibilities.[76] But lack of access did not mean a lack of desire, as many yearned to move beyond the mysterious, symbolic nature of the Bible.

Harriet Jacobs told the story of "Uncle Fred," who went from learning his alphabet to reading through the entire New Testament in six months, driven by a passionate belief that he would know God better if he could just read the Bible.[77] He was not alone, as Jacobs reflected: "There are thousands, who, like good uncle Fred, are thirsting for the water of life; but the law forbids it, and the churches withhold it."[78] Indeed, in his second autobiography (1855) Douglass included an account, omitted from the 1845 edition, of his conversion and his desire to read Christianity's sacred text: "My desire for knowledge increased, and especially did I want a thorough acquaintance with the contents of the bible. I have gathered scattered pages from this holy book, from the filthy street gutters of Baltimore, and washed and dried them, that in the moments of my leisure, I might get a word or two of wisdom from them."[79]

Douglass's collection from the gutter was, in Sterling Stuckey's words, "a telling indication of the inaccessibility of the Bible to slaves. There was sad irony in his exposure to its pages, for he treated them,

---

75. The quote is from James Pennington, *Fugitive Blacksmith* (London: Charles Gilpin, 1849), 68*. See Henry Bibb, *Narrative of the Life and Adventures of Henry Bibb, An American Slave, Written by Himself* (New York: Author, 1849), 119*; Frederick Douglass, *Narrative of the Life of Frederick Douglass, an American Slave. Written by Himself* (Boston: Anti-Slavery Office, 1845), 122*; Harriet Jacobs, *Incidents in the Life of a Slave Girl. Written by Herself* (Boston: Published for the Author, 1861), 113*.

76. Stuckey imagines the following: "Let us remember that Douglass was for a whole year in the midst of illiterate field hands, some of whom were gifted poets and easily capable of putting to use biblical images and heroes for their own purposes. Other slaves who could read and possessed knowledge of the Bible were also in the company of field hands, working beside them or in contact with them at other times in other places and might have recounted biblical stories later used in the creation of slave songs. There were means by which slaves had contact with the Bible, opening to them varied possibilities for biblical influences in their spirituals" (Stuckey, "'My Burdened Lightened,'" 256–57). Apparently the high point of the spirituals was also during this period, 1830–1865. See Wilma Ann Bailey, "The Sorrow Songs: Laments from Ancient Israel and African American Diaspora," in *Yet with a Steady Beat: Contemporary U.S. Afrocentric Biblical Interpretation*, ed. Randall C. Bailey, Semeia Series (Atlanta: Society of Biblical Literature, 2003), 66.

77. Jacobs, *Incidents*, 111–13*.

78. Jacobs. *Incidents*, 113*.

79. Frederick Douglass, *My Bondage and My Freedom* (New York: Miller, Orton & Mulligan, 1855), 167*.

soiled as they were, as the rarest of finds."[80] Yet a few, like Henry Bibb, had a copy (small enough to fit into one of his pockets), although it was one of a list of items stolen from him by members of the Methodist Episcopal Church, after he reentered the slave states with plans to locate his wife and child.[81] Accessibility must not have been limited only by cost, as Bibb lists the expense of the Bible at only $0.62 "and one half cents," compared to his $10 silver watch and $0.75 pocket knife. Of course, what funds some of the enslaved may have had would have been negligible.

Furthermore, the physical accessibility to the Bible, or lack thereof, was supported by legal stipulations, as many of the enslaved were well aware. Examples abound in the narratives themselves of the illegal nature of reading or learning to read the Bible, even though many like Jacobs and Uncle Fred were willing to suffer the legal consequences.[82] Samuel Ward relayed the following story about a representative of the American Bible Society who was, surprisingly, ignorant of the literacy laws in Louisiana:

> In 1841 I knew of an agent of an auxiliary to that Society who was distributing Bibles in Louisiana, and, being ignorant of the laws upon the subject, asked a free coloured man if he could read, with the intention of giving or selling him a Bible if he could. Some one overheard him, and informed against him. He was arrested, tried, found guilty, but leniently discharged, on account of his ignorance of the law which he had violated. Slaveholders and their abettors belong to and are officers of the American Bible Society, and they control it. That slavery forbids the searching of the Scriptures, which Christ enjoins, is to them not even a matter of complaint. Albeit, they pledge themselves to give the Christian Scriptures to every family in the Union.[83]

In addition, a number of the authors expressed sincere gratitude to the person who first taught them to read.[84] Lydia Maria Child, editor of Harriet Jacobs's *Incidents*, even repeated Jacobs's story as part of her introduction: "the mistress with whom she [i.e., Jacobs] lives till she

80. Stuckey, "'My Burdened Lightened,'" 253.

81. The list of items included $14, a silver watch (worth $10), a pocket knife (worth $.75), and a Bible ($.62 "and one half cents") (Douglass, *Narrative*, 46*).

82. Cf. Douglass, *Narrative*, 122*; Bibb, *Narrative*, 21*; Douglass, *My Bondage and My Freedom*, 167–69*.

83. Samuel Ward, *Autobiography of a Fugitive Negro: His Anti-Slavery Labours in the United States, Canada, & England* (London: John Snow, 35 Paternoster Row, 1855), 65*.

84. Mary Prince, *The History of Mary Prince, A West Indian Slave. Related by Herself. With a Supplement by the Editor* (London: Published by F. Westley and A. H. Davis, 1831), 17*; Douglass, *Narrative*, 33*.

was twelve years old, was a kind, considerate friend, who taught her to read and spell."[85] Although Jacobs also acknowledged this kindness, a "privilege, which so rarely falls to the lot of a slave," she struggled with her "bitterness" toward this mistress, who had committed a severe "act of injustice" by breaking the promise to Jacobs's mother that they would be released upon the mistress's death. More important than the illegality of teaching the enslaved to read, Frederick Douglass provided an excellent example of the ideology behind such a viewpoint by describing an account of his former slave owner's position, which was representative of the position of many Southern slaveholders: "[Mr. Auld said that] if you teach that nigger . . . how to read, there would be no keeping him. It would forever unfit him to be a slave. He would at once become unmanageable, and of no value to his master. As to himself, it could do him no good, but a great deal of harm. It would make him discontented and unhappy."[86] This "special revelation" drove Douglass to learn in every possible instance, because he believed the truth of what Mr. Auld spoke. He would repeat this truth claim again later in the narrative.[87] Learning would be Douglass's way to freedom, as he remembered: "From that moment, I understood the pathway from slavery to freedom."[88]

One final story is in order, because it came closer to the earlier century's trope of the Bible as the Talking Book than any other account within the extant antebellum narrative tradition. Sojourner Truth had arrived before the grand jurors in a local court to plead her case about the fraudulent sale of her son (she was, at this time, a free black woman):

> She then went in, where she found the Grand Jurors indeed sitting, and again commenced to relate her injuries. After holding some conversation among themselves, one of them rose, and bidding her follow him, led the way to a side office, where he heard her story, and asked her "if she could *swear* that the child she spoke of was her son?" "Yes," she answered, "I *swear* it's my son." "Stop, stop!" said the lawyer, "you must swear by this book"—giving her a book, which she thinks must have been the Bible. She took, and putting it to her lips, began again to swear it was her child. The clerks, unable to preserve their gravity any longer, burst into an

85. "Introduction by the Editor," in Jacobs, *Incidents*, 8*.
86. Douglass, *Narrative*, 33*.
87. Douglass. *Narrative*, 38*.
88. Douglass, *Narrative*, 33*.

uproarious laugh; and one of them inquired of lawyer Chip of what use it could be to make *her* swear. "It will answer the law," replied the officer. He then made her comprehend just what he wished her to do, and she took a lawful oath, as far as the outward ceremony could make it one.[89]

In this account, we find, once again, the symbolic use of the Bible. It is not as surprising that this example derives from one of the *dictated* narratives and not from one written by the formerly enslaved person herself.[90] For Truth, like those in the previous century's narrative tradition, the "Book" was personified.[91] In the earlier tradition, it "spoke" to Gronnisaw's master. Here, Truth felt obligated to speak or, more correctly, to "swear" *to the Book itself.* Whatever she thought about the value of this object for these jurors at this point (that is, whether it "talked" to them), she planned—in light of her desperate situation—to follow whatever process was necessary to secure legal support to obtain the immediate return of her son.

EXAMPLES OF ENCOUNTERING THE "BIBLE" (CONTENT) AS READ AND INTERPRETED

The freedom narratives cited most books of the Bible. Even within the representative narratives receiving focused attention for this chapter, we find explicit citations, paraphrased references, or allusions to many of the biblical books, with specific significance given to the following: Genesis, Exodus, 1 Kings, Job, Ecclesiastes, Isaiah, Jeremiah, Daniel, Matthew, Mark, Luke, John, Acts, Ephesians, Colossians, and 1 Thessalonians.[92]

89. *Narrative of Sojourner Truth*, 48*.
90. Though a fluent speaker in Dutch and English, Sojourner Truth was probably unable to read or write (Nell Irvin Painter, *Sojourner Truth: A Life, A Symbol* [New York: W. W. Norton & Co., 1996], 3).
91. As Sojourner Truth said, "You read books, I talk to God" (Margaret Washington, "Introduction," in *Narrative of Sojourner Truth*, ed. Margaret Washington [New York: Vintage Books, 1993], xxviii). As Washington and Nell Painter recognize, notions of Spirit (or spirituality) provided the impetus, for many nineteenth-century African American women, to talk back to the talking book.
92. Genesis (Douglass, Bibb, Pennington); Exodus (Bibb); 1 Kings (Bibb); Job (Douglass, Pennington, Jacobs); 1 Kings (Bibb); Ecclesiastes (Jacobs); Isaiah (Douglass, Pennington, Jacobs); Jeremiah (Douglass); Daniel (Jacobs); Matthew (Douglass, Bibb); Mark (Jacobs); Luke (Bibb, Pennington); John (Prince); Acts (Jacobs); Ephesians (Jacobs); Colossians (Bibb); and 1 Thessalonians (Douglass). In conversation, Margaret Aymer has informed me that a richer resource for wrestling with Douglass's interpretation of the Bible occurs in his speeches. For this list, I am grateful to a former graduate assistant, Beth Ritter, who assisted me in scanning through the University of North Carolina's online collection, "North American Slave Narratives," http://docsouth.unc.edu/neh/.

First Encounters with the Bible
in the Narrative Tradition: The "Book" Talks

Within these African American autobiographical narratives, the initial "encounters" with the Bible were generally *negative*. This is not surprising in light of the cultural milieu that established an ideological reading of sacred texts to inform a bias against the humanization of persons of African descent. The Bible was simply one means to carry out this agenda. Frequently the slaveholding opposition controlled these "encounters," as reported by the formerly enslaved.

In Frederick Douglass's 1845 *Narrative*, the first allusion to the Bible was to the mythological tradition of the "curse of Ham," in the context of Douglass's description of the increasing mulatto slave population. The curse of Ham was a common ideological racist theory derived from Genesis 9. Noah cursed Canaan, Ham's son, because Ham saw Noah's nakedness (Gen. 9:18–27). In the biblical world, this story furnished a literary provenance for Canaan, a land inhabited by the Canaanites, who became Israel's enemy. From Israel's perspective, it was understandable that the Canaanites should be their hated opponent, since they lived under Noah's curse. In Douglass's day, Noah's curse provided justification for racism and the enslavement of African people, since many considered Africans to be the ancestors of Ham.

Apparently someone had predicted "the downfall of slavery by the inevitable laws of population." For Douglass, the "mulatto" population, at least, "will do away the force of the argument, that God cursed Ham, and therefore American slavery is right. If the lineal descendants of Ham are alone to be scripturally enslaved, it is certain that slavery at the south must soon become unscriptural; for thousands are ushered into the world, annually, who, like myself, owe their existence to white fathers, and those fathers most frequently their own masters."[93] Douglass recognized a much more complex history of racial identity than any of the proslavery proponents would attest. This biblical myth should be categorically dismissed by the practicality of racial mixing common in Douglass's experience of slavery. It may be significant, however, that Douglass did not attempt to argue *against* the myth based on any historical, exegetical analysis. In this instance, Douglass chose not to engage biblical interpretation directly.

---

93. Douglass, *Narrative*, 5*.

Douglass's friend and fellow popular abolitionist speaker, Henry Bibb, also provided, early in his narrative, a *negative* encounter with the content of the Bible. At first, his description suggested a way forward. In a report on the function of the Sabbath, Bibb mentioned that many of the enslaved desired to learn more about the Bible, but slaveholders viewed "Sabbath schools" as part of "an incendiary movement."[94] As part of this discussion, Bibb revealed that a "pro-slavery doctrine" was frequently preached, which drove "thousands into infidelity" and included the specific passages, "Servants be obedient to your masters;— and he that knoweth his masters will and doeth it not, shall be beaten with many stripes" (Col. 3:22 and Luke 12:47).[95] These specific passages were commonly cited throughout the narrative tradition (see chap. 5).[96]

In one other example, Jacobs illustrated a story from early childhood about the Bible and, as Jacobs's editor described her, Jacobs's "kind, considerate" mistress. Let me cite the entire passage:

> After a brief period of suspense, the will of my mistress was read, and we learned that she had bequeathed me to her sister's daughter, a child of five years old. So vanished our hopes. My mistress had taught me the precepts of God's Word: "Thou shalt love thy neighbor as thyself." "Whatsoever ye would that men should do unto you, do ye even so unto them." *But I was her slave, and I supposed she did not recognize me as her neighbor.* I would give much to blot out from my memory that one great wrong. As a child, I loved my mistress; and, looking back on the happy days I spent with her, I try to think with less bitterness of this act of injustice. While I was with her, she taught me to read and spell; and for this privilege, which so rarely falls to the lot of a slave, I bless her memory.[97]

In the paragraph immediately preceding the one above, Jacobs discussed her "suspense," as she expressed optimistic thoughts on the possibility of a "future." The promise made to her mother, that she would be freed upon the death of her mistress, had been broken. This first encounter with the Bible became Jacobs's written explanation of an interpretive dispute, one she had within her own mind and now with her public audience. Jacobs provided insight into a very different

---

94. Bibb, *Narrative*, 21*.
95. Bibb, *Narrative*, 24*.
96. Douglass, *Narrative*, 55*.
97. Jacobs, *Incidents*, 15–16* (emphasis added).

understanding of the biblical text.[98] For Jacobs's "kind mistress," "neighbor" did *not* include a slave; it is evident (from later in the narrative) that Jacobs understood "neighbor" to be connected to a biblical reference to the Samaritan.[99] If an ancient Jew should treat a Samaritan kindly, as Jesus' parable implies, then surely "owners" should show honesty and fair treatment to the enslaved. This was not the case in Jacobs's experience.[100]

This account, she admitted, had left an indelible mark on her memory. The psychological implications of this event lingered, as Jacobs described her lifelong "bitterness" toward this clear "act of injustice" and the broken promise. She concluded this segment, nonetheless, with thankfulness for the gift of literacy, which she gained from this same mistress; a gift that allowed her not only to interpret the Bible for herself (i.e., the neighbor *should include* the enslaved), but also to tell her story, indeed the first slave narrative authored by a *female* writer.[101]

Talking Back to the Talking Book (Other Narrative Encounters)

These initial negative encounters do not last throughout these political treatises, whose task was to reclaim selfhood and dignity and to struggle against the persistent enslavement of their fellow human beings. So, by means of a literacy that gave them access to the Bible, they began to "talk back" to (or signify on) the biblical text.

As Allen Callahan recently concluded in the publication of *The Talking Book*, "African Americans were learning en masse to read the Bible as a book both opened and closed. . . . As a written text, it greeted them with silence." But as they continued to wrestle with the biblical text, in light of the multifaceted and convoluted conditions surrounding them, they would eventually "make the Talking Book their own."[102] In fact, we find numerous examples of claiming the Talking

98. On the commonness of the appropriation of the "love neighbor" (Mark 12:31 and par.) and so-called "golden rule" (Matt. 7:12) passages, see Callahan, *Talking Book*, 35–36. Although Yuval Taylor suggests that Jacobs drew on Mark 12:31, it is clear later in the narrative that Jacobs was (also?) aware of the Lukan version of the "love neighbor" passage (*Incidents*, 107*).

99. Jacobs, *Narrative*, 107*.

100. Nor did Jesus' teaching go far enough, since—in his day—a "neighbor" apparently did *not* include the slave. Many of Jesus' parables assume the master/slave relationship of first-century life. See Jennifer Glancy, *Slavery in Early Christianity* (Oxford/New York: Oxford University Press, 2002), chap. 4.

101. One exception to this experience of literacy during enslavement was Pennington. Later in his narrative, Pennington reflected on his encounter, or lack thereof, with the Bible during the first twenty-one years of his life: "Up to this time, I recollected to have seen one copy of the New Testament, but the entire Bible I had never seen, and had never heard of the Patriarchs, or of the Lord Jesus Christ" (*Fugitive Blacksmith*, 43*).

102. Callahan, *Talking Book*, 20.

Book as their own within the freedom-narrative tradition, this unique genre in the larger literary tradition of American autobiography. Since we will take up fuller discussions in the following chapters, here we offer just a few examples.

Douglass did not hesitate to apply Isaiah 53:3 to fellow slaves: "They were in very deed men and women of sorrow, and acquainted with grief. Their backs had been made familiar with the bloody lash, so that they had become callous."[103] Was Douglass alluding to the larger verses surrounding Isaiah 53:3 as well: "a man of sorrows, and acquainted with grief" (v. 3); "he was wounded for our transgressions" (v. 5); "with his stripes we are healed" (v. 5); "all we like sheep have gone astray" (v. 6)?

Even as Douglass expanded Isaiah's vision to include "men and women," far removed from Douglass's thinking were any ideas of "redemptive suffering" for the enslaved, a theological concept that may possibly account for some of Bibb's reflection on his own life, "I could indeed afford to crucify my own flesh for the sake of redeeming myself from perpetual slavery."[104] Perhaps there was a closer association between this biblical allusion and Douglass's sensitivity to theodicy issues found elsewhere (e.g., "Does a righteous God govern the universe?").[105] In Isaiah 53:10, "it was the will of the LORD to crush him with pain." Even if Douglass had such thoughts, would it have been wise to broach these theological topics in this "public transcript"?[106] Standing behind the allusion, most strikingly, was the association of Jesus (and Isaiah's "suffering servant") with the battered bodies of his enslaved companions.

Can anyone imagine a more powerful appropriation (or "history of effect")[107] of Matthew 25 than Bibb's conclusion to his narrative? The scene was a slave auction in which it was common for families to be broken apart, never to meet again on earth. Right in the middle of his description, Bibb exclaimed, "Christ shall say to the slaveholding professors of religion, 'Inasmuch as ye did it unto one of the least of these little ones, my brethren, ye did it unto me.'"[108]

---

103. Douglass, *Narrative*, 46*.

104. Bibb, *Narrative*, 163*.

105. Douglass, *Narrative*, 82*.

106. In fact, Douglass omitted the Isaian allusion from *My Bondage and My Freedom* (1855), even though he retained most of the passage. This may have been an attempt to distance his thinking from the possibility of redemptive suffering in the suffering of the enslaved.

107. For the concept of *Wirkungsgeschichte*, see Hans-Georg Gadamer, *Truth and Method*, 2nd rev. ed. (New York: Continuum, 2004).

108. Bibb, *Narrative*, 202–3*. Douglass utilized Matt. 25:31–46 to describe the generous hospitality Nathan Johnson showed him in New Bedford (*Narrative*, 114*).

Samuel Ward also connected Christ to freedom by utilizing this same familiar passage as one of liberation. Ward too appealed to the latter portion of Matthew 25—the judgment of the nations—and found in it a hearty critique of slaveholders and affirmation of his enslaved siblings: "They hear Christ say, 'Inasmuch as ye did it (or did it not) to the least of these my brethren, ye did it (or did it not) unto me.' Black men are, in the estimation of these brethren who oppose the anti-slavery cause, 'the least.' Should not religious men tremble, lest the Son of Man should denounce these terrible words against them?"[109]

Ward's appropriation of this passage was telling for several reasons. First, it showed his careful attention to the text, emphasizing how treatment (or lack thereof) of the least was significant for their final evaluation. Second, with this passage he was able to muster theological support to level his invective against his tormentors. Finally, by employing this particular passage, like Douglass he identified Christ with the enslaved. Christ became a manifestation of the enslaved and, again, the antithesis of the slaveholding community.

One other such declaration that resonated with this group was an otherwise insignificant and notoriously problematic verse from the Psalms. Psalm 68:31 proclaims, "Princes shall come out of Egypt; Ethiopia shall soon stretch out her hands unto God" (KJV). This text would form the basis of the Ethiopianist movement, which from the mid-nineteenth to the early-twentieth century served as a ground for African American identity formation (see chap. 1). Because of this passage, those once viewed as chattel could see themselves as African princes upon whom the fate of the world rested. Wrested from its context, this single verse became paradigmatic for African peoples, providing them a lens through which to see themselves as vital members of the family of God. It was also typologically useful to them, for it enabled them to recast the horrors of enslavement and brutality as a necessary step in God's overall plan to evangelize the world.

In this regard, this otherwise innocuous passage became the lynchpin for a larger theological drama in which Africans could see themselves and their homeland as crucial to God's unfolding plan to redeem the entire world and all people. But the Ethiopianist movement would be a later, more fully formed expression of engagement with this text, an engagement that actually began in fleeting references in the first literary genre of this people, the narratives of the formerly enslaved.

---

109. Ward, *Autobiography of a Fugitive Negro*, 68*.

In these documents we can find several early attempts to plumb this passage for meaning. It provided a basis for those who had themselves been enslaved to imagine themselves in God's plan as a royal people who were not just receiving, but taking God's word throughout the world with "outstretched hands." For example, in his 1833 autobiography Richard Allen recalled this verse at the end of an address occurring in the latter part of his narrative:

> I feel an inexpressible gratitude towards you who have engaged in the cause of the African race; you have wrought a deliverance for many from more than Egyptian bondage; your labours are unremitted for their complete redemption from the cruel subjection they are in. . . . you make the tyrants tremble; you strive to raise the slave to the dignity of a man; you take our children by the hand to lead them in the path of virtue, by your care of our education; you are not ashamed to call the most abject of our race brethren, children of one Father, who hath made of one blood all the nations of the earth. You ask for this, nothing for yourselves, nothing but what is worthy the cause you are engaged in [sic]; nothing but that we would be friends to ourselves, and not strengthen the bands of oppression by an evil conduct, when led out of the house of bondage. May He who hath arisen to plead our cause, and engaged you as volunteers in the service, add to your numbers, until the princes shall come forth from Egypt, and Ethiopia stretch out her hands unto God.[110]

Here this passage seems a fitting end to Allen's special note to his white abolitionist friends, entitled, "A short address to the friends of him who hath no helper." After a lengthy description of the audience of this address, which seems as much to motivate them to support his cause by moral force as it is to thank them, we find his reference to Psalm 68. Framed in the midst of a prayer, Psalm 68:31 serves to express his desired outcome of their collective efforts. Should God "add to [their] numbers," Rev. Allen envisioned the end result to be that "princes shall come forth from Egypt, and Ethiopia stretch out her hands unto God."[111]

We should note how this verse was employed in this context. Technically, Psalm 68:31 is part of a much longer eclectically themed song, yet Allen read it as a prophecy that would inevitably be fulfilled in the near future. In this context it is not clear if the goal Allen sought

---

110. Allen, *The Life, Experience, and Gospel Labours of the Rt. Rev. Richard Allen* (Philadelphia: Martin & Boden, Printers, 1833), 48–49*.

111. This brief section on the use of the Psalms comes from Rodney Sadler's research on the narratives.

was the manumission of enslaved Africans, achieved by the increase in numbers of abolitionists, or the evangelism of Africans that will bring forth prophesied intervention by God. But what is clear was that Allen viewed this verse to be a crucial prophecy announcing an impending moment of divine intervention in the status of African peoples.

Finally, we once again return to Jacobs's narrative. One startling distinction from her male counterparts was Jacobs's insistence to report the psychological repercussions of the abusive sexual encounters that enslaved females experienced.[112] Some white women slaveholders lived in daily tension with their enslaved black women, not only because of the cultural demands of their respective positions in life, but because of the abusive sexual encounters white male slaveholders initiated on what they considered to be their property.

As the *first* African American *female* writer of one of these accounts, Harriet Jacobs, unlike most of her (male) predecessors in the freedom-narrative tradition, aimed to record the experiences, exposure, and challenges of this part of the story! The Bible in particular played an important (symbolic?) role in her account. In a chapter entitled "The Church and Slavery," she reported the following conversation the day after the slaveholder joined the church:

> In answer to some of his usual [i.e., sexual] talk, I reminded him that he had just joined the church. "Yes, Linda," said he. "It was proper for me to do so. I am getting in years, and my position in society requires it, and it puts an end to all the damned slang. You would do well to join the church, too, Linda."
>
> "There are sinners enough in it already," rejoined I. "If I could be allowed to live like a Christian, I should be glad."
>
> "You can do what I require; and if you are faithful to me, you will be as virtuous as my wife," he replied. [clear sexual innuendo]
>
> I answered that the *Bible* didn't say so. [emphasis added]
>
> His voice became hoarse with rage. "How dare you preach to me about your infernal Bible!" he exclaimed. "What right have you, who are my negro, to talk to me about what you would like, and what you wouldn't like? I am your master, and you shall obey me."
>
> No wonder the slaves sing,—
>> "Ole Satan's church is her below;
>> Up to God's free church I hope to go."[113]

---

112. Not all male authors ignored such atrocities, although their reports were often less explicit, e.g., Bibb, *Narrative*, 44*, 199*; Pennington, *Fugitive Blacksmith*, v–vi*.

113. Jacobs, *Incidents*, 116*. This final dialogue was part of Jacobs's chapter on "The Church and Slavery," in which she addressed the common freedom-narrative theme of "Christianity vs. Slave-holding Religion" (105–16*).

Earlier female narratives (e.g., Mary Prince [1831] and Sojourner Truth [1850]) were constrained by the thoughts and the pens of their white editors. A number of scholars, including Jean Fagan Yellin and Margaret Washington, have noted how these earlier *dictated* narratives rarely discussed issues of sexual violence. In Sojourner Truth's case, Washington explains, "It is peculiar that Olive Gilbert's censoring of Isabella's story is strongest in the female 'sphere' and in sexuality. Gilbert decided (or perhaps was told) to omit certain details about Isabella's life. The *Narrative* is silent on many of Isabella's 'long series of trials,' says Gilbert, 'not for want of facts' but 'from motives of delicacy.'"[114] Yet we know from other accounts of Truth's life that she "was not modest about the sexual politics of slavery." As Washington concludes, "[Truth] scoffed at white ideals of womanhood and challenged the patriarchal nature of American society. Sexuality was for her an open issue because she, like many enslaved women, separated the physical body from the spiritual self. This separation represented a means of resisting the effects of sexual exploitation."[115]

Sexual violence and abuse was a key motif in Jacobs's narrative. She was able to write, in her own voice, about the nature of the most intimate form of humiliation. This was evidently one reason she wrote to fill in the gap of female *degradation*, as she highlights on her title page. She had read a number of accounts written by her male counterparts, who had chosen to avoid this delicate but psychologically debilitating aspect of the evil institution. In the narrative itself, the appropriation of this book, as symbol and more, allowed her to defend her humanity and maintain her dignity. In this final scene, the book (i.e., the Bible), voice, and gender intermingle to signify a clear and direct reappropriation of the Talking Book of the previous generation. On issues as delicate (for the public arena) as sexuality in the Victorian age in the antebellum states of the North, she desired to convince her audience that the Bible functioned as a nongendered book, one with capacity to determine agency, if interpreted correctly as a (womanist?) response to this male power game of interpretation and sexual exploitation. And Harriet Jacobs appropriated her "infernal Bible" to make it so!

She set up this section as a response to a recent publication by an unnamed Northerner, called "South-Side View of Slavery" (114*). See Nehemiah Adams, *A South-Side View of Slavery, or, Three Months in the South in 1854*, 4th ed. (Boston: Ticknor & Fields, 1860).

114. Washington, "Introduction," xxix–xxx.

115. Washington, "Introduction," xxxii.

CONCLUSION: "WE CAN MAKE THE BOOK 'TALK' TOO"

Literacy, for many authors of the slave narratives, meant the beginning of basic freedom. *Biblical* literacy, and the ability to "talk back" to the talking book, meant the beginning of the deconstruction of a hermeneutical ideology that had dehumanized black identity and black humanity. Biblical literacy meant facility with the hermeneutical exchange to claim one's own reorientation and revisioning of a new humanity before God. It was also, as Wimbush has suggested, an attempt "to enter the mainstream of American society."[116] Their hermeneutical decisions were not determined by any historical support, as if such would benefit their present situation (i.e., they were not in a fair rhetorical argument on equal footing with their opposition), but rather their experience, and the dehumanization associated with it, forced them to signify on this "foundational" text as if it were the very constitution upon which society was grounded. In reality, in many Northern (especially Garrisonian) abolitionist circles, these African American abolitionists knew that the Bible and its *just* appropriation may have been *more* significant than any interpretation of the US Constitution.[117]

As Henry Louis Gates Jr. concludes, "The (former) slave wrote not only to demonstrate humane letters but also to demonstrate his or her own membership in the human community." If true, then the formerly enslaved interpreted and appropriated the biblical text to validate his or her hermeneutical sensitivity to and capability with the Bible, in order, in the words of Frederick Douglass, "to promote the moral, social, religious, and intellectual elevation of the free colored people . . . [and] to advocate the *great and primary work* of the universal and unconditional emancipation of [the] entire race."[118]

The *symbolic function* of the Bible can be traced through the freedom narratives, and this sketch expresses the larger cultural expectations about its usefulness as a book of the Divine. So, as one anonymous author writes, "Aaron has a great knowledge of the Bible but cannot read a word." Even when left unread, many of these authors assumed

---

116. Wimbush, "The Bible and African Americans," 90.

117. On Douglass's "love" for *The Liberator*, Garrison's paper, see *My Bondage and My Freedom* (354): "From this time I was brought in contact with the mind of William Lloyd Garrison. His paper took its place with me next to the bible. *The Liberator* was a paper after my own heart."

118. Douglass, *My Bondage and My Freedom*, 406*. The "elevation of the free colored people" was one of Douglass's more prominent emphases in the second edition of his autobiography in 1855.

the prominence of a symbolic Bible that would function positively on behalf of their dignity.

On the other hand, once the formerly enslaved began to read and write critically (and these narratives are representative of the latter), an engagement with the texts of the Bible (and the interpretations that surrounded its words) began to produce some popular but critical assessments of the words of its pages. These stories then enlightened an immediate generation of the need to talk back to the "talking book" for purposes of survival, community shaping, and uplift.

3

The Sabbath and the Freedom Narrative

"We remembered what our brothers told us—when we were able to run away, to try it on some favorable Sunday."

The Life and Sufferings of Leonard Black (1847)

INTRODUCTION

Formerly enslaved authors attempted to report, among other themes, periods of rest and respite for the enslaved on Southern plantations. Aware of the debilitating effects religion had on slave life, many authors addressed the theme of the Sabbath as they experienced it during captivity. Because it was difficult for an audience to feel the physical and psychological strain of the loss of time, the narratives tackle this religious theme, a practice that should symbolize what was good and just about thinking of one's self as part of an active religious community. For those burdened by the physical toils of servitude, driven by the rigors of slave life, with its incessant demands on time and the burden of having no space in life for thought, action, and/or self-care, the theoretical idea of a Sabbath was attractive. Within the freedom narratives, we find descriptions of (1) what slaveholders wanted the enslaved to do on the Sabbath, (2) what the enslaved actually did on the Sabbath, and (3) what the enslaved hoped to achieve on the Sabbath.

On Southern plantations, overseers controlled the time and labor of the enslaved. This was no less true of the arrangement on the Sabbath—if a Sabbath was granted. Some slaveholders managed the religious instruction of the enslaved, in order to minimize prayers longing for freedom. Others wanted to avoid religious instruction altogether; so they developed other activities for the enslaved during this "day of rest." Frequently they encouraged gambling, drinking, and organized fighting, as a way to provide entertainment. This may have been an attempt to prevent the enslaved from engaging in sincere worship experiences. As converted, baptized, and catechized believers, the enslaved could have possibly contested their status. Or perhaps the activities revealed the thoughts enslavers held about the enslaved, that is, that African Americans were simple, immoral brutes. The freedom narratives point in both directions.

When granted more autonomy over their own time and activities on the Sabbath, the enslaved engaged in a variety of activities. While many rested, some secured work off of their enslaver's clock to make additional money, and still others participated in religious services managed by the white community. Finally, others planned their own worship meetings, sometimes privately under the threat of danger. We hear about all of these examples within the narratives of the formerly enslaved, as they attempted to represent the broader community.

In light of this book's primary concern, this chapter in particular will tackle the final category more thoroughly, attempting to explore the activities associated with the more independent gatherings of the enslaved. On this side of freedom, it is difficult to imagine what these moments of respite meant in a society in which time and labor were not one's own. How would religious worship in such a context inevitably be more than just an abstract, ritualized reflection on God for spiritual formation, but also a deeply engaged, pathos-laden encounter with God incarnate in their brothers and sisters who (only in this time and space) were able to be freely functioning spiritual, moral, and intellectual beings?

A Sabbath among themselves would afford them the time to study the text—through oral interpretive traditions (like the spirituals) or through the text itself—most available to them. The authors of our narratives frequently connected the Sabbath to literacy. They reflected on how the successes of learning to read and teaching others to do so buoyed the spirits of those bombarded with cultural signs of their inferiority. The occasions of independent worship on the Sabbath also made space for some to imagine liberation and to ponder what it might look like. In this regard, how many hatched plans of escape on the Sabbath? How did the space provided on this day embolden the people to believe that they could be free and could exercise autonomy and self-determination?

Within these narrative settings, we gain access, if only indirectly, to how the Bible may have functioned for these black hermeneuts. When the enslaved were allowed to meet—or, clandestinely met—independent of white control and sponsorship, what themes marked these gatherings? When they assembled to solidify the bonds of community and to exert their own autonomy in the brush-arbor worshiping communities, what was the content of their prayers? What did their songs mean to them? Most importantly for our larger project, how did they interpret the Bible?

BIBLICAL LAW AMONG AFRICAN AMERICANS: A GENERAL UNDERSTANDING

Sabbath law was an important concern for early enslaved men and women, for they too had their own understanding of God's laws, which, to the best of their abilities, they enacted in their lives.[1] Born enslaved in 1815, Henry Highland Garnet gave "An Address to the Slaves of the United States of America" in 1843 in order to discuss what he deemed "divine commandments."[2]

> The divine commandments you are duty bound to reverence and obey. If you do not obey them, you will surely meet with the displeasure of the Almighty. He requires you to love Him supremely, and your neighbor as yourself, to keep the Sabbath day holy, to search the Scriptures, and bring up your children with respect for His laws, and to worship no other God but Him. But slavery sets all these at nought and hurls defiance in the face of Jehovah. The forlorn condition in which you are placed does not destroy your moral obligation to God. You are not certain of Heaven, because you suffer yourselves to remain in a state of slavery, where you cannot obey the commandments of the Sovereign of the universe.[3]

The inclusion of Sabbath legislation in this short list signified its significance. In Garnet's mind, Sabbath law followed closely love for God and for neighbor—that which Jesus deemed most important (see Mark

---

1. Debates surrounding proper activity on Sunday—economic, cultural, and religious—were popular in US society during this period. See Alexis McCrossen, *Holy Day, Holiday: The American Sunday* (Ithaca, NY: Cornell University Press, 2000).

2. Henry Highland Garnet, "An Address to the Slaves of the United States of America," in *Lift Every Voice: African American Oratory 1787–1900*, ed. Philip S. Foner and Robert James Branham (Tuscaloosa: The University of Alabama Press, 1998), 198–204.

3. Garnet, "An Address to the Slaves," 201.

12:29–31). Mary Ann Shadd offered a similar arrangement in which, again, Sabbath law was second only to the law of love (see below).[4]

Some of these authors argued, however, that the very existence of slavery represented a deliberate nullification of God's laws. In June 1839, Daniel Payne noted this explicitly in "Slavery Brutalizes Man":[5]

> But what saith slavery? "they are my property, and shall be brought up to serve." They shall not *even learn to read his word,* in order that they may be brought up in his nurture and admonition. If any man doubts this, let him read the slave code of Louisiana and see if it is not death to teach slaves. Thus saith the Lord, "Remember the Sabbath day, to keep it holy." Does not slavery nullify this law, and compel the slave to work on the Sabbath?[6]

Payne also highlighted how slavery forced the enslaved to violate other laws, like marriage, adultery, and so forth. The mandates of American slavery inevitably compelled African men and women to live contrary to God's laws. For some more theologically minded, like Garnet, the disobedience would have eternal consequences.

THE AUTOBIOGRAPHICAL FREEDOM NARRATIVES AND THE SABBATH

The History of Mary Prince (1831) and the Decade of the 1830s

In the 1830s, within the narratives, attention to issues surrounding the Sabbath day increased. Although the religious idea was not completely absent from earlier narratives, it occurred sparingly. Increasing interest in Sabbath regulations was due to broader debates occurring in North American and British societies.[7] We begin our account with Mary Prince's 1831 *The History of Mary Prince, A West Indian Slave. Related by Herself,* the first narrative by an African female in the Americas.[8] Prince did not write her own account, but—according to her

---

4. Mary Ann Shadd, "Break Every Yoke and Let the Oppressed Go Free," in *Lift Every Voice,* 319–20.
5. Born free in 1811, Payne was well educated in the South at a school for free blacks (*Lift Every Voice,* 173).
6. Daniel Payne, "Slavery Brutalizes Man," in *Lift Every Voice,* 176; Payne's italics.
7. McCrossen, *Holy Day.*
8. Mary Prince, *The History of Mary Prince, A West Indian Slave. Related by Herself. With a Supplement by the Editor* (London: Published by F. Westley and A. H. Davis, 1831).

editor—"it is essentially her own."[9] She offered two primary, albeit short, passages on the Sabbath.[10]

> It is very wrong, I know, to work on Sunday or go to market; but will not God call the Buckra [i.e., "white"] men to answer for this on the great day of judgment—since they will give the slaves no other day?[11]
>
> They hire servants in England; and if they don't like them, they send them away: they can't lick them. Let them work ever so hard in England, they are far better off than slaves. If they get a bad master, they give warning and go hire to another. They have their liberty. That's just what we want. We don't mind hard work, if we had proper treatment, and proper wages like English servants, and proper time given in the week to keep us from breaking the Sabbath. But they won't give it: they will have work—work—work, night and day, sick or well, till we are quite done up; and we must not speak up nor look amiss, however much we be abused. And then, when we are quite done up, who cares for us, more than for a lame horse? This is slavery.[12]

The end of her story, which provided the literary context of the second quote, highlighted the comparison between slavery in the Western Hemisphere and the servant workforce in early nineteenth-century England. Evident in this contrast was the political nature of her story.

While Prince offered no substantial treatment of the subject, or any mention of the concept of rest, her remarks reveal awareness that slaveholding society had abrogated the Sabbath law. In fact, her first passage presented a clear definition of Sabbath breaking: working and buying/selling on the Sabbath broke the law. The context of the second passage implied the same. Prince also carefully suggested a solution to the problem: "proper treatment" and "proper wages," with time to fulfill requisite chores, would allow folks the ability to carry out proper Sabbath-law observance. From her perspective, judgment for this act of

9. As Thomas Pringle stated in the preface, "No fact of importance has been omitted, and not a single circumstance or sentiment has been added. It is essentially her own, without any material alteration farther than was requisite to exclude redundancies and gross grammatical errors, so as to render it clearly intelligible" (*History*, i*). See Andrews, *To Tell a Free Story: The First Century of Afro-American Autobiography, 1760–1865* (Urbana: University of Illinois Press, 1988), iii.

10. She also mentions incidentally a brush-arbor meeting, without stating that it occurred specifically on a Sabbath day. Apparently, she was unable to visit the service herself, since whites had discovered its whereabouts and shut down the gathering (Prince, *History*, 13*).

11. Prince, *History*, 16*.

12. Prince, *History*, 23*.

disobedience will fall upon the "Buckra men" and not on the enslaved individuals who have no personal choice in the matter.

Though there is no clear evidence of literary dependence, Mary Prince's work was a precursor of more in-depth discussions of the Sabbath in later freedom narratives. Nevertheless, we know that African Americans read and shared stories of their experiences with one another, as in the case of Frederick Douglass, who read accounts of others within abolitionists' newspapers,[13] or the siblings Harriet and John Jacobs, who helped to revitalize the antislavery reading room that was established above the office of the *North Star* (Douglass's abolitionist newspaper).[14]

In addition to familiarity with the stories of the formerly enslaved, African American authors of the 1840s were heeding the call of Theodore Weld's *American Slavery as It Is*, published in 1839, in which Weld, a leading white abolitionist, advocated for more testimonies from those who had escaped the immoral institution.[15] Benjamin Quarles calls Theodore Weld "the driving spirit behind the organized abolitionist movement" before 1840.[16] With his summons, Weld's specifications included a need for the description of "hours of labor and rest"—in addition to a description of food, clothing, and lodging.[17] One final striking reference should be mentioned here. At the end of the decade (in 1838) and prior to Weld's public appeal, Moses Roper recorded an account of the twisted brutality of one individual that even the religious Sabbath could not protect: "Thus, Mr. Bell flogged this poor boy even to death; for what? for breaking the Sabbath, when he (his master) had set him a task on Saturday which it was not possible for him to do, and which, if he did not do, no mercy would be extended towards him. So much for the regard of this Methodist for the observance of the Sabbath."[18]

13. Evidence of this dependence can be found in Douglass's speeches from 1841 to 1845. See John Blassingame, "Introduction," in *The Frederick Douglass Papers, Series 2: Autobiographical Writings*, vol. 1, *Narrative*, ed. John W. Blassingame, John R. McKivigan, and Peter P. Hinks (New Haven/London: Yale University Press, 1999), xxiii.

14. Jean Fagan Yellin, *Harriet Jacobs: A Life* (New York: Basic Civitas Books, 2004), 101–3.

15. Theodore Weld, *American Slavery as It Is: Testimony of a Thousand Witnesses* (New York: American Anti-Slavery Society, 1839). According to Blassingame, Weld's announcement of the American Anti-Slavery Society's intention to publish more testimonies and narratives about slavery may have instigated Douglass's own story (Blassingame, "Introduction," xxiv–xv).

16. Benjamin Quarles, *Lincoln and the Negro* (New York: Oxford University Press, 1962), 46.

17. Weld, *American Slavery*, iv. What Weld did not call for—yet many African Americans provided—was attention to the biblical text with respect to Sabbath law.

18. Moses Roper, *A Narrative of the Adventures and Escape of Moses Roper, from American Slavery* (Philadelphia: Merrihew & Gunn, 1838), 24–26*.

The discourse among *free* African Americans (e.g., Shadd and Payne), among whom these authors lived when they wrote their abolitionist texts, supported extensively the expected peaceful nature the Sabbath day intended, despite the abuse many experienced during their enslavement.[19]

The 1840s: Douglass, Bibb, and Pennington

The 1840s witnessed the heyday of African American narratives of the formerly enslaved. Frederick Douglass wrote a classic example of a story of individual freedom, a theme that he later modified in his 1855 narrative over which he exerted greater autonomy.[20] Within the genre, Henry Bibb published one of the most striking examples of a love story among the enslaved, in which he reentered slave territory on several occasions because of a deep longing to be with his wife, Malinda, and daughter.[21] Finally, James Pennington's narrative provided an excellent portrayal of the necessary role of "deception"—and the theological crisis it can cause—in order to gain one's freedom.[22] These individual narratives were representative of many others and emphasize significant themes of the genre, including the recurrent religious ideal of the Sabbath day.

Two motifs predominate these discussions of the Sabbath day. First, on this day, the potential existed for the establishment of Sabbath-day schools, which would allow for crucial humanizing opportunities for securing literacy and developing community. Both Frederick Douglass (writing about life in Maryland) and Henry Bibb (writing about life in Kentucky) included passages in which they examined the organization of such schools by *named* white sympathizers.[23] Unfortunately, in both instances, the actual "schools" lasted only for a season. According to Franklin and Moss, the rise of the abolitionist crusade in the North

---

19. In the 1850s, depictions of this physical violence continued. See Solomon Northup's moving account of Patsey's brutal whipping on the "Sabbath of the Lord," followed by further reflections on the meaning of rest, in *Twelve Years a Slave* (Auburn, NY: Derby & Miller, 1853), 254–62*. See also William Wells Brown, *Narrative of William W. Brown, A Fugitive Slave. Written by Himself* (Boston: The Anti-Slavery Office, 1847), 38*.

20. Frederick Douglass, *Narrative of the Life of Frederick Douglass, an American Slave. Written by Himself* (Boston: Anti-Slavery Office, 1845); *My Bondage and My Freedom* (New York: Miller, Orton & Mulligan, 1855).

21. Henry Bibb, *Narrative of the Life and Adventures of Henry Bibb, An American Slave, Written by Himself* (New York: Author, 1849).

22. James Pennington, *Fugitive Blacksmith* (London: Charles Gilpin, 1849).

23. Mr. Wilson, the white sympathizer in Douglass's story, was a Quaker, who taught in a local school for whites, and who represented those "who continued to argue against slavery and for teaching the slaves to read the Scriptures" ("Historical Annotation," in *The Frederick Douglass Papers*, ed. Blassingame, 138).

caused a tightening of white control over religious gatherings in the Southern states.[24] In Douglass's community, the school was disrupted by "class-leaders" from the local Methodist church.[25] In Bibb's case, Sabbath schools were illegal, so that it was soon disbanded. In both cases, slaveholders considered these meetings to be part of, in Bibb's words, "an incendiary Movement."[26]

As Raboteau highlights, the slaveholding community generally insisted on religious instruction by the "oral method," so as not to challenge anti-literacy laws in many states.[27] Sabbath schools attempted to rearrange the status quo and were frequently opposed by white majorities, including many local religious leaders. Charles Colcock Jones, a white minister and missionary to the African American community, provided a view from the 1840s on literacy, the law, and the enslaved black community:

> Shall we speak of access to the Scriptures? The statutes of our respective slave States forbid all knowledge of letters to the Negroes; and where the statutes do not custom does. It is impossible to form an estimate of the number of Negroes that read. My belief is that the proportion would be expressed by an almost inconceivable fraction. The greatest number of readers is found in and about towns and cities, and among the free Negro population, some two or three generations removed from servitude. There are perhaps in all the larger cities in the South, schools for the education of colored children, supported chiefly by the free Negroes, and kept generally in the shade. On the one hand, therefore, the Negro children cannot be "hearers of the law," for oral instruction is but sparingly afforded to the mass of them; and on the other, they cannot "search the Scriptures," for a knowledge of letters they have not, and legally, they cannot obtain.[28]

In addition to a brief description of one initial effort, Douglass also included an account of a more successful and substantial Sabbath school, one that he himself led! Douglass attributed partial credit for

24. "In most states, black preachers were outlawed between 1820 and 1835, and thereafter slave religious services were presided over by a white person. More and more, however, slaves were required to attend the churches of their masters" (John Hope Franklin and Alfred A. Moss Jr., *From Slavery to Freedom: A History of African Americans*, 8th ed. [New York: Alfred A. Knopf, 2006], 153).

25. Douglass, *Narrative*, 55*.

26. Bibb, *Narrative*, 21*.

27. Albert J. Raboteau, *Slave Religion: The Invisible Institution in the Antebellum South* (New York: Oxford University Press, 1978), 161. This method may account for inexact quotations from the Bible.

28. Charles Colcock Jones, *The Religious Instruction of the Negros. In the United States* (Savannah, GA: 1842), 115*. Leonard Black described the threat of whipping if he were discovered with a book (*The Life and Sufferings of Leonard Black, a Fugitive from Slavery. Written by Himself* [New Bedford: Benjamin Lindsey, 1847], 18–19*).

the success of this school to the more lenient Mr. Freeland, who Douglass considered to be "the best master I ever had, *till I became my own master*."[29] In contradistinction from Douglass's severe critique of professing slaveholders, Mr. Freeland "made no pretensions to, or profession of, religion; and this, in my opinion, was truly a great advantage."[30] This Sabbath school "society of my fellow-slaves," Douglass emphasized was a community, men and women,[31] in which "we would have died for each other."[32] In this setting, they were "behaving like intellectual, moral, and accountable beings," yet they had to be constantly aware that many would view such positive humanistic activities as contrary to slaveholding designs.[33] Their secret society met in the home of a free, intentionally unnamed African American, whose action must have placed his own status in jeopardy.[34]

The success of this mission affected both Douglass and individual members. David Blight thinks it had a direct impact on Douglass's rhetorical skills in writing his autobiographies.[35] For Douglass, "it was the delight of my soul," he stated, "to be doing something that looked like bettering the condition of my race."[36] Of the forty "scholars," several members learned to read, and "one, at least is now free through my agency," Douglass wrote.[37] One decade later, in his 1855 edition, Douglass reported that others had since escaped enslavement.[38] Apparently, Douglass was able to maintain contact with at least some members of this gathering in Maryland after he escaped to the North. The success of this early flirtation with religious autonomy may well have served as a foreshadowing of a flourishing independent African American church movement.[39]

29. Douglass, *Narrative*, 82*; Douglass's italics.
30. Douglass, *Narrative*, 77*.
31. In *My Bondage and My Freedom* (1855), Douglass omits the more inclusive phrase "and women" of the 1845 edition (*My Bondage and My Freedom* [New York: Miller, Orton & Mulligan, 1855], 265*).
32. Douglass, *Narrative*, 83*.
33. Douglass, *Narrative*, 81*.
34. Enslaved blacks kept contacts with free blacks to a minimum (see Franklin and Moss, *From Slavery to Freedom*, 141). Douglass named him—James Mitchell—in the later edition (*My Bondage and My Freedom*, 199*).
35. "The book is imbued with biblical reference, imagery, and metaphors, and it owes much to the black sermonic tradition from which Douglass had learned a great deal about the use of language and its powers. His exhortative tones and rhythms not only were modeled on the Old Testament prophets that Douglass read. They were undoubtedly the ones he had practiced among his band of brothers at the Sabbath school on Freeland's farm, as he and his charges learned to plot their own deliverance, as well as to keep faith in one another and in God" (David Blight, "Introduction," in *Narrative of the Life of Frederick Douglass: An American Slave, Written by Himself: With Related Documents*, 2nd ed., ed. with intro. by David W. Blight [Boston/New York: Bedford/St. Martin's, 2003], 8–9).
36. Douglass, *Narrative*, 82*.
37. Douglass, *Narrative*, 82*.
38. Douglass, *My Bondage and My Freedom*, 267*.
39. Douglass's description hints at the fact that freedom, to some extent, was predicated on Sabbath practice! See Andrews, *To Tell a Free Story*, 230.

As part of his discussion, although a theme absent from Douglass, Bibb highlighted that "[t]he Sabbath is not regarded by a large number of the slaves as a day of rest." This was not due to any fault of the enslaved, as Mary Prince and Henry Highland Garnet previously observed. For Bibb, as for others, "Sabbath" and "literacy" correlate extensively.[40] There was nothing incompatible with rest on the Sabbath and education despite state regulations. Yet, with no schools to attend and no moral or religious instruction, breaking the Sabbath was a common occurrence. Those actions that hindered the intellectual and spiritual development of the human being—gambling, fighting, and drunkenness—Bibb considered Sabbath breaking. As Bibb noted, many slaveholders actually encouraged these behaviors on the Sabbath.[41] He explained part of the slave-owning rationale later in the narrative. During slave auctions intelligence was a significant offense:

> If they are found to be very intelligent, this is pronounced the most objectionable of all other qualities connected with the life of a slave. In fact, it undermines the whole fabric of his chattelhood; it prepares for what slaveholders are pleased to pronounce the unpardonable sin when committed by a slave. It lays the foundation for running away, and going to Canada. They also see in it a love for freedom, patriotism, insurrection, bloodshed, and exterminating war against American slavery.[42]

Although Bibb only hinted at implicit agreement with this "rationale," Douglass recognized the truth of this explanation in the words of his former master Thomas Auld, who in forbidding his wife from teaching Douglass anything, offered the following explanation: "[Learning] would forever unfit him to be a slave. He would at once become unmanageable, and of no value to his master. As to himself, it could do him no good, but a great deal of harm. It would make him discontented and unhappy."[43]

Ironically, this "special revelation" drove Douglass to learn to read on every possible occasion after this moment, because he believed that Mr. Auld spoke the truth. Learning would be his way to freedom.[44] He also found, as mentioned earlier, great comfort in leading "fellow

---

40. Bibb, *Narrative*, 21–24*.

41. Bibb, *Narrative*, 23–24*. Douglass also highlighted that slaveholders sponsored "degrading sports" (*Narrative*, 81*).

42. Bibb, *Narrative*, 101–2*.

43. Douglass, *Narrative*, 33*.

44. Solomon Northup discussed the tension in the white community over the slaveholder's (William Ford's), willingness to offer Bibles to the enslaved (Northup, *Twelve Years a Slave*, 97–98*).

slaves" along the path of literacy. For Bibb, the "unpardonable sin" was an offense worth pursuing, and he too saw the interconnectedness between literacy and liberty and literacy and the Sabbath.

The second major motif that emerges in the narratives is that the Sabbath day was viewed as a day for physical escape. James Pennington, in one of the more lucid examples of this view of the Sabbath, wrote: "It was the Sabbath: the holy day which God in his infinite wisdom gave for the rest of both man and beast."[45] A few sentences after this statement of confession, Pennington discussed his escape from slavery. The Sabbath day provided sufficient time (in some states) to organize escape routes, prepare emergency supplies for the journey, and (when the day arrived) establish distance between the escapee and the slaveholder. Pennington was aware that, at least in Maryland, "the slaves generally have the Sabbath" legally.[46] This was not the case in Kentucky in the 1840s, for example, as far as Bibb knew; he believed that a Georgia law passed in 1770 against religious instruction for blacks was enforced throughout the entire United States.[47]

Widespread awareness of this idea was best summed up in a lesser known narrative, *The Life and Sufferings of Leonard Black*, "written by himself" in 1847: "We remembered what our brothers told us—when we were able to run away, to try it on some favorable Sunday."[48] Several of Black's brothers had escaped slavery when he was a young boy, and they gave him this advice. The Sabbath was a day when, in Black's context (also in Maryland), the enslaved were allowed to attend religious services in the nearby village, so escapees could distance themselves several miles from the plantation.[49] Ten years later, Black would successfully run away as well, an event that he connected intimately to his religious conversion: "When God had opened my eyes, I grew very uneasy reflecting upon the condition of my brothers, who were enjoying their liberty in a land of freedom. I wanted also to be free. I resolved to be free. I made up my mind to run away in the year 1837."[50] In the ongoing cultural debate among white slaveholders whether religion would make the enslaved more compliant, Black's experience testified otherwise.

45. Pennington continued, highlighting what normally happened on the Sabbath: "In the state of Maryland, the slaves generally have the Sabbath, except in those districts where the evil weed, tobacco, is cultivated; and then, when it is the season for setting the plant, they are liable to be robbed of this only rest" (*Fugitive Blacksmith*, 12*).
46. Pennington, *Fugitive Blacksmith*, 12*.
47. Bibb, *Narrative*, 31–32*.
48. Black, *Life and Sufferings*, 17*.
49. Black, *Life and Sufferings*, 15–18*.
50. Black, *Life and Sufferings*, 22*.

Both motifs can be viewed under the larger umbrella of "freedom," spiritually, emotionally, intellectually, *and* literally. For authors of the autobiographical slave narratives, the Sabbath, if practiced correctly, was a symbol for freedom in all of its manifestations. The narratives of the 1840s demonstrate, even more than Prince's 1831 treatise, the significance of a just appropriation of the Sabbath law. It was an attempt by African Americans to persuade their generally white abolitionist audiences that not even this biblical commandment was followed consistently within the slaveholding communities of the South and British West Indies. Yet when "rest" was allowed, the enslaved could take advantage of the opportunity for self-preservation—spiritually and physically—and, occasionally, could seek out avenues to flee for safer lands.

Adjustments to the "Pattern": The 1850s (Randolph and Douglass)

Nell Irvin Painter describes the 1850s as the most "desperate decade" in African American history,[51] as authors of these narratives maintained a strong emphasis on the significance of the Sabbath day for the enslaved. According to William Andrews, it was during this decade that these authors "would move further outside the margins of propriety in search of greater narrative freedom and more usable truth."[52] We now turn to two representatives of the genre in the 1850s: Randolph and Douglass.

In his 1855 *Sketches of Slave Life*,[53] Peter Randolph described the nature of life for the enslaved in Virginia. He referred to the Sabbath in several different contexts, as part of his narrative attempt to stress this day as the only time that the enslaved had for themselves. Hence, they engaged in a range of activities, from making traps and capturing

---

51. Painter, *Sojourner Truth*, 132. Painter highlights significant events of the period, including several of the following: the Fugitive Slave Law Act of 1850; the regional splits, over slavery, in both the Democratic (1848) and the Whig parties (1854); the abolition of the slave trade, *not slavery*, in Washington, DC (1850); the appearance of Harriet Beecher Stowe's *Uncle Tom's Cabin* (1852); the Dred Scott case of 1857; and economic shifts, e.g., the rise in cotton production and profits, which increased the demand for slaves.

52. "[B]y the end of the 1840s, the slave narrative had begun to make its first tentative steps away from its white readership, whose embrace meant suppression as well as success. The most self-conscious black autobiographers were beginning to wonder openly whose truth they were to speak, thus revealing the strains to which the genre's traditional social and moral proprieties subjected them. In the next decade their successors would move further outside the margins of propriety in search of greater narrative freedom and more usable truth" (Andrews, *To Tell a Free Story*, 166).

53. Peter Randolph, *Sketches of Slave Life: Or, Illustrations of the "Peculiar Institution"* (Boston: The Author, 1855).

"possums" to supplement their meager food rations,[54] to visiting friends and family on other plantations,[55] to engaging in recreational activities, to participating in religious services.[56]

In a section entitled "Sabbath and Religious Meetings," Randolph highlighted worship as the most important part of the holy day, a religious experience that took place in two distinct contexts for the enslaved. Many enslaved people met secretly, slipping away to the swamps where they were free to worship as they pleased. Randolph reported on activities that resemble contemporary worship in some African American congregations, including therapeutic and cathartic interactions of members and singing, climaxing in preaching that leads to an ecstatic experience where "there fall to the ground twenty or thirty men and women," which was punctuated by a passing of the peace. They also had what appeared to be a fatalistic surrender, but can best be described as an apocalyptic hope, as expressed in the statement "Thank God, I shall not live here always." In this regard their focus was on heaven, "where all is joy, happiness and *liberty*."[57]

The other typical context for worship was in sanctioned and sanitized buildings on plantations. Slaveholders subjected the enslaved to a gospel of servitude centered on texts like Ephesians 6, "Servants, obey your masters."[58] Plantation owners employed their own ministers, who would warn the captive congregation, "It is the devil . . . who tells you to try to be free."[59] The plantation community sanctioned these messages, but the enslaved interpreted them as attempts to thwart the spread of Christ's gospel. Recall Randolph's words, "[L]et no one say that the slaves have the Gospel of Jesus preached to them." In effect, slaveholding community members denied the enslaved, even on the Sabbath, access to the authentic gospel. Thus, as a rule, enslaved people had restricted access to God, on the Sabbath, as though such contact was dangerous to the interests of their tormentors. Reminiscent of Bibb's words almost a decade earlier, Randolph noted that "if the slaves

---

54. Randolph, *Sketches*, 19–20*.

55. Randolph, *Sketches*, 28*.

56. Randolph, *Sketches*, 30–33*. Absalom Jones delivered "A Thanksgiving Sermon," on January 1, 1808, which also addressed the Sabbath as a time when enslaved Africans were able to forage for food, partly because they were denied spiritual nourishment on this day. He continued:

He [God] has seen them return to their smoky huts in the evening, with nothing to satisfy their hunger but a scanty allowance of roots; and these, cultivated for themselves, on that day, which God ordained as a day of rest for man and beast. He has seen the neglect with which their masters have treated their immortal souls; not only in withholding religious instruction from them, but, in some instances, depriving them of access to the means of obtaining it (*Lift Every Voice*, 76).

57. Randolph, *Sketches*, 31*; emphasis added.

58. See chap. 5 for a thorough discussion of these slaveholding-sponsored sermons.

59. Randolph, *Sketches*, 32*.

were caught praying to God, they are whipped more than if they had committed a great crime. The slaveholders will allow slaves to dance, but do not want them to pray to God."[60]

The white slaveholding community offered mixed reactions to religious instruction for the enslaved. Debates continued from the early decades in the century. Many thought religion would benefit the enslaved community and encourage passivity and a willingness to continue their service.[61] As Solomon Northup wrote, one plantation owner, Peter Tanner, would frequently read Luke 12:47 during Sabbath gatherings, in an attempt to maintain control over the minds and actions of the enslaved: "And that servant, which knew his lord's will, and prepared not himself, neither did according to his will, shall be beaten with many stripes" (KJV).[62]

Yet occasionally white-led religious instruction was depicted positively, as in Northup's description of Bible instruction under slave owner William Ford, who allowed for the distribution of Bibles, an action opposed by many in the local community.[63] Hearing about the formation of formal Sabbath schools to encourage Christian instruction and, sometimes, literacy upset many citizens in the community, including Master Nattie:

> A few benevolent individuals, about this time, established a Sabbath School in Lexington, for the instruction of such slaves as might be permitted by their masters to learn.
>
> At this proceeding Master Nattie was indignant. He would not have his niggers spoiled by getting Learning—no, indeed! Niggers were bad enough, without being set up by such rascals as these Sunday School teachers. They'd better not meddle with his property; and if he heard of one of his boys going near the school, he'd give him such a flogging that he'd never need any more education.[64]

---

60. Randolph, *Sketches*, 31*. In Randolph's 1893 edition, *From Slave Cabin to the Pulpit. The Autobiography of Rev. Peter Randolph: The Southern Question Illustrated and Sketches of Life* (Boston: J. H. Earle, 1893), he rehearsed much of the earlier account in *Sketches of Slave Life*. One notable exception was the inclusion of a section entitled "Religious Instruction"; he provocatively began, "Many say the Negroes receive religious education—that Sabbath worship is instituted for them as for others, and were it not for slavery, they would die in their sins—that really, the institution of slavery is a benevolent missionary enterprise" (196*). After that he reproduced reflections similar to those noted above, about the hypocritical and self-serving nature of the "slaveholding gospel" that was thrust on enslaved people by the plantation owners. Thus, for Randolph, the Sabbath could be viewed as a time of either temporary escape from the rigors of slavery to the beatific secret worship in the swamps or a time of sacralized ideological violence whereby the domination system gave the inhumane conditions under which enslaved people lived.

61. See Mitchell Snay, *Gospel of Disunion: Religion and Separatism in the Antebellum South* (Cambridge: Cambridge University Press, 1993).

62. Northup, *Twelve Years a Slave*, 128*.

63. Northup, *Twelve Years a Slave*, 97–98*.

64. *Kate Pickard, The Kidnapped and the Ransom: Recollections of Peter Still and his Wife "Vina" after Forty Years of Slavery* (Syracuse, NY: William T. Hamilton, 1856), 40*.

Additionally, others attempted to manage their own affairs by providing "spiritual" instruction themselves, yet occasionally went well beyond the Bible to include theological concepts foreign to orthodox Christian teaching. Henry Box Brown recorded the following account of one Sunday school superintendent, a leader in the community:

> As I have stated, Mr. A. was a devout attendant upon public worship, and prayed much with the pupils in the Sabbath school, and was indefatigable in teaching them to repeat the catechism after him, although he was very particular never to allow them to hold the book in their hands. But let not my readers suppose on this account, that he desired the salvation of these slaves. No, far from that; for very soon after thus exhorting them, he would tell his visiters [*sic*], that it was "a d—d lie that colored people were ever converted," and that they could "not go to heaven," for they had no souls; but that it was his duty to talk to them as he did.[65]

Among other things, it is intriguing that Mr. A. would not allow blacks even to "hold the book." Furthermore, Mr. Allen's belief that African Americans "had no souls" was not unique to him and had more widespread support (even from the mid-nineteenth century "scientific" community) than is frequently assumed (see the discussion in chap. 4). Despite his religious belief, he viewed it as a "duty" to provide religious instruction as a way to encourage passivity among the enslaved and supposedly to strengthen the status quo.

In 1855, ten years after his initial publication, Frederick Douglass developed his autobiography further, writing another, revised, freedom narrative, which he titled *My Bondage and My Freedom*.[66] Several scholars have offered detailed analyses of the distinctions between the two versions.[67] For this chapter, we wish to draw only on Douglass's alterations to the Sabbath-day motif in the 1855 edition.

According to the author of the preface to the new edition, James McCune Smith, a physician and leading African American abolitionist of the day, Douglass's updated version appealed to a different kind of

65. Henry Box Brown, *Narrative of the Life of Henry Box Brown, Written by Himself* (Manchester, England: Printed by Lee & Glynn, 1851), 46*.

66. By this point, Douglass had also published a work of fiction, *The Heroic Slave: From Autographs for Freedom* (Boston: John P. Jewett & Co., 1853).

67. See William Andrews, "*My Bondage and My Freedom* and the American Literary Renaissance of the 1850s," in *Critical Essays on Frederick Douglass*, ed. William L. Andrews (Boston: G. K. Hall & Co., 1991). Andrews discusses a number of Douglass's "contradictions" in the 1855 narrative in another publication; see *To Tell a Free Story: The First Century of Afro-American Autobiography, 1760–1865* (Urbana: University of Illinois Press, 1988), 228.

audience, one whose ideology understood more clearly than their white Garrisonian counterparts the interrelationship between the enslaved of the South and the "free" blacks of the North. Douglass's explicit move away from Garrison exposed a significant development in his thinking.[68] We find evidence of this shift even in the altered descriptions of the stories about the Sabbath schools; for example, in the new edition he acknowledged the existence of schools for free African American children *in the South* in an analogy to Nat Turner.[69] The latter reference to Turner and his insurrection highlighted a noteworthy change in Douglass's view as well, since it had taken Douglass a few years to accept the viability of violent slave insurrection, proposed by Henry Highland Garnet and others, as an option if necessary (see chap. 2).[70] (Garrison was a committed pacifist.)

Equally striking was Douglass's 1855 expanded explanation of the ideology behind the slaveholders' disruption of the school, which is particularly pertinent to our discussion. As he stated, "if slavery be right, Sabbath schools for teaching slaves to read the Bible are wrong."[71] Douglass rightfully reasoned that this ideology placed the Protestant principle, of people searching the Scriptures for themselves, in jeopardy.[72] His expanded edition dealt with a number of contradictions, both in the slaveholders' religious views and in his own role.[73] One could imagine how these "contradictions" also impacted Northern

68. Douglass's split with Garrison was permanent by 1851. See Andrews, "*My Bondage and My Freedom* and the American Literary Renaissance," 138.

69. In the account on the Sabbath school initiated by the white Quaker, Mr. Wilson, Douglass provided additional pertinent information in the 1855 edition: (1) in Baltimore, there were Sabbath schools for *free* African American children; (2) Mr. Wilson invited Douglass to assist in the teaching of the Sabbath school; (3) in addition to the New Testament (1845 edition), spelling books were also utilized; (4) Douglass included his former master, Thomas Auld, as one of the "mob" who disrupted and disbanded the school; (5) he shared the story that one of the mob compared Douglass to Nat Turner, forewarning him that he would end up like him; (6) Douglass addressed "the reader" directly, stressing how this disbandment weakened his faith.

In his account on the Sabbath school on Mr. Freeland's farm, Douglass also expanded his 1855 version to include the following: (1) he listed Webster's dictionary and the *Columbian Orator* as additional textbooks to the Bible; (2) he specifically mentioned reading the "word of God" (*not* the "will of God"); (3) he provided an extended explanation on the ideology behind the slaveholders' strategy; (4) he mentioned that more than one slave from this band of learners had secured freedom; (5) he addressed the reader directly again, to consider the lengths to which the enslaved went to secure this type of minimal educational experience.

70. The disbandment by white slaveholders was one more attempt to control the lives of the enslaved. It was insurrections like Denmark Vesey's and Nat Turner's, and the interrelationship between "religion and rebellion," that "probably alerted Southern slaveholders to the need for white control of Afro-American religion" (Snay, *Gospel of Disunion*, 90, also 93). Southern clerics, especially in the lower South, also participated in this system of "control" (91).

71. Douglass, *My Bondage and My Freedom*, 266*.

72. Douglass, *My Bondage and My Freedom*, 266*.

73. "In 1845 Douglass led his readers to believe that the Sabbath school he opened at Freeland's was the result of pressure from fellow slaves who longed to learn to read. *My Bondage and My Freedom* brings out Douglass's selfish motives; he "wanted a Sabbath school, in which to exercise my gifts," as well as to teach his brother slaves their letters. *My Bondage and My Freedom* also does not neglect to mention Douglass's preference for self-interest over the welfare of those he would have to leave behind in the slave quarters, people he knew were likely to suffer to some extent, whether he succeeded or failed in his escape. In sum, the second autobiography deliberately brings to the

perceptions of African American society. Peter Randolph's extensive description of the brush arbor meetings and Douglass's later edition serve as examples of a more comprehensive and complicated view of the thoughts among the formerly enslaved on the significance of the Sabbath for literacy, freedom, *and community* (a much stronger emphasis in the 1855 edition).

CONCLUSION

Dynamic discussions and public debates surrounding proper observance of the Sabbath day filled the air of the nineteenth century. General reformers in the North, including Lyman Beecher, Arthur and Lewis Tappan, and other ministers, in 1828 formed the General Union for Promoting the Observance of the Christian Sabbath.[74] Yet apparent economic realities (greed?) and political tensions were reasons (excuses?) that slaveholders used to continue to enforce labor on the Sabbath unevenly throughout the Southern states.

From the perspective of the enslaved, the Sabbath functioned as a slaveholders' tool by which they deliberately attempted to maintain the status quo. Most enslavers preferred an unorganized, but highly intentional, reprieve, instead of opportunities for the development of the enslaved's intellectual, moral, and religious well-being. What was available was either (1) to hear the preaching of the white slaveholders' gospel or (2) to engage in activities, like "drinking" and "gambling," that did not aid in intellectual development.

Yet the African American appropriation of Sabbath law derived from a self-affirming hermeneutic. The Sabbath for these persons represented a time for liberation, as manifest in the activities of worship, religious education, literacy programs, and even escape. Despite slaveholder intentions to provide structured worship that supported the status quo or encouraged morally questionable activities, enslaved and free Africans interpreted the Sabbath as the moment during the week in which they encountered the liberating God of Jesus, who mandated the cessation of business as usual and provided opportunities for escape (whether temporary or permanent) from their circumscribed existences. Recognizing the mutual benefits of these gatherings, Douglass

---

fore the contradictions in Douglass's role at the turning point of his life, which are at most only hinted at in the first autobiography" (Andrews, *To Tell a Free Story*, 228).

74. See McCrossen, *Holy Day*, 24.

could write about one such encounter: "I could teach him 'the letter,' but he could teach me 'the spirit.'"[75]

We end with a consideration of the work of Mary Ann Shadd,[76] who argued against slavery in a 1858 sermon, "Break Every Yoke and Let the Oppressed Go Free." In a creative modification of traditional views of Sabbath, she advocated for liberative Sabbath labor, an obedient response to God that is literally a labor of love.[77] She then utilized Jesus' reinterpretation of Sabbath law, advocating a similar hermeneutic.

> There is too a fitness of time for any work for the benefit of God's human creatures. We are told to keep Holy the Sabbath day. In what manner? Not by following simply the injunctions of those who bind heavy burdens, to say nothing about the same but as a man is better than a sheep, but combining with God's worship the most active vigilance for the resurrector from degradation violence and sin of his creatures [sic]. In these cases particularly is the Sabbath made for man and *woman* if you please as there may be those who will not accept the term man in a generic sense. Christ has told us as it is lawful to lift a sheep out of the ditch on the Sabbath day, i[f] a man is much better than a sheep [sic].[78]

Despite the challenging syntax of the final sentence, it is clear that she was applying Jesus' liberating rereading of Sabbath law here, suggesting the necessity of engaging in abolitionist work on the Sabbath.

The sense of "rest" that Jesus had is one that the enslaved would have shared. As Frederick Douglass and Henry Bibb implied in their writings, rest on the Sabbath was not at all incompatible with the establishment of schools for the purpose of moral and religious instruction. The opposite of rest—that is, to "break the Sabbath," in Bibb's words—was to act in ways opposite to the attainment of literacy and knowledge. Nor was this sense of rest incompatible with an opportunity to escape on the Sabbath, as James Pennington so aptly described.

75. Douglass, *My Bondage and My Freedom*, 83*.

76. Shadd was a freeborn African American woman, born in 1823 to an affluent African American family, an integrationist and the "first black woman newspaper editor" (*Lift Every Voice*, 318).

77. "We must then manifest love to God by obedience to his will—we must be cheerful workers in his cause at all times—on the Sabbath and other days. The more readiness we Evince the more we manifest our love, and as our field is directly among those of his creatures made in his own image in acting as themselves who is no respecter of persons we must have failed in our duty until we become decided to waive all prejudices of Education birth nation or training and make the test of our obedience God's Equal command to love neighbor as ourselves (Shadd, "Break Every Yoke," 319*).

78. Shadd, "Break Every Yoke," 320*.

Despite this apparent link between Jesus' view and the enslaved's view of the Sabbath, African Americans rarely recalled Jesus' own actions and teaching on the Sabbath. Rather, they redefined the First Testament concept of rest as activity that involved the well-being of the human person. The Sabbath day was, for all intents and purposes, the only potential day for such liberating and communal activity.

Many narratives support the idea of a Sabbath for the enslaved and observed the lack of one as indicative of the unchristian nature of the institution as a whole. In contradistinction, some white abolitionists—for example, William Lloyd Garrison—argued against the authority of the Bible for contemporary practices, whether Sabbath observance or slavery itself.[79] Many black abolitionists, particularly the formerly enslaved, did not share this sentiment. They did not view it as hermeneutically inconsistent to uphold an authoritative Bible on one topic (i.e., Sabbath observance) while rejecting its authority on separate practices (i.e., slavery). They could be selective with their biblical literalism and its application. They had no problem exclaiming God's intentional benefit in the one while believing God's absence from the other.[80] With the topos of the "Sabbath," one intention the narratives desired was to incite in their audience, particularly Christian abolitionists, a deep disgust for slaveholding communities, a people who even disregard God's holy Sabbath law.

Perhaps the enslaved of the nineteenth century did not follow Jesus' words on Sabbath practices, but they at least intuit his pragmatic hermeneutical practice. For just as Jesus reclaims the precursor (Old Testament) text in order to express his attempt to co-opt the biblical text for his own use, nineteenth-century African Americans chose the biblical ideology that best suited their desires and practices for liberation of the mind and body, and thereby sought to secure a sacred moment wherein they could reclaim pieces of their stolen humanity. Whatever else the Sabbath day may have meant to African Americans, it was also intended to be a time for liberation and a time for community. In fact, Sabbath ideology, which facilitated the development of the early black church and corporate autonomy, may just be the birth of African American independence!

79. See McCrossen, *Holy Day*, 30–31.

80. In a similar vein, Douglass (in opposition to Garrison) was unwilling to give up the practical use of the Constitution, as he was the practical use of the Bible, for arguments to support the injustice of the peculiar institution. On Douglass's personal reflections, in 1855, on his break with the Garrisonians, see *My Bondage and My Freedom*, 398*.

4

The Origins of Whiteness and the Black Biblical Imagination

"What happens to the writerly imagination of a black author who is at some level *always* conscious of representing one's own race to, or in spite of, a race of readers that understands itself to be "universal" or race-free?"

(Toni Morrison)[1]

INTRODUCTION

Peculiar to slavery in the Americas, in the history of slavery, was the phenomenon of race.[2] Even as arguments in support of the peculiar institution mounted, the notion of ethnic groups was less systematically explored within religious circles. Nevertheless, enslavement of people of African descent sustained the practice in the United States. Many began to turn to the Bible to buttress their cultural perspectives on race, even as they utilized the holy book to justify the tradition of holding other humans in bondage. Interpreters highlighted a number of passages to defend differences among people groups, but the predominant support text for debates surrounding racial divisions was a passage from Genesis, the first book in the Bible.[3]

Following the end of the flood in the Genesis account (Gen. 6–8), the narrator introduces Noah's sons, Shem, Ham, and Japheth. Noah plants a vineyard as a sign of the future productivity of the land. From the vine, he gets drunk and falls asleep. Ham witnesses his father's

---

1. Toni Morrison, *Playing in the Dark: Whiteness and the Literary Imagination* (New York: Vintage Books, 1992), xii.

2. See David Brion Davis, *The Problem of Slavery in Western Culture* (Ithaca, NY: Cornell University Press, 1996); Robin Blackburn, *The Making of New World Slavery: From the Baroque to the Modern, 1492–1800* (London: Verso, 1997); Page duBois, *Slavery: Antiquity and Its Legacy* (New York: Oxford University Press, 2009).

3. See Sylvester Johnson, *Myth of Ham in Nineteenth-Century American Christianity: Race, Heathens, and the People of God* (New York: Palgrave MacMillan, 2004); Stephen Haynes, *Noah's Curse: The Biblical Justification of American Slavery* (New York: Oxford University Press, 2002).

nakedness, the implied sin of the story (Lev. 18:6–7). When he awakes from his stupor, Noah announces a curse on Canaan, Ham's son, including the indictment that he would be his brothers' servant (Gen. 9:18–27).[4] Within ancient Israel, the story functioned as an etiological account for the downfall of Canaan, which in turn provided justification for Israel's "eventual" (following the biblical time line) entry and destruction of the land of Canaan.

Yet in the nineteenth century, this story became one of the most popular myths promulgated for the purpose of shaping popular perceptions—among religious people—and developing the ideology necessary for maintaining the peculiar social institution. The so-called "curse of Ham" tradition was widely appropriated as a biblical warrant to maintain the link between race and the prevailing slavocracy.[5] For example, the popular white writer Josiah Priest suggested that the *character* of Ham was like the color of Ham's black skin. In response to such views, African American authors would occasionally refute Genesis 9's implications for coloration, especially with respect to the ties between "blackness" and "enslavement." Since the biblical narrative omits racial designation, African American interpreters responded to conjectures of coloration in Genesis 9. Rarely, however, was Genesis 9 utilized by the formerly enslaved to discuss the origins of "whiteness."[6]

Rather than discuss the image of blackness in the white mind (on which much has been written),[7] we want to explore the image of *whiteness* in the black mind. Fundamental to this historical discussion is the broader notion of identity and the appropriation of the biblical tradition. For nineteenth-century African Americans, as Sylvester Johnson has shown, "[t]his also meant constructing a Negro past—that is, racialized history—where there was previously none; Africans were not 'Africans' or 'Negroes' before the emergence of whiteness and colonization."[8]

---

4. Crucial for interpreting Genesis 9 in this manner was its narrative link to Genesis 10, the so-called "Table of Nations" (see Haynes, *Noah's Curse*, 41–61).

5. Of course, this is one of the major differences between nineteenth-century enslavement and its counterpart in antiquity. In antiquity, anyone could be enslaved; in its nineteenth-century US version, only dark-skinned peoples could be enslaved. See Finkelman, "Introduction: Defending Slavery," in *Defending Slavery: Proslavery Thought in the Old South: A Brief History with Documents* (Boston/New York: Bedford/St. Marting's, 2003), 8.

6. White interpreters utilized this text to explore racial origins (see Virgil Peterson, *Ham and Japheth: The Mythic World of Whites in the Antebellum South*, ATLA Monograph Series 12 [Lanham, MD: Scarecrow Press, 1978]).

7. Winthrop D. Jordan, *White over Black: American Attitudes toward the Negro, 1550–1812* (Chapel Hill: University of North Carolina Press, 1968); George M. Fredrickson, *The Black Image in the White Mind: The Debate on Afro-American Character and Destiny, 1817–1914* (New York: Harper & Row, 1971).

8. Johnson, *Myth of Ham*, 52; see Mia Bay, *The White Image in the Black Mind: African-American Ideas about White People, 1830–1925* (New York: Oxford University Press, 2000).

More specifically, in this chapter we will take up this discussion from the perspective of the earliest collection of the African American literary tradition, the narratives of the formerly enslaved. The nineteenth-century freedom-narrative accounts provided various challenges to the curse of Ham myth: (1) they observed contemporary experience and the phenomenon of black skin color in the Americas; (2) they employed the "one blood" tradition from the Bible as a counterstory; (3) occasionally they appropriated less common biblical passages in order to explore alternative origins. Within the literary tradition, this third challenge stands out. William Anderson's 1857 account of 2 Kings—a passage he claimed as support for the origins of whiteness—comes to the forefront. After an analysis of the "curse of Ham" motif in representative freedom narratives and the prominence of Acts 17 as a countertext, we will situate Anderson's interpretation within the broader ideological context of the period. We will conclude this chapter with some suggestive hermeneutical implications of this African American approach to the biblical text, in light of the discussion on racial origins, or what we might call "whiteness and the black biblical imagination."

THE "CURSE OF HAM" MYTH
AND CONTEMPORARY EXPERIENCE

As popular as the "curse of Ham" passage was in the public discourse of the nineteenth century, it failed to attract the same kind of attention within the antebellum freedom narrative tradition. Frederick Douglass was the first (among the formerly enslaved) to include it within the narrative tradition.[9] In the 1845 account, Ham appeared in the opening pages as his first allusion to the Bible. In the context of Douglass's description of the increasing mulatto slave population, he referenced the tradition of the curse of Ham from Genesis and the ideological racist theory associated with this myth common during the antebellum period. For many whites, this curse justified the enslavement of African people, since most Americans considered people of African descent to be descendants of Ham.

Prominent proslavery advocate Josiah Priest published his popular *Slavery, as It Relates to the Negro* in 1843, a couple of years before

---

9. Even though Ottobah Cuguano did not mention Ham in his narrative (in 1787), he discussed the Genesis 9 passage (focusing attention on Canaan) in his public refutation of slavery, in *Thoughts and Sentiments on the Evil of Slavery*, ed. Vincent Carretta (orig. 1787; New York: Penguin Books, 1999), 33, 48.

Douglass's widely distributed narrative.[10] Priest concluded that slavery was a biblical practice; therefore, it was "not sinful" to enslave African Americans, if performed in a manner that was Christian, that is, "tender, fatherly and thoughtful."[11] Indeed, for Priest and others, Genesis 9 was the anchor text for more than slavery. He believed that the original human being was "red"; so he explained the "supernatural manner" in which God developed both the black *and* white races through Noah as follows:

> Those two sons were Japheth and Ham. Japheth He caused to be born white, differing from the color of his parents, while He caused Ham to be born black, a color still farther removed from the red hue of his parents than was white, events and products wholly contrary to nature, in the particular of animal generation, as relates to the human race. It was therefore, by the miraculous intervention of the divine power that the black and white man have been produced, equally as much as was the creation of the color of the first man, the Creator giving him a complexion, arbitrarily, that pleased the Divine will.[12]

This "miraculous intervention," for Priest, was a second creative moment, and Ham's black skin, as random as it was, was an act of the Divine. In a slightly different direction, many Southern ministers propagated the idea that the curse of Canaan was a curse of blackness as well as enslavement.[13] Augustin Calmet's (d. 1757) French dictionary of the Bible became widely popular in English as *Calmet's Dictionary*; Calmet passed on the legend that Ham's skin turned black when Noah cursed Canaan and Ham's descendants.[14] Many cite this secondary source, considered learned and well reasoned, as one of the leading academic guides on the topic. Sylvester Johnson forcefully argues that the "primary concern" surrounding the myth of Ham tradition was "racial origins," not "slavery apologetics," as many assume. The fundamental issue "was not slavery but identity and existence."[15] In popular white

10. Josiah Priest, *Slavery, As It Relates to the Negro, Or African Race, Examined in the Light of Circumstances, History and the Holy Scriptures* (Albany, NY: C. Van Benthuysen & Co., 1843). This volume was published in 1851 as *Bible Defence of Slavery*.

11. Cited in Scott Williamson, *The Narrative Life: The Moral and Religious Thought of Frederick Douglass* (Macon, GA: Mercer University Press, 2002), 87.

12. Priest, *Slavery*, 27–28.

13. Finkelman, "Introduction: Defending Slavery," in *Defending Slavery*, 26, 32. This differed from the prevailing science of the day, which *rejected* monogenesis (i.e., creation from *one* human being/source).

14. Augustin Calmet, *Calmet's Great Dictionary of the Holy Bible*, trans. Charles Taylor (London: Charles Taylor, 1797). Calmet attaches Indian descendants as well as African descendants to Ham's lineage.

15. Johnson, *Myth of Ham*, xiii, 5.

imagination and conversation, the two issues were not easy to distinguish from one another.

Many nineteenth-century blacks, nonetheless, accepted Ham as the progenitor of the descendants of Africa, even while questioning the language of perpetual oppression. Thomas Smallwood, in his 1851 account, provided one example of this common assumption:

> In like manner the rulers of the United States are acting. When the wise men, the sorcerers, the magicians, and astrologers of the United States were assembled at Washington, casting their rods in opposition to the servants of God, to see how they could further oppress the children of Ham, by opening a way through Mason's and Dixon's sea, that they might recapture those that had crossed, they attempted to expel from their hall a servant of God, the Hon. Mr. Seward, for telling them that there was a higher power than their constitution. But many of the children of Ham, like the children of Reuben, Gad, and Manasseh, who took their inheritance beyond Jordan, Joshua xiii. 8, have taken inheritance beyond lake Ontario: the result is, their oppressors are in hot pursuit to carry them back into bondage; but I believe that it will end in their overthrow, as it did the Egyptians at the Red Sea.[16]

Smallwood accepted the classification "children of Ham" as an identification marker for African Americans even while he opposed the government's application of the Fugitive Slave Act of 1850, especially the desire of many Northerners to capture folks who had escaped bondage. A proponent of the African Colonization Society, Smallwood was a member of the growing number of African Americans living in Canada.[17]

Frederick Douglass acknowledged the impact of his contemporary experience on any exegetical analysis of the biblical text. In Douglass's words, a person (whom he left unnamed) had predicted "the downfall

---

16. Thomas Smallwood, *A Narrative of Thomas Smallwood, (Coloured Man)* (Toronto: Smallwood; James Stephens, 1851), 49*.

17. Smallwood, in one of the clearest passages in the antebellum freedom-narrative tradition, addressed the exodus story as a paradigm for the peculiar institution; this narrative became much more prominent in the postbellum period. Contrary to the findings of Sylvester Johnson—who argues for the prominence of the exodus story in the *postbellum* period—Callahan concludes that "the story of the Exodus has been the most influential of all biblical narratives among American slaves" (Allen Callahan, *The Talking Book: African Americans and the Bible* [New Haven, CT: Yale University Press, 2006], 48). For this assessment, Callahan draws mainly on the spirituals, as the oldest testimony, in the antebellum period (*Talking Book*, 85). Strikingly, the exodus motif is absent from *most* antebellum narratives of the formerly enslaved. Smallwood, of course, was an exception. Also compare Douglass, who calls Garrison a modern-day Moses, even while establishing intellectual and political distance from Garrison (*My Bondage and My Freedom* [New York: Miller, Orton & Mulligan, 1855], 355*; see, also, 278*, 281*); see Henry Bibb, *Narrative of the Life and Adventures of Henry Bibb, An American Slave, Written by Himself* (New York: Author, 1849), 29*. Douglass's exodus motifs were not included in the 1845 *Narrative*.

of slavery by the inevitable laws of population." For Douglass, this population shift (i.e., the rising numbers of mulattos) at least "will do away the force of the argument that God cursed Ham, and therefore American slavery is right." As the son of a mixed-race rape, Douglass recognized the irony of the presence of these offspring who made the enslavement institution "unscriptural": "for thousands are ushered into the world, annually, who, like myself, owe their existence to white fathers, and those fathers most frequently their own masters."[18] Douglass omitted the explicit language of rape and skillfully chose words appropriate for the public performance of his story.[19] He narrated a much more complex racial history than any proslavery proponent would attest. Certainly it was one that Josiah Priest preferred to avoid. The practicality of racial mixing common in Southern plantation life should easily, for Douglass, dismiss the ideology associated with the biblical myth.[20]

Harriet Jacobs also used this common experience to respond to the simplistic racial categories surrounding an interpretation of the so-called biblical curse. Her question was less about the curse than about her theological conviction that God created all humans from "one blood," a clear allusion to Acts 17:[21] "They seem to satisfy their consciences with the doctrine that God created the Africans to be slaves. What a libel upon the heavenly Father, who 'made of one blood all nations of men!' And then who *are* Africans? Who can measure the amount of Anglo-Saxon blood coursing in the veins of American slaves?"[22]

Drawing on Acts 17 as well, Austin Steward appropriated the example of interracial sexual activity to address the issue of the "pure African": "How many pure Africans, think you, can be found in the whole slave population of the South, to say nothing of their nativity? Native

18. Douglass, *Narrative*, 5*.

19. In the 1855 edition, he subtly alludes to the crime, "The slave-woman is at the mercy of the fathers, sons or brothers of her master. The thoughtful know the rest" (Douglass, *My Bondage and My Freedom*, 60*). See Callahan, *Talking Book*, 23.

20.Austin Steward suggested that "three-fourths of the colored race" had European blood (*Twenty-two Years a Slave, and Forty Years a Freeman* [Rochester, NY: William Alling, 1857], 331*). The number was not as high as Steward imagined. According to Franklin and Moss, almost 8 percent of the enslaved population was mulatto (246,000 out of 3.2 million) in 1850. By 1860, that number had surpassed 10 percent (411,000 out of 3.9 million); see John Hope Franklin and Alfred A. Moss Jr., *From Slavery to Freedom: A History of African Americans*, 8th ed. (New York: Alfred A. Knopf, 2006), 158.

21. The KJV reads as if God took "all nations" and made them *into* "one blood." The NRSV seems to suggest that the origins of "all nations" stems *from* (or *out of*) "one ancestor." The Greek has "out of one" without any noun (either "blood" or "ancestor") to follow. Either translation would create a theological problem in some nineteenth-century contexts, suggesting that God made "one nation/blood" by allowing white men to abuse their power over black bodies.

22. Harriet Jacobs, *Incidents in the Life of a Slave Girl. Written by Herself* (Boston: Published for the Author, 1861), 69*.

Africa, indeed! Who does not know, that in three-fourths of the colored race, there runs the blood of the white master,—the breeder of his own chattels! Think you, that a righteous God will fail to judge a nation for such flagrant sins?"[23]

This biblical allusion confronted the US reality of the crimes that regularly occurred—for example, rape—in addition to enslavement. Of course, during this period, it was not considered a crime to rape a black woman.[24] Jacobs's story, *Incidents in the Life of a Slave Girl*, detailed examples of the true nature of the blood that flowed through the veins of many so-called Africans.[25] Her critique specifically condemned the leaders of the white church: "If a pastor has offspring by a woman not his wife, the church dismiss [*sic*] him, if she is a white woman; but if she is colored, it does not hinder his continuing to be their good shepherd."[26]

A decade later, Douglass rewrote this section of his narrative in order to account for a missing dimension in his initial assessment.[27] On the one hand, Noah's curse is a biblical story about an ancient family; on the other hand, as Douglass confessed (in 1855), "[s]lavery does away with fathers, as it does away with families."[28] He emphasized the impact of these forced "unions" on the interpretation of the Hamite myth, in addition to its effect on the situation of women, both white and black women.[29] In *My Bondage and My Freedom*, Douglass included an additional discussion on the negative effect the mulatto "offspring" have on the complex emotional state of white women:[30]

> What is still worse, perhaps, such a child is a constant offense to the wife. She hates its very presence, and when a slaveholding woman hates, she wants not means to give that hate telling effect.

23. Steward, *Twenty-two Years a Slave*, 331–32*.

24. See Jeffrey J. Pokorak, "Rape as a Badge of Slavery: The Legal History of, and Remedies for, Prosecutorial Race-of-Victim Charging Disparities," *Nevada Law Journal* 7/1 (2006), 6.

25. In the case of Jacobs's children, she *chose* to have children with a white lawyer, as part of her strategy to avoid the sexual advances of Dr. Flint, the slaveholder. For more on her interpretation of the Bible, see Emerson Powery, "'Rise Up Ye Women': Harriet Jacobs and the Bible," *Postscripts: The Journal of Sacred Texts and Contemporary Worlds* 5.2 (2009): 171–84. Austin Steward acknowledged that occasionally interracial choice and love sparked some of these mutual relationships (*Twenty-two Years a Slave*, 331*).

26. The fuller context of the quote above is as follows: "There is a great difference between Christianity and religion at the south. If a man goes to the communion table, and pays money into the treasury of the church, no matter if it be the price of blood, he is called religious" (Jacobs, *Incidents*, 115*).

27. In the 1845 narrative, the discussion occurred early in the narrative on page 5*, shortly after Douglass introduced his mother and his separation from her at an early age; in the 1855 narrative, albeit in conjunction with the introduction of his mother, the account occurred on page 59*.

28. Frederick Douglass, *My Bondage and My Freedom* (New York: Miller, Orton & Mulligan, 1855), 51*.

29. Attention in the 1855 edition to the impact on women may be due to Douglass's increasing involvement in women's rights issues in the 1850s.

30. He omitted any discussion of the psychological challenges on the white master-fathers, which he included in the earlier account.

Women—white women, I mean—are IDOLS at the south, not WIVES, for the slave women are preferred in many instances; and if these idols but nod, or lift a finger, woe to the poor victim: kicks, cuffs and stripes are sure to follow. Masters are frequently compelled to sell this class of their slaves, out of deference to the feelings of their white wives; and shocking and scandalous as it may seem for a man to sell his own blood to the traffickers in human flesh, it is often an act of humanity toward the slave-child to be thus removed from his merciless tormentors.[31]

Furthermore, in the 1855 account, Douglass did not fail to consider the impact these interracial children had on the black women who bore them, in general, and his own mother, in particular.[32] As a male, he could not fully experience the emotional attachment a mother had for her child. But he attempted to grapple with his own origins through a heartening rendition of his mother's circumstances. He concluded the section with a short account of his mother's death—one that framed his chapter—and her unmarked grave.[33]

Finally, other African American interpreters took a more critical approach to Genesis 9 altogether, concentrating attention on the specific content of the passage itself. Along with Smallwood (above) and other African Americans, Samuel Ringgold Ward concurred with the cultural assumption that Genesis 9 provided insight into the racial divisions present in the nineteenth century. Yet he turned a critical gaze on to the details of the passage itself:

In the sacred Scriptures, no mention is made of the son of Ham which in any respect represents him as at all inferior to the sons of Shem or Japhet [sic]. I know that "cursed be Canaan" is sometimes quoted as if it came from the lips of God; although, as the Rev. H. W. Beecher says, and as the record reads, these are but the words of a newly awakened drunken man. There was about as much inspiration in these words, as there might have been in anything said by Lot on two very disgraceful nights in his existence. I admit, of course, that the descendants of Canaan have since been the "servants of servants"; but I do deny that God is responsible for the words of Noah at that time, and I also deny that there is any sort of connection between his prediction and the enslavement of the Negro. The Scriptures nowhere allude to it in that sense: indeed, I see no more

31. Douglass, *My Bondage and My Freedom*, 59*.
32. There are no references to this passage in Douglass's later editions (1881, 1892).
33. Douglass, *My Bondage and My Freedom*, chap. 3.

sanction to that prediction than I see approval of his debauch, in the Scriptures. Besides, how many other than Africans have been enslaved, oppressed, and made "servants of servants," since the time of that prediction![34]

Ward accepted the designation "son of Ham" as an identifying marker of African Americans, even as he argued for Ham's equality with his kin, Shem and Japheth. Throughout his narrative, Ward continued to use the label "race of Ham" as a satisfactory description for people of African descent.[35] Acknowledgment of this biblical ("racial") equivalent, however, did not transfer to an acceptance of Noah's curse. Following the Rev. Henry Ward Beecher, prominent Congregationalist pastor of Plymouth Church in Brooklyn, New York, Ward critically questioned the divine sanction of the curse, since it derived from "a newly awakened drunken man."[36] Plus, as he acknowledged, many other ethnic groups had been enslaved throughout world history in addition to Africans. For Ward, Noah's curse was simply the scourge of a drunk, divorced from any divine sanction, an exegetical decision Ward made based on a close reading of the biblical story.

Despite these critical explanations of the Hamite curse, none of these African American interpreters attempted to argue against this biblical myth as a source for explaining the origins of *racial* identity.[37] Apparently, along with many of their white contemporaries, they accepted the *blackness* of Ham's (and Canaan's?) skin despite the lack of exegetical evidence within the biblical narrative itself. They tacitly shared the larger cultural assumption that Genesis 9 provided a statement about origins. It would have been "exceptional," according to Sylvester Johnson, for any African American to have questioned this basic assumption in the nineteenth century.[38] Douglass and Jacobs (and Steward, by implication) did not concede, however, that "Ham" was an uncomplicated identification of contemporary African Americans.[39]

---

34. Samuel Ward, *Autobiography of a Fugitive Negro: His Anti-Slavery Labours in the United States, Canada, & England* (London: John Snow, 35 Paternoster Row, 1855), 270–71*.

35. Ward, *Autobiography of a Fugitive Negro*, 209*, 246*.

36. Ward, *Autobiography of a Fugitive Negro*, 271*. Ward was not simply attempting to elevate the "Negro race"; he also reminded his readers of "the wickedness" of some "ancient Negroes" (273*).

37. Douglass also failed to recognize that Noah's curse fell on *Canaan* and not Ham, a point that James Pennington made, in *A Textbook of the Origin and History of the Colored People* (Hartford, CT: L. Skinner, 1841), 14.

38. Johnson, *Myth of Ham*, 10. Along with William Anderson, Alexander Crummel argued, in 1862, that blacks did *not* descend from Canaan, in "The Negro Race Not under a Curse: An Examination of Genesis ix.25" (cited in Haynes, *Noah's Curse*, 194).

39. A decade later, in a speech titled "The Composite Nation," Douglass broadened his argument to include observations about the influx of Asians onto the American soil: "The Chinese are likely to be even more difficult to deal with than the negro. The latter took his pay in religion and the lash. The Chinaman is a different article, and will want the cash. He has notions of justice that are not to be confused or bewildered by any of our 'Cursed

As Jacobs asserted, using Acts 17, God has "made of one blood all nations." Furthermore, Genesis 9:25–27 may support enslavement but, as Douglass and Ward argued, it did *not* support the enslavement of American blacks! For Douglass and Jacobs, Genesis 9 did *not* support the enslavement of the types of blacks, racially speaking, who live in the United States. Their common experience attested otherwise. For Ward, Noah's curse had no divine authorization. These authors indicated that a complex color arrangement existed in the Americas that would not allow for the simplistic assertion that enslaved Africans in the Americas were "black" Hamites, instead suggesting that they were an elaborate admixture that necessitated a more nuanced reading of Genesis 9, especially in relation to slavery.

THE "CURSE OF HAM" MYTH
AND THE "ONE BLOOD" TRADITION (ACTS 17)

Harriet Jacobs's citation of Acts 17 provided one early example of a long African American tradition of viewing Acts 17:26 ("[God] hath made of one blood all nations") as the pinnacle of God's original creative activity, what eventually became known as the "one blood" doctrine.[40] One of her contemporaries in the narrative tradition, William Craft, began his preface in the following way, one year prior to Jacobs's publication: "Having heard while in Slavery that 'God made of one blood all nations of men.'" As a common memory among the enslaved, Craft reclaimed this passage as a summons, along with the Declaration of Independence, to freedom. He and his wife, Ellen, took this passage to heart as they escaped to the North in one of the most inventive escapes from the institution.[41]

As attractive as this passage was to nineteenth-century African Americans, a number of authors in the freedom narrative tradition appealed to Acts 17 for other purposes besides addressing issues of origins.

---

be Canaan' religion" (cited in Frederic May Holland, *Frederick Douglass: The Colored Orator* [New York: Funk & Wagnalls, 1895], 321*).

40. The tradition goes back as far as the famous mathematician and astronomer Benjamin Banneker, who died in 1806. See Demetrius Williams's excursus "The African American Protest Tradition and the 'One Blood' Doctrine," in "The Acts of the Apostles," in *True to Our Native Land: An African American New Testament Commentary*, ed. Brian K. Blount et al. (Minneapolis: Fortress Press, 2007), 236–38. In a speech before congress, Henry Highland Garnet also used Acts 17 to hold up the irony of Christians supporting slavery (see Abraham Smith, "Paul and African American Biblical Interpretation," in *True to Our Native Land*, 35).

41. William Craft, *Running a Thousand Miles for Freedom: Or, The Escape of William and Helen Craft from Slavery* (London: William Tweedie, 1860), iii*; also, James Mars, *Life of James Mars, A Slave Born and Sold in Connecticut* (Hartford, CT: Case, Lockwood & Co., 1864), 21*.

Generally, they utilized this passage to attend more to the future, that is, the needs of social uplift (from their white supporters?) and equality. Richard Allen concluded his very short 1833 account with "A short Address to the friends of him who hath no helper," recognizing white comrades who accepted their common humanity: "[Y]ou strive to raise the slave to the dignity of a man; you take our children by the hand to lead them in the path of virtue, by your care of our education; you are not ashamed to call the most abject of our race brethren, children of one Father, who hath made of one blood all the nations of the earth."[42]

Although there were many white Christians who acknowledged the sentiment of Acts 17, there are just as many who refused to find in it a statement challenging the inequality of the peculiar institution. Charles Hodge, for example, one of the most influential biblical theologians of the day, could affirm his belief in the "common brotherhood of men" as he argued against the idea of an "inferior race" yet still conclude that the enslaved were not "equal with their masters in authority, or station, or circumstances."[43] On the other hand, when African Americans preached on this passage, they discovered a word of impartiality from the Creator of equality. J. D. Green claimed that he heard a different type of preaching when he heard the "colored ministers" expound on this passage:

> I was a regular attendant at the Methodist Free Church, consisting entirely of colored people; at which place I heard the scriptures expounded in a different way by colored ministers—as I found that God had made colored as well as white people: as *He had made of one blood all the families of the earth*, and that all men were free and equal in his sight; and that he was no respecter of persons whatever the color: but whoever worked righteousness was accepted of Him. Being satisfied that I had not sinned against the Holy Ghost by obtaining my freedom, I enlisted in the church, and became one of the members thereof.[44]

Green joined this church in which he heard the message of liberation, because these sisters and brothers did not condemn his escape from

---

42. Richard Allen, *The Life, Experience, and Gospel Labours of the Rt. Rev. Richard Allen* (Philadelphia: Martin & Boden, Printers, 1833), 49*.

43. Charles Hodge, *Commentary on Ephesians* (New York: Robert Carter & Bros., 1856), 362, 369. Hodge believed in a voluntary, gradual emancipation process in which the institution of enslavement would slowly fade away with legal assistance.

44. J. D. Green, *Narrative of the Life of J. D. Green, a Runaway Slave* (Huddersfield: Printed by Henry Fielding, Pack Horse Yard, 1864), 27*; emphasis added.

slavery as a "sin." Furthermore, in this community was a "Holy Ghost" he could believe in.[45]

The popularity of Acts 17 as a support text for a belief in the common origins of humans was commonplace, but writers in the narrative tradition employed it more often as a statement reinforcing the *equality* of all human beings. The passage allowed interpreters to look forward rather than backward, to signify on the Bible for progress in the present rather than simply describe the historical situation of the past. More importantly, Acts 17 was utilized as a direct response to Genesis 9, in arguments in which this Old Testament passage was upheld as the dominant biblical passage supporting the distinctions among nineteenth-century ethnic groups.[46]

"A GREAT DEAL HAS BEEN SAID ABOUT COLORS"

The Cultural Context of "Race Origins"

In an extensive study of the period, Sylvester Johnson concludes that an ideological conflict of identifying the racial origins of blackness solely through the tainted image of the biblically cursed Ham cornered nineteenth-century African Americans.[47] Admittedly, this was generally true. Genesis 9–10 was the dominant mythic-origin paradigm of the day for determining the classifications of racial histories. And those who had access to the pen and the press made it the public discourse of the land. Even early black attempts to narrate the "historical" discussion—by James Pennington (1841) and Robert Lewis (1843)—found themselves reacting to this national paradigm that was already set in motion by white ethnologists, biblical scholars, and scientists who had developed theories of racial origins based on hierarchical presuppositions.

The exceptions to this general discourse, however, will require our attention in the remainder of this chapter. During this period, readers of the Bible commonly read themselves into the story.[48] We find

---

45. This theological language is particularly intriguing in light of Charles Hodge's own claim about the Spirit, in his *Commentary on Ephesians*: "It is thus that the Holy Spirit deals with slavery" (370).

46. Acts 17 and Genesis 9 are not necessarily incompatible. God has made out of "one blood" (i.e., Noah) all "nations" (i.e., Shem, Ham, and Japheth), if the interpreter believes that Noah's sons represented the "nations" of the world, which may be implied in the so-called "table of nations" chapter of Genesis 10.

47. Sylvester Johnson, *Myth of Ham*.

48. Johnson, *Myth of Ham*, 52. E.g., Charles Hodge called his former colleague at Princeton Theological Seminary, James Waddell Alexander, a "Christian, an *Israelite* without guile" at his funeral service (*New York Times*, August 5, 1859; emphasis added).

examples of this kind of application within the freedom-narrative tradition itself. For some white interpreters, like Priest (discussed earlier), the origin of "whiteness" was Japheth, not Adam. This line of interpretation opened the door for "free thinkers" like William Anderson, whose narrative we will discuss below.

References to "Whiteness" in the Freedom Narratives

The authors of the narratives had to be careful, since they wrote primarily for the consumption of the Northern white public. The audience expected prescribed accounts of the lives of former enslaved existences, even if smaller details differed. An explanation of the origins of racial groups in the United States was not on Theodore Weld's list for what was expected in this type of narrative.[49] Weld insisted on detailed accounts of the everyday experiences of the enslaved, for example, stories about food and rest—or the lack thereof. But Weld did not insist on hearing the thoughts of the enslaved with respect to issues like racial origins. Nevertheless, some narrators—like Douglass, Jacobs, and many others—simply could not help themselves.

Many white interpreters, on the other hand, offered contrived theories of racial histories, using various hermeneutical approaches to the Bible, as the decade of the 1850s experienced a proliferation of such interpretations. During this decade, Paul Finkelman concludes, the "Southern defense of slavery had reached its most mature and sophisticated form."[50] By 1860, many in the North and most in the South, according to Mark Noll, believed that the Bible sanctioned slavery.[51] Even if Northern white interpreters disapproved of the South's particular practice of the institution, many still believed that the Bible supported the idea of human bondage.[52] These so-called "moderates"—including prominent biblical scholars Moses Stuart and Charles Hodge[53]—believed, taught, and published that slavery was a "biblical"

---

49. Theodore Weld, *American Slavery as It Is: Testimony of a Thousand Witnesses* (New York: American Anti-Slavery Society, 1839), iv*.

50. Finkelman, ed., *Defending Slavery*, viii; also, Mark Noll, *The Civil War as a Theological Crisis* (Chapel Hill: University of North Carolina Press, 2006), 22.

51. Mark Noll, *America's God: From Jonathan Edwards to Abraham Lincoln* (New York: Oxford University Press, 2005), 17. Nevertheless, as Noll also discovers, "no body of Protestants elsewhere in the English-speaking world agreed that the Bible sanctioned slavery" (17).

52. Noll, *The Civil War as a Theological Crisis*, 45.

53. Moses Stuart, *Conscience and the Constitution* (Boston: Crocker and Brewster, 1850); Charles Hodge, "Slavery," in *Essays and Reviews: Selected from the Princeton Review* (Broadway, NY: Robert Carter & Bros., 1857). Even so, Bishop Daniel Payne, at the end of the century, describes Hodge as "the greatest theologian

practice, even while they advocated for a gradual, voluntary emancipation of the enslaved in the United States. The institutional practice with its specific abuses and dissolution of black families, they argued, was not representative of the biblical mandate.

Despite Noll's claim that "proslavery advocates had largely succeeded in winning the battle for the Bible,"[54] the most important battle of the century was not over the authority of the Bible. That was one theological crisis among many. Other wars being fought were more central to the humanization of all people. The history and origin of the division of races was one of these pivotal concerns, and the Bible was a weapon in these wars. So the decade leading up to the Civil War was a time of hermeneutical activity unlike any other decade of the nineteenth century. And some (African Americans) entered the public conversation on the complexities of "race."

For example, Dr. James McCune Smith, a free black physician who wrote the preface to Douglass's 1855 edition of his narrative, responded to white assumptions that Douglass's literary gifts must have derived from his "Caucasian" heritage (that is, his unknown white slaveholding "father") by challenging the ethnic origins of Caucasian as a pure race:

> These facts show that for his energy, perseverance, eloquence, invective, sagacity, and wide sympathy, [Douglass] is indebted to his negro blood. The very marvel of his style would seem to be a development of that other marvel,—how his mother learned to read. The versatility of talent which he wields, in common with Dumas, Ira Aldridge, and Miss Greenfield, would seem to be the result of the grafting of the Anglo-Saxon on good, original, negro stock. If the friends of "Caucasus" choose to claim, for that region, what remains after this analysis—to wit: combination—they are welcome to it. They will forgive me for reminding them that the term "Caucasian" is dropped by recent writers on Ethnology; for the people about Mount Caucasus, are, and have ever been, Mongols. The great "white race" now seek paternity, according to Dr. Pickering, in Arabia—"Arida Nutrix" of the best breed of horses &c. Keep on, gentlemen; you will find yourselves in Africa, by-and-by. The Egyptians, like the Americans, were a mixed race, with some negro blood circling around the throne, as well as in the mud hovels."[55]

---

which America has yet produced, in *Recollections of Seventy Years* (orig. 1890; New York, 1969), 248; cited in Noll, *America's God*, 548.

54. Noll, *America's God*, 393.

55. James McCune Smith, "Preface," *My Bondage and My Freedom*, xxx–xxxi*.

Despite McCune Smith's own "versatility of [writing] talent" and strong defense of Douglass's "black" intellectual gifts, Douglass did not reflect on the issue himself in the 1855 account almost two decades following his escape from slavery. He waited until much later in life; in his *final* narrative, in 1892, he offered reflections on the American curiosity with respect to his ancestral composition and its influence on intelligence:

> There is no disguising the fact that the American people are much interested and mystified about the mere matter of color as connected with manhood. . . . I have often been bluntly and sometimes very rudely asked, of what color my mother was, and of what color was my father? In what proportion does the blood of the various races mingle in my veins, especially how much white blood and how much black blood entered into my composition? Whether I was not part Indian as well as African and Caucasian? Whether I considered myself more African than Caucasian, or the reverse? Whether I derived my intelligence from my father, or from my mother, from my white, or from my black blood? Whether persons of mixed blood are as strong and healthy as persons of either of the races whose blood they inherit?[56]

Inherent to Douglass's example was a prevailing view of the superiority of whiteness. These views flooded the North American landscape, both South and North. Prior to the Civil War, President Lincoln himself could not imagine a country in which blacks and whites would live equally and peaceably together following emancipation, partly because of his view of the superiority of the white race.[57] These prevailing ideas influenced a number of tales created to promote the advantages of whiteness. The freedom narratives provided a few examples of these stories that circulated among the enslaved.

In his 1851 appendix to his account, Henry "Box" Brown wrote the following interesting "tale" that was circulating among some (nontraditional?) slaveholding whites. In this mythic account of origins, God created four people at the beginning of the world, with two blacks to serve the needs of their white counterparts. As a side note, without elucidation, this tale included a statement that blacks were created without

56. Douglass, *Life and Times* (1892), 621–22*.
57. See George Fredrickson, "A Man but Not a Brother: Abraham Lincoln and Racial Equality," *The Journal of Southern History* 41/1 (Feb. 1975): 39–58; Eric Foner, "Abraham Lincoln, Colonization, and the Rights of Black Americans," in Follett, Foner, and Johnson, *Slavery's Ghost: The Problem of Freedom in the Age of Emancipation* (Baltimore: Johns Hopkins Press, 2011), 31–49.

souls, which we may assume was the rationale for their servant status. God's soul-less human creation was an essential point of contention among whites during the early nineteenth century. According to this story, the black couple delivered sufficient service but annoyed their masters by their constant presence, so the white couple prayed to God (since they had souls) to arrange activities to keep their servants preoccupied. And God answered their prayers:

> [I]mmediately while they stood, a black cloud seemed to gather over their heads and to descend to the earth before them! While they gazed on these clouds, they saw them open and two bags of different size drop from them. They immediately ran to lay hold of the bags, and unfortunately for the black man—he being the strongest and swiftest—he arrived first at them, and laid hold of the bags, and the white man, coming up afterwards, got the smaller one. They then proceeded to untie their bags, when lo! in the large one, there was a shovel and a hoe; and in the small one, a pen, ink, and paper; to write the declaration of the intention of the Almighty; they each proceeded to employ the Instruments which God had sent them, and ever since the colored race have had to labor with the shovel and the hoe, while the rich man works with the pen and ink![58]

What the white man discovered in his bag allowed him "to write the declaration of the intention of the Almighty," that is, by implication, the words of sacred Scripture. In this oral tale, the white man assumed responsibility for the "divine instructions" all Christians had to obey. Support of the peculiar institution would, of course, proceed from this line of storytelling. Though Brown omitted any direct reproach, the subtle implications of a *white*-sponsored (biblical?) text may have opened the way for a perceptive critique of the received text: why should African Americans, in particular, read the "intention of the Almighty" if it was sifted through the interpretation of "the rich man" who used "the pen and ink" for "his" own benefit.

One other interesting related tale was also recorded in the narratives of the formerly enslaved. The day after his mother was sold, J. D. Green (1864) recalled a childhood story he had heard from a slaveholder. This moment of immense human tragedy and isolation was coupled, in this

---

58. Henry Box Brown, *Narrative of the Life of Henry Box Brown, Written by Himself* (Manchester, England: Printed by Lee & Glynn, 1851), i–ii*. This appendix is absent from the earlier account of his life, which Brown had dictated to Stearns; see Charles Stearns, *Narrative of Henry Box Brown, Who Escaped from Slavery, Enclosed in a Box 3 Feet Long and 2 Wide, Written from a Statement of Facts Made by Himself* (Boston, MA: Brown & Stearns, 1849). This is an excellent example of the occasional differences encountered when the formerly enslaved have more control over the content of their own accounts.

young boy's life, with the master's explanation of the separate origins of whites and blacks. Green reflected:

> Why was I born black? It would have been better had I not been born at all. Only yesterday, my mother was sold to go to, not one of us knows where, and I am left alone, and I have no hope of seeing her again. At this moment a raven alighted on a tree over my head, and I cried, "Oh, Raven! if I had wings like you. I would soon find my mother and be happy again." Before parting she advised me to be a good boy, and she would pray for me, and I must pray for her, and hoped we might meet again in heaven, and I at once commenced to pray, to the best of my knowledge, "Our Father art in Heaven, be Thy name, kingdom come.—Amen" But, at this time, words of my master obtruded into my mind that God did not care for black folks, as he did not make them, but the d—l did. Then I thought of the old saying amongst us, as stated by our master, that, when God was making man, He made white man out of the best clay, as potters make china, and the d—l was watching, and he immediately took some black mud and made a black man, and called him a nigger.[59]

Another enslaver passed along this biblically sounding tale constructed to promulgate the ideology of the superiority of whiteness. Most striking, from this perspective, was that God played no creative role in the creation of this secondary human being, but the "d—l" (i.e., devil) did. Presumably, this allowed proponents of this fable to retain belief in the soul-less nature of African American people. As long as black people did not possess souls and thereby had no capacity for spiritual flourishing, harsh treatment would be perceived as no different from severe treatment of any other animal.[60] Of course, to derive this account from the Genesis narrative exegetically, white interpreters would have needed to provide creative hermeneutical feats in order to support this imaginative (and denigrating for marginalized people) interpretation. To sustain this kind of ideological control, the stakeholders had to preserve their systems of illiteracy. And many states enforced this system legally.[61]

---

59. J. D. Green, *Narrative*, 5–6*.

60. See Albert J. Raboteau, *Slave Religion: The Invisible Institution in the Antebellum South* (New York: Oxford University Press, 1978), 220. On the other hand, some white Christians—influenced by the Great Awakening—argued that "[i]f all souls are worth saving, then surely there is something wrong with enslaving the bodies that contain those souls" (Finkelman, "Introduction: Defending Slavery," in *Defending Slavery: Proslavery Thought in the Old South: A Brief History with Documents* [Boston/New York: Bedford/St. Martin's, 2003], 19).

61. Despite state regulations, there were many instances in which individual slaveholders taught the enslaved to read. Literacy statistics are difficult to ascertain, but guesstimates place literacy rates among the enslaved around

Henry "Box" Brown and J. D. Green each reported a story—initiated by white slaveholders—that provided glimpses into the oral traditions circulating among the enslaved. Members of the majority population developed these tales in order to maintain the hierarchical structures in society and the ideological arguments that supported the myths surrounding the privileges of whiteness. The leading, contemporary "scientific" explanations reinforced these extrabiblical tales. Josiah Nott, a prominent white physician and well-respected racial theorist, propagated a view of a "separate" creation and distinct origins of the races.[62] By the 1840s, as Thomas Peterson shows, these ethnologists "made belief in the innate inferiority of the black race scientifically respectable."[63]

Part of the conclusions from the American School of Ethnology, founded by George Glidden, included the "discovery" that Egyptians were Caucasians, not Africans.[64] (Prior to the heyday of the freedom narratives, African Americans [e.g., Pennington and Lewis] had responded publicly to attempts to distinguish the ancient fame of Egypt from its African neighbors.) Largely overlooked was Glidden's argument that the ancient Canaanites were part of the Caucasian race.[65] Due to this latter discovery, Glidden avoided the Bible and forcefully argued against its usefulness in general. He was an early proponent of the advancing historical-critical approaches to the biblical text. But Glidden was also ignored or challenged by white Southern Christians who defended the authority of the biblical account, despite the benefits of Glidden's racialized arguments (with the exception of his conclusions about the Canaanites) for their cause.[66] By 1850, most American scientists endorsed polygenism.[67] And the folklore in support of the superiority of whiteness received its scientific backing.

Despite the direction of some of the leading white scientists of the day, many religious whites—including James Henley Thornwell, one

---

1–2 percent of the enslaved population prior to the Civil War (see Franklin and Moss, *From Slavery to Freedom*, 155–56).

62. Apparently, Nott was the first American to do so, according to Donald Swan, "American School of Ethnology," *The Mankind Quarterly* (1971): 85. See Josiah C. Nott, George R. Gliddon, Samuel G. Morton, Louis Agassiz, William Usher, and Henry S. Patterson, *Types of Mankind* (Lippincott, Grambo & Co., 1854); Nott, *Instincts of Races* (L. Graham, 1866). Cf. William Stanton, *The Leopold's Spots: Scientific Attitudes towards Race in America, 1815–1860* (Chicago: University of Chicago Press, 1960).

63. Thomas Virgil Peterson, *Ham and Japheth: The Mythic World of Whites in the Antebellum South*, ATLA Monograph Series 12 (Lanham, MD: Scarecrow Press, 1978), 65.

64. His research was based on cranial evidence; see Swan, "American School of Ethnology," 83.

65. Peterson, *Ham and Japheth*, 105.

66. According to Peterson, those who rejected the authority of the Bible, like Nott and Glidden, were more effective than those who attempted to marry their scientific conclusions with the Bible (Peterson, *Ham and Japheth*, 70).

67. Swan, "The American School of Ethnology," 90.

of the South's respected religious thinkers—held firm to the belief that all humans derived from the original biblical couple,[68] despite the eventual curse of enslavement. The so-called "scientific" discoveries simply "did not conform to biblical truth," as Thornwell and his ilk argued.[69] Of course, this did not mean that these same whites believed in the equality of races in their day. But these white interpreters desired to uphold the integrity of the creation account of Genesis 1. The tradition surrounding the common ancestry in Genesis was one of the primary reasons, as Eddie Glaude has shown, for rare "assertions of permanent inferiority" before the 1830s.[70]

Following congressional fights over the Fugitive Slave Law of 1850, the decade of the 1850s involved rising intense arguments surrounding slavery. Most religious people in the United States, though not all, believed that the Bible was of primary import for defending the theological rationale for enslavement and ethnic difference.[71] Intimately related to this debate was the underlying racial ideology that surfaced. By 1850, the majority of American scientists, as Donald Swan argued, held to "the principle tenets of the doctrine of polygenism."[72]

As diligent as white interpreters were about providing biblical support for the slavocracy of the day, they were much less engaged in biblical interpretation for an analysis of "race." As Mark Noll concisely claims, interpreters used a commonsense approach when locating biblical passages on slavery but "relied on common sense" only when thinking about race.[73] This so-called common sense knowledge was supported by institutional structures (i.e., educational, economic, legal) to maintain the superiority of the white race. For many of them the issue of race was settled by the biblical Ham and the ensuing curse on his family.[74] Despite little to no concentrated focus on a "biblical perspective" on race (if you will) by white exegetes, this gap was occasionally filled by black exegetes who frequently engaged the Bible with "race" at the forefront of their analyses. In 1855, Douglass reacted, "Shall we . . .

---

68. See Noll, *America's God*, 399.
69. Peterson, *Ham and Japheth*, 4.
70. Eddie Glaude, *Exodus! Religion, Race, and Nation in Early Nineteenth-Century Black America* (Chicago: University of Chicago Press, 2000), 65.
71. See Noll, *The Civil War as a Theological Crisis*.
72. Swan, "The American School of Ethnology," 90.
73. Noll, *America's God*, 418.
74. Peterson claims that there was only *one* Southern clergyman in the antebellum South who "unequivocally rejected Ham as the progenitor of the black race"; this Lutheran pastor in Charleston, John Bachman, asserted that "environmental factors" were the cause for different racial groups in America (Peterson, *Ham and Japheth*, 102).

fling the Bible away as a pro-slavery book?"[75] With respect to the Bible, Douglass himself was more interested in slavery than race. But in 1857 William Anderson proposed an alternative biblical narrative to account for the origins of race. Rather than attempting to offer an account for the curse of blackness, Anderson turned the question on its head: How did whiteness occur?[76]

William Anderson and the Disease of Whiteness: A Theory on the Origin of "Whiteness"

The year was 1857 and this decade, following the congressional fights over the Fugitive Slave Law of 1850, witnessed rising tensions leading up to the first shots of the Civil War. The Fugitive Slave Act, in Nell Irvin Painter's words, "turned the whole country into the enemy of black people."[77] Even free African American leaders in the North realized that their own status was tenuous at best and that their "new legal status was in no essential sense different from that of slaves."[78] Many of these debates were religious in nature. Many people in the United States, though not all, believed in the central role the Bible played in determining the theological rationale for enslavement, ethnic difference, and freedom.[79] Any statement about racial origins was particularly important, since the 1850s saw a proliferation of such views among white advocates for Southern life and slavery.[80]

Anderson's title revealed his objectives clearly and directly: *Life and Narrative of William J. Anderson, Twenty-four Years a Slave; Sold Eight Times!! In Jail Sixty Times!! Whipped Three Hundred Times!!! Or The Dark Deeds of American Slavery Revealed. Containing Scriptural Views of the Origin of the Black and of the White Man. Also, A Simple and Easy Plan to Abolish Slavery in the United States, Together with An Account of the Services of Colored Men in the Revolutionary War—Day and Date, and Interesting Facts.* The number of words in his title was barely

75. Speech in Boston, Massachusetts, Feb. 8, 1855; cited in Albert Harrill, "Use of the New Testament in the American Slave Controversy: A Case History in the Hermeneutical Tension between Biblical Criticism and Christian Moral Debate," *Religion and American Culture* 10 (2000): 160.

76. In Toni Morrison's words, "What happens to the writerly imagination of a black author who is at some level *always* conscious of representing one's own race to, or in spite of, a race of readers that understands itself to be 'universal' or race-free?" (*Playing in the Dark: Whiteness and the Literary Imagination* [New York: Vintage, 1993], xii).

77. Nell Irvin Painter, *Sojourner Truth: A Life, A Symbol* (New York: W. W. Norton & Co., 1996), 132.

78. William Andrews, "*My Bondage and My Freedom* and the American Literary Renaissance of the 1850s," in *Critical Essays on Frederick Douglass*, ed. William L. Andrews (Boston: G. K. Hall & Co., 1991), 136.

79. See Noll, *The Civil War as a Theological Crisis.*

80. See Peterson, *Ham and Japheth.*

surpassed by the length of his narrative (only fifty-seven pages). Born free, Anderson was kidnapped and sold off against his legal "rights" as a child in the 1820s.[81] After detailing his personal story, Anderson tackled the significant trifecta in his appendices: freedom (plan to abolish slavery), race (ethnic origins), and war (contributions of "colored men" in the war).[82]

Like many freedom narratives (though not all), the author emphasized that this account was "written by himself." Unlike some other narratives, Anderson's narrative has no prefatory comments from (usually white) dignitaries either to recommend it, acknowledge the high caliber of the lead character of the story, or offer a statement about the relative value of such a project. But this independence allowed him to carry out his objective unhindered, to do what he called "free thinking." Of particular interest is his relatively short analysis of "scriptural views of the origin of the black and of the white man."

Anderson ignored the widely held view that Ham was the "father of the black race." Using Genesis 2:7, Anderson believed instead that originally all people were black, since "the ground was quite black or dark."[83] In a search through the antebellum narratives, we found Anderson to be the only formerly enslaved writer who appropriated Genesis 2:7 in a discussion of racial origins.[84] But he was not the first African American to do so; others (e.g., Robert Lewis, a freeborn black) interpreted the book of Genesis in this manner more than a decade before Anderson (see below).[85]

Since Anderson presupposed blackness as the default race of all original humanity, he proposed a theory of racial origins that addressed whiteness as the aberration! To support this idea, he turned his attention to 2 Kings 5, the story of Naaman's healing. In the biblical account, the

---

81. William Anderson, *Life and Narrative of William J. Anderson, Twenty-four Years a Slave; Sold Eight Times! In Jail Sixty Times!! Whipped Three Hundred Times!!! Or The Dark Deeds of American Slavery Revealed. Containing Scriptural Views of the Origin of the Black and of the White Man. Also, A Simple and Easy Plan to Abolish Slavery in the United States, Together with An Account of the Services of Colored Men in the Revolutionary War—Day and Date, and Interesting Facts* (Chicago: Daily Tribune Book and Job Printing Office, 1857), 5*, 11*.

82. Of less interest to this chapter, Anderson proposed compensation to slaveholders and colonization for African Americans, although he envisioned the setting aside of US land for this purpose.

83. Anderson, *Life*, 61. "And the LORD God formed man of the dust of the ground, and breathed into his nostrils the breath of life; and man became a living soul" (Gen. 2:7 KJV).

84. Others—e.g., Henry Box Brown (in Charles Stearns, *Narrative of Henry Box Brown*) and David West (in Benjamin Drew, *A North-Side View of Slavery* [Boston: J. P. Jewett & Co., 1856])—provided oral statements (to white narrators) reflecting on this biblical passage, but it was utilized to discuss status rather than race. Without reference to Genesis, Leonard Black wrote about the common knowledge among the enslaved regarding the blackness of King Solomon (Leonard Black, *The Life and Sufferings of Leonard Black, a Fugitive from Slavery. Written by Himself* [New Bedford: Benjamin Lindsey, 1847], 52–53*).

85. See Robert Benjamin Lewis, *Light and Truth: From Ancient and Sacred History* (Augusta, ME: Severance & Dorr, 1843; repr., Lexington, KY: Cornell University Library Digital Collections, 2012).

Syrian captain Naaman was inflicted with a skin disease. Hearing of the prophet Elisha's healing power, Naaman sought him out, secured his healing (though reluctant to heed the prophet's advice), and attempted to offer a payment. Elisha refused payment. The biblical narrator then introduced Gehazi, Elisha's servant.[86] Gehazi disagreed (secretly) with Elisha's refusal to benefit financially from this wealthy Syrian (and rival) captain. So he tracked down Naaman without Elisha's permission. He told Naaman a lie, secured goods, and hid them. But Elisha was not to be fooled. (He was a prophet after all!) Elisha discovered Gehazi's deception and cursed him with the same disease that Naaman once had. Not only was Gehazi punished, but his descendants would also carry this disease forever. And Gehazi, originally black, "went out from Elisha's presence," in the King James Version, "a leper as white as snow."[87]

Anderson classified Naaman's "leprosy" (2 Kgs. 5:1, 3, 6, 7 KJV) as a "certain bad disease."[88] Though central to the biblical account, Naaman's healing was of much less interest to Anderson than Gehazi's actions and eventual disease.[89] In Anderson's retelling of the story, he ignored a few details.[90] Most significantly, he omitted the words "menservants, and maidservants" from Elisha's list of items that one should not accept from others at that time (2 Kgs. 5:26; during a war?). Anderson kept his focus on race without complicating it with the issue of status. Many of his white counterparts in the nineteenth century recited this story, and Gehazi's sin in particular, to enforce the status quo of the peculiar institution.

Most early nineteenth-century white biblical expositors (between 1801 and 1850) avoided any racialized exegetical possibilities for Gehazi turning, in the King James Version's phraseology, "white as snow." They concentrated their efforts on other factors within the story to emphasize themes related to (im)piety: (1) Gehazi's sin of greed;[91]

---

86. Gehazi was introduced earlier in the biblical narrative in the story of the Shunamite woman (2 Kgs. 4).

87. The Hebrew text does not include the adjective "white"; nevertheless the KJV continues to influence many translations, including the NRSV translation of 2 Kgs. 5:27: "So he left his presence leprous, as white as snow." One recent translation, the Common English Bible, alters the color analogy: "And Gehazi left Elisha's presence, flaky like snow with skin disease."

88. Anderson, *Life*, 61.

89. In Anderson's description, Naaman received 2.5 lines; Gehazi received 14.5 lines. In the KJV text, Naaman is described as a Syrian (2 Kgs. 5:1–2, 20) who—as captain of the Syrian army—had captured an Israelite girl to serve his wife.

90. Anderson omitted the following: (1) Gehazi's request is for "two prophets"; in Anderson's retelling, it sounds as if the clothes were for Elisha himself; (2) Naaman's "two servants" carry the goods back; in Anderson, Gehazi carried the items away himself.

91. In nineteenth-century secondary sources on the Bible, Gehazi was frequently associated with Achan in OT and Judas in NT as preeminent biblical thieves.

(2) Gehazi's lie to cover up his greed; (3) Gehazi's sin, as an outgrowth of Adam's sin; (4) Elisha's "prophetic" foresight (to observe Gehazi's true actions); (5) Elisha's frugality and disinterest in worldly goods (i.e., lack of greed).[92]

Surprisingly, William Anderson neglected to link Gehazi's "greed" with his newfound "whiteness." Yet such a connection would seem relevant in light of the nineteenth-century arguments surrounding the economic value of the peculiar institution. White, pious interpreters exposed plenty of greed in the passage; Anderson discovered whiteness (i.e., the curse of whiteness).[93] Neither combined the two.[94] Most interpreters avoided *race*. More attuned to *status* than race, antebellum white interpreters—in the North and South—utilized Gehazi's failure and condemnation as an example to teach servants in their midst to read their Bibles, as in the widely popular "Tracts of the American Tract Society" in the North (in 1825), which included "An Address to Persons in Different Stations of Life, on the Duty of Studying the Bible": "There you will find an account of pious servants; you will see how faithfully Abraham's servant obeyed his master, Gen. 24; how a servant-maid was useful to Naaman, the captain of the king of Assyria's army; you will see the punishment of a lying servant in Gehazi."[95] Or we find examples of the common arguments in the South in support of the institution of enslavement, such as J. B. Thrasher's pamphlet *Slavery: A Divine Institution*:

> Also the prophet Elisha, on whom the mantle of Elijah fell—the man of God who performed so many miracles, and among others, that of raising the dead to life—was a slave holder, and punished his slave Gehazi, by afflicting him with leprosy. . . . [just a few paragraphs later] So that we find God ever after entering into the covenant with Noah and his sons, constantly punishing sin and sinful nations, whether Jew or Gentile, with slavery, captivity and death.

---

92. Extremely rare is a focus on the leprosy as God's "theocratic punishment."

93. In contemporary biblical scholarship, Randall Bailey (unaware of William Anderson's account) also recognized that the phrase "white as snow," which also appears in Num. 12:10, represented an intentional curse within biblical literature, in "They Shall Become as White as Snow: When Bad Is Turned into Good," in *Race, Class, and the Politics of Bible Translation*, ed. Randall C. Bailey and Tina Pippin (Atlanta: Scholars Press, 1996), 99–113. More positive association is attached to the literary phrase elsewhere (Dan. 7:9; Rev. 1:14; Isa. 1:18; Ps. 5:7).

94. Legh Richmond, a British abolitionist, connected Gehazi's greed with England's avarice, in *The Fathers of the English Church* (London: Printed for John Hatchard, 1810), 450.

95. In *Tracts of the American Tract Society: General Series*, vol. 6 (New York: American Tract Society, 1825). No author is listed. Digital Presentation in the Theological Commons, http://commons.ptsem.edu/ (subsequently abbreviated DPTC).

Hence we believe that the slavery of the negro is of God, which we can trace back to the curse of Caanan [sic].[96]

While Thrasher linked, implicitly, the notion of coloration and slavery in 2 Kings, he completely ignored the ending of 2 Kings, with its explicit reference to coloration, and turned his attention to Genesis. Anderson, on the other hand, omitted (intentionally?) the label of the disease as "leprosy" (in the KJV of 2 Kgs. 5:27) in order to concentrate on its coloration. Anderson referred to it simply as a "disease," what we might call the *disease of whiteness*. As the King James Version states and Anderson reiterated, Gehazi departed from Elisha's presence as "white as snow." (Commonsense interpretation of the Bible was the prevailing hermeneutical approach of the day.) If there was ever a commonsense interpretation in the nineteenth century, this was it.[97]

For Anderson, Gehazi's curse is the biblical beginning of "whiteness." Apparently he had presented this exegesis, as he reported, "a thousand times in the hearing of the learned" and had never been challenged or questioned.[98] Even if exaggerating the number of his hearers, what Anderson claimed about the decade was true, as we know from multiple sources that "a great deal has been said about colors" during the 1850s. The period provided heightened intense debate over the origins of races, and interpreters mined the Bible as a central resource to help people discern how things came to be. Anderson shared what most people thought before 1860: "we have to do the best we can with the writings that are left for our instruction."[99]

As arguments surrounding the origins of racial identification increased in the decade, the Bible was not excluded from such racialized interpretive discourse. One need only search the entries on "Ham," "Japheth," and "Shem" in the Bible dictionaries of the day for prevailing sentiments about contemporary racial divisions.[100] On the other hand, white interpreters rarely commented on Gehazi's miraculous alteration (to "white as snow") in a racialized manner.[101] But it did

---

96. *Slavery: A Divine Institution* (Port Gibson, MS: Southern Reveille Book & Job Office, 1861); DPTC.

97. See Mark Noll on the preponderance of commonsense hermeneutics in the nineteenth century. The only addition Anderson made to the biblical account was to discuss Gehazi's feelings when he departed from Elisha; according to Anderson, Gehazi was "scared" (Anderson, *Life*, 62).

98. Anderson, *Life*, 62. Other traditions—surrounding Cain, e.g.—circulated among African Americans that accounted for the "invention of whiteness" (Callahan, *Talking Book*, 28).

99. Anderson, *Life*, 62.

100. For example, in one popular dictionary, John Brown concluded with respect to Japheth, "Their posterity peopled the north half of Asia, almost all the Mediterranean isles, all Europe, and I suppose, most of America," in *Dictionary of the Holy Bible* (Edinburgh: Murray & Cochrane, 1797), 2:10; DPTC.

101. Occasionally the phrase "white as snow" was utilized, among white writers of fiction, as a reference to skin color. E.g., Martha Griffith Browne, *Autobiography of a Female Slave* (New York: Redfield, 1857), 79* and 291*.

occur, even though reluctantly, as the decades leading up to the Civil War mounted.

In his popular commentary on the Bible (published in New York), Adam Clarke (d. 1832) mentioned the speculation of some who thought Gehazi had contemporary descendants: "Some have thought, because of the prophet's curse, . . . that there are persons still alive who are this man's real descendants, and afflicted with this horrible disease. Mr. Maundrell when he was in Judea made diligent inquiry concerning this, but could not ascertain the truth of the supposition. To me it appears absurd."[102]

Clarke's commentary was published "for the Methodist Episcopal Church" and centered on the debate over the meaning of "forever" (that the leprosy would be on Gehazi and descendants). Some understood this adverb as "until the end of his immediate family"; others interpreted it as a reference to Gehazi's line *forever*. Although Clarke's suggestion, with which he himself disagreed, did not seem to have racialized overtones, it was a common interpretive assumption to label contemporary groups as the descendants of ancient personages. These types of hermeneutical decisions partially explain the attempts to trace the ancestry of antebellum African Americans to Ham.

A more explicit exploration of coloration appeared in *Illustrations of the Holy Scriptures*, from Rev. George Bush (apparently, a distant relative of the former US presidents),[103] who was in 1839 Professor of Hebrew and Oriental Literature in New York City University. In a reflection on the phrase "leper as white as snow," the author wrote the following about Indian culture:

> There are many children born white, though their parents are quite black. These are not lepers, but albinos; and are the same as the white negroes of Africa. To see a man of that kind almost naked, and walking among the natives, has an unpleasant effect on the mind, and leads a person to suspect that all has not been right. . . . The natives do not consider this a disease, but a BIRTH, i.e. produced by the sins of a former birth.[104]

102. Adam Clarke, *The Holy Bible, Containing the Old and New Testaments: Authorized Translations, Including the Marginal Readings and Parallel Texts, with a Commentary and Critical Notes*, vol. 2 (New York: G. Land & P. P. Sandford, 1843); DPTC.

103. I am grateful to a member of the audience at the University of Detroit Mercy, who pointed this out to me (see https://web.archive.org/web/20081112171741/http://usinfo.state.gov/media/Archive_Index/Life_of_Mohammed_Book_NOT_Authored_by_Grandfather_or_Ancestor_of_President_Bush.html).

104. *Illustrations of the Holy Scriptures, Derived Principally from the Manners, Customs, Rites, Traditions and Works of Art and Literature, of the Eastern Nations . . . with Descriptions of the Present State of Countries and Places Mentioned in the Sacred Writings*, ed. George Bush (Brattleboro, VT: Brattleboro Typographic Company, 1839).

Unlike some of his contemporaries (e.g., Adam Clarke), Bush thought it logical to locate ancient biblical "white lepers" in contemporary settings, even if as "albinos" in India or "white negroes" in Africa. This racialized discourse magnifies what Edward Said described as the Western gaze on the "Orient," with its fierce—and usually distorted—description of the "other."[105]

William Anderson had a different interpretive objective in mind. The Gehazi narrative provided a black countermyth to the prevailing racialized tradition surrounding Noah's sons. Anderson's exegetical conclusion—leprosy equals whiteness—became logical only if the interpreter presumed the blackness of humans at the origins of creation and whiteness—not blackness—as the product of sin! Anderson, of course, upheld such a position based on his reading of Genesis 2:7.

Although he chose not to acknowledge any interpretive forerunners, Anderson had predecessors for this idea in the black interpretive tradition. In 1843 Robert Lewis, in his pamphlet *Light and Truth from Ancient and Sacred History*, advocated for God's original creation of black human beings, which he deduced to be Ethiopians.[106] For Lewis, "Adam" meant "earthy" etymologically, and the earth was a "dark substance."[107] Following Genesis 2:7, Lewis concluded that Adam must have been "black," since "[t]he soil of Eden was very rich, and *black*."[108] What Lewis did not account for, unlike Anderson, was the origin of whiteness. It simply was not part of his objective, since his goal was to explore the greatness of ancient Ethiopia to counter contemporary claims to the contrary.

Anderson's independence from others, unlike other formerly enslaved authors, allowed him to stake an interpretive claim on the biblical narrative to explore the racial identities of the peoples who populated his United States. Apparently he had no need for such financial (and editorial) support. He owned three farms and ran other successful businesses in Indiana and simply had the means to carry out this

---

The statement was republished in the 1856 edition, DPTC. Most of this description, if not all, Bush derived from Joseph Roberts, *Oriental Illustrations* (London, 1829).

105. See Edward Said, *Orientalism* (New York: Vintage Books, 1979).

106. See Lewis, *Light and Truth*. It does not seem that Lewis or Pennington (*Textbook*) account for "whiteness," though Lewis was also interested in reporting on the origins of Native Americans. Initially, Lewis concluded that Adam must have been "black," based on the color of the soil (*Light and Truth*, 1), but a few pages later he also suggested that Adam was "reddish in color" (*Light and Truth*, 7). Lewis's goal was to explore the greatness of ancient Ethiopia to counter contemporary claims to the contrary. For Josiah Priest, the origins of whiteness, like blackness, began at Genesis 9, since Noah and his wife were originally red, as were the first created humans.

107. Lewis, *Light and Truth*, 6.

108. Lewis, *Light and Truth*, 1; Lewis's italics. James Pennington turned to Genesis 2:7 to make his case for the human intellect of African Americans, without privileging any racial identification (*Textbook*, 57).

literary project unencumbered by the political necessities of his formerly enslaved colleagues.[109] In many ways, his appendix offered a rare glimpse into the biblical imagination of the black mind to account for the color of whiteness in the contemporary world. If a lot was "said about color" in his day, it was really what whites wrote and advocated about the origins of blackness, as a way of organizing their social institutions in antebellum America. What was not widely available—because the institutions of politics, economics, religion, and media would not allow for it—was what African Americans thought, said, and wrote about the origin of whiteness.

Anderson decided to explore the racial identities of his country's people groups and fill in an interpretive gap in black hermeneutical history. Of course, he did not go far enough. He offered no ideas about Native Americans or the small (but growing) pockets of Asian and Latino Americans who were part of the increasingly diverse landscape of the 1850s.[110] (The later Douglass did provide a more global vision.[111]) But what Anderson recommended—a theory of whiteness—was sufficient to challenge the dominant myth of the day that blackness was secondary, inferior, and later in the creative order. Furthermore, he accomplished this feat by using the primary religious source for Christian readers of his day, simply trying "to do the best we can with the writings that are left for our instruction."

CONCLUSION

No matter how we adjudicate the legitimacy of Anderson's racialized understanding of 2 Kings 5, his interpretation served as a potent critique of white interpretive tendencies. Why was it that white interpreters failed to see this narrative—that concludes with the offender and

---

109. Anderson, *Life*, 37–38*. Whether other narratives may have been enslaved to the (abolitionist prescribed) form of the storyline of the "slave narrative," Anderson's independence—like Douglass's own in 1855—allowed him literary opportunities to explore topics more relevant to himself and other African Americans.

110. E.g., the numbers of Chinese immigrants remained small relative to the US population. Larger numbers began arriving in the 1860s, primarily due to the transcontinental railroad and other building projects. The 1870 census listed 63,199 ethnically Chinese Americans. The 1880 census listed 105,465; more than 70 percent of them lived in California. These numbers exclude the significantly smaller arrivals of Japanese (first arriving in 1869) and Korean immigrants (see Roger Daniels, *Coming to America*, 2nd ed. [New York: Harper Perennial, 2002], 238–64). On Hispanic immigration, the situation is more complex, due to land acquisition. See James S. Olson and Heather Olson Beal, *The Ethnic Dimension in American History*, 4th ed. (Malen, MA: Wiley-Blackwell, 2010), 218–29. E.g., there were 50,000 Nuevos Mexicanos in New Mexico (which included Arizona in the nineteenth century), who cultivated a strong sense of Hispanic identity. I owe a special thanks to Steve Nolt at Goshen College for these sources and information.

111. See also Robert Lewis, who briefly attempted to account for Native Americans (i.e., what he called "red" people groups).

his descendants being perpetually cursed to be as "white as snow"—as an etiology of the white race? Clearly 2 Kings has far more explicit content that can be considered "racialized" than does the "curse of Ham" account in Genesis 9, which never mentions skin color and curses only the eponymous ancestor Canaan, with no explicit statement of genealogical perpetuation. Yet the Genesis narrative supported the ideological basis of Southern enslavement and the subsequent denigration of African peoples from the 1820s until the 1960s, and the myth still holds sway in some congregations.

Anderson's argument is thus helpful, if only to shine a light on the (deliberate?) inconsistencies of the hermeneutical traditions of the proslavery school, which readily chose texts to support their larger economic and political goals but ignored others that could be perceived as detrimental to those in their social location. Had Anderson's reading of 2 Kings 5 prevailed, the understanding of "whiteness" as a curse on Gehazi and his "seed forever" brought about because of greed might have served as a potent condemnation of a system that dehumanized darker peoples for the financial benefit of lighter peoples and perhaps even fostered conversation about such economic exploitation. Suffice it to say that a significant hermeneutical opportunity offered by Anderson's distinctive interpretive move was missed, as white proslavery advocates were never forced to reconcile their interpretive biases with regard to Genesis with the text in 2 Kings, whose plain meaning should have challenged their assumptions about Scripture's bases and what they thought of as God's bases for racial divisions.[112]

These formerly enslaved individuals lifted up the pen to write and raised the voice to speak about an experience of enslavement that included a religious setting in which the Bible was frequently interpreted to enforce and maintain their status and condition. For the most part, they sifted through these theological perspectives to reclaim the Bible for themselves and placed it on the side of the oppressed. In light of the conditions of the day, this took an unimaginable ingenuity. They took a text—used against them—and made it their own, often reversing the implications of normative mainline interpretive conclusions.

These public narratives left behind a legacy of their commitment, a snapshot of their lives, a challenge to the system of bondage, and a critical engagement with the sacred texts of the Christian religious tradition that the dominant race marshaled to read against the marginalized and

---

112. I am grateful to Rodney Sadler for the reflections in this paragraph, ideas generated in response to an earlier draft.

the minoritized. Anderson's interpretive approach called for more than simply the right textual choice, since the Bible was a contested site. It placed at the forefront attention to identity, in light of an ideological presupposition in which he took stock of the margins—that is, a hermeneutical approach that positioned the text and himself, simultaneously, on the side of minoritized populations. This was Anderson's utilization of what we might call (since Delores Williams) a hermeneutics of survival and the best of the black biblical imagination![113]

---

113. See Delores Williams, *Sisters in the Wilderness: The Challenge of Womanist God-Talk* (Maryknoll, NY: Orbis Books, 1993), 1–6.

5

Reading Paul with the Formerly Enslaved

Emancipation from the "Master's Minister"

INTRODUCTION

In *Jesus and the Disinherited*, Howard Thurman argued that the fundamental core of Jesus' religion was found in his care for the less fortunate in society. Contemporary Christianity had become, he claimed, a religion of the hereafter, with little regard for the reality of everyday life. This kind of religion had little value for human existence, much less for the poor and the oppressed. True Christian faith, inspired by Jesus' teachings and life, should supply "a technique of survival for the oppressed."[1] Yet the teachings of the modern Church failed to include this survival technique. Thurman's goal was to recover this essential message for contemporary exploited people. As he put it, "For years it has been a part of my own quest so to understand the religion of Jesus that interest in his way of life could be developed and sustained by intelligent men and women who were at the same time deeply victimized by the Christian Church's betrayal of his faith."[2] It is in this 1949 publication that Thurman related his grandmother's lesson about reading the Pauline letters, which shaped his life and thought.

Howard Thurman's grandmother, Nancy Ambrose, was born enslaved. Little is known about the details of her early life, either before

---

1. Howard Thurman, *Jesus and the Disinherited*, foreword by Vincent Harding (orig. Nashville: Abingdon Press, 1949; Boston: Beacon Press, 1996), 29.
2. Thurman, *Jesus and the Disinherited*, 30.

or immediately after emancipation.[3] When Howard was born in 1899, she helped raise him. She exercised a profound influence on all aspects of Howard's life, even how he interpreted the Bible—in particular, her preference for which biblical texts to read. Her choice of biblical readings would have a tremendous impact on his approach to the Bible. Perhaps this influence can be seen especially on his understanding of the Pauline corpus. Thurman narrated this childhood memory:

> My regular chore was to do all of the reading for my grandmother—she could neither read nor write. Two or three times a week I read the Bible aloud to her. I was deeply impressed by the fact that she was most particular about the choice of Scripture. For instance, I might read many of the more devotional Psalms, some of Isaiah, the Gospels again and again. But the Pauline epistles, never—except, at long intervals, the thirteenth chapter of First Corinthians. My curiosity knew no bounds, but we did not question her about anything.[4]

Several years later, when Thurman was in college, his bravery finally matched his curiosity; so he asked the matriarch

> why it was that she would not let me read any of the Pauline letters. What she told me I shall never forget. "During the days of slavery," she said, "the master's minister would occasionally hold services for the slaves. Old man McGhee was so mean that he would not let a Negro minister preach to his slaves. Always the white minister used as his text something from Paul. At least three or four times a year he used as a text: 'Slaves, be obedient to them that are your masters . . . , as unto Christ.' Then he would go on to show how it was God's will that we were slaves and how, if we were good and happy slaves, God would bless us.' I promised my Maker that if I ever learned to read and if freedom ever came, I would not read that part of the Bible.'"[5]

Part of Thurman's response to the omission of Paul's letters was the publication of *Jesus and the Disinherited*. First, Thurman provided a psychological analysis of Paul's situation to explain the first-century dilemma of this apostle. Saddened by the fact that Jesus' disciples did not accept him, because he had never met Jesus, Paul developed a distinctive message that was not easily welcomed by other followers of

---

3. See Howard Thurman, *With Head and Heart: The Autobiography of Howard Thurman* (San Diego/New York/London: Harcourt Brace & Co., 1979), 13.
4. Thurman, *Jesus and the Disinherited*, 30.
5. Thurman, *Jesus and the Disinherited*, 30–31.

Jesus.[6] Second, Thurman analyzed the Pauline letters through a post-colonial lens, decades before this approach would become common parlance in biblical studies. Paul's hybrid identity included his Jewishness (that is, he was a member of the minority class) and his Roman citizenship. As a member of the "privileged class" (i.e., as a Roman citizen), Paul "was of a minority but with majority privileges."[7] From this perspective, Paul could advocate obeisance to the ruling government in Romans 13 and maintain the master/slave relationship within ecclesial settings.[8] On the other hand, Paul advanced a universal appeal to the commonality of all persons in his writings. This collection of letters presented contradictory ideas. What distinguished Jesus from Paul, for Thurman, was Jesus' formal distance from Rome: "Now Jesus was not a Roman citizen. He was not protected by the normal guarantees of citizenship—that quiet sense of security which comes from knowing that you belong and the general climate of confidence which it inspires. If a Roman soldier pushed Jesus into a ditch, he could not appeal to Caesar; he would be just another Jew in the ditch."[9]

The distinction was crucial for Thurman's thesis. Despite the two-thousand-year chasm, Jesus and "American Negros," for Thurman, shared the same human psychological milieu within their respective societal contexts. Because of this common experience, Jesus' life could model the "survival technique" for people with their "backs against the wall."[10] Despite Thurman's more formal and critical engagement with Paul, he shared his grandmother's general opinion. Incorporating the ideas and methods of the biblical Paul would not be the way forward for the African American Christian community. The first-century apostle did not share the social insecurities of blacks, and others who lived in a postindustrialized capitalistic system in which they were only partially protected by the legal and judicial institutions in place. Thurman's Paul was not like them.[11]

Nancy Ambrose, therefore, operates as a hermeneutical witness to an approach to the Bible that has left a legacy on African American

---

6. Thurman, *Jesus and the Disinherited*, 31.

7. Thurman, *Jesus and the Disinherited*, 32.

8. Thurman accepted Pauline authorship of the "later" (non-Pauline) letters, contrary to proponents of historical criticism in his day. See Werner Georg Kümmel, *Introduction to the New Testament*, rev. and enlarged, trans. Howard Clark Kee (Nashville: Abingdon Press, 1975), 250–52.

9. Thurman, *Jesus and the Disinherited*, 33.

10. Thurman, *Jesus and the Disinherited*, 11.

11. Not all of Thurman's contemporaries shared his opinion. Within the African American interpretive tradition, others found Paul useful. E.g., Martin Luther King Jr.'s "Paul's Letter to American Christians" (published in 1956) serves as one example from a (late?) contemporary of Thurman.

interpretation.[12] In this chapter we want to contextualize a part of that legacy by looking more carefully at Ambrose's contemporaries. Like her, they endured abusive religious settings in which the "master's minister" appropriated select passages from the Pauline letters in order to maintain the status quo and keep the enslaved bound physically, emotionally, and spiritually. Unlike her, many of these authors could read and write and chronicle their own stories. Furthermore, this larger contextual story, set in the antebellum period, has consequences for how all oppressed groups in general, and African Americans in particular, negotiate their interpretive relationships with the letters of Paul, encompassed within a Bible that was (and is) expected to present a God of resistance, freedom, and reconciliation.

A REVIEW OF THE NINETEENTH-CENTURY CONTEXT: "THE MASTER'S MINISTER"

Undoubtedly, the "master's minister" was frequently at work. The narratives of the formerly enslaved detailed numerous accounts in which a white minister—the "master's minister," usually one hired by the enslaver—invoked specific Pauline texts in order to proclaim God's blessings for those who would remain "good and happy slaves." While white slaveholders would occasionally allow a black/slave minister to preach to the enslaved,[13] when the white minister preached, "Slaves, obey your masters" was a frequently cited passage imposed on black audiences. The selected text, from the King James Version, was usually Ephesians 6:5 or Colossians 3:22:[14]

> Servants, be obedient to them that are [your] masters according to the flesh, with fear and trembling, in singleness of your heart, as unto Christ; not with eyeservice, as menpleasers. (Eph. 6:5–6)

> Servants, obey in all things [your] masters according to the flesh; not with eyeservice, as menpleasers; but in singleness of heart, fearing God. (Col. 3:22)

---

12. See Allan Callahan, *The Talking Book: African Americans and the Bible* (New Haven, CT: Yale, 2006), 33–34; Brad Braxton, *The Tyranny of Resolution: 1 Corinthians 7:17–24* (Atlanta: Society of Biblical Literature, 2000), 240–41.
13. Some Southern white communities occasionally allowed the influence of black preaching. See Kenneth K. Bailey, "Protestantism and Afro-Americans in the Old South: Another Look," in *Religion and Slavery*, ed. Paul Finkelman (New York: Garland Pub., 1989), 33–54.
14. See also Titus 2:9; 1 Pet. 2:18.

The decade of the 1850s witnessed increased attention to the biblical arguments surrounding the enslavement institution. The Fugitive Slave Law, passed in 1850, altered the debates in specific ways. As part of the "compromise measures" of 1850, as Frederick Douglass would label them,[15] this law legislated that all enslaved persons who escape must be returned to their respective masters, even by citizens within free states. Paul's short letter to Philemon became a widely utilized biblical warrant interpreted in support of this law.[16] On the other hand, the formerly enslaved increased their efforts to provide firsthand oral and written accounts of their recent experiences in the slaveholding South. While Paul's letter to Philemon was rarely cited within these black sources (see below), other Pauline texts received prominent attention within the freedom narratives.

Henry Bibb offered, in 1849, the standard formulation of the Pauline obedience texts present in communities among the enslaved:

> This is where they have no Sabbath Schools; no one to read the Bible to them; no one to preach the gospel who is competent to expound the Scriptures, except slaveholders. And the slaves, with but few exceptions, have no confidence at all in their preaching because they preach a pro-slavery doctrine. They say, "Servants be obedient to your masters;—and he that knoweth his masters will and doeth it not, shall be beaten with many stripes—means that God will send them to hell, if they disobey their masters.' This kind of preaching has driven thousands into infidelity.[17]

Most of the enslaved, "with but few exceptions," did *not* trust in this type of white appropriation of the Bible. Despite the lack of religious education, many of the enslaved believed differently. They could not accept their condition as divinely ordained. Some undeniably walked away from a religion that sponsored a lifetime of bondage. Others found another way to think through this oppressive presentation, in order to locate an uplifting message within the Christian faith. Bibb,

15. Frederick Douglass, "The Anti-Slavery Movement: Extracts from a Lecture before Various Anti-Slavery Bodies, in the Winter of 1855." Douglass included this speech as an appendix, in Frederick Douglass, *My Bondage and My Freedom* (New York: Miller, Orton & Mulligan, 1855), 465*.

16. Albert Harrill, "Use of the New Testament in the American Slave Controversy: A Case History in the Hermeneutical Tension between Biblical Criticism and Christian Moral Debate," *Religion and American Culture* 10 (2000): 151.

17. Henry Bibb, *Narrative of the Life and Adventures of Henry Bibb, An American Slave, Written by Himself* (New York: Author, 1849), 23–24*. The theological conclusion—"that God will send them to hell" if the enslaved disobeyed—is intriguing as well. In first-century Christianity, the idea may be implicit in Col. 3:24–25, since the language of "reward" and "penalty" may imply future actions beyond earthly existence. (The negative aspect of Col. 3:25 was missing from Eph. 6 and 1 Pet. 2.)

among many others, was an advocate of "Sabbath Schools," a potential space for meaningful African American Christian education and literacy (see chap. 3).[18]

As Bibb asserted at the end of this brief account, large numbers simply turned away from Christianity altogether. Charles Ball's grandfather provided one example. In 1859, Ball related the following story about his grandfather's lifelong tension with white Christian religion: "He had singular religious notions—never going to meeting or caring for the preachers he could, if he would, occasionally hear. He retained his native traditions respecting the Deity and hereafter. It is not strange that he believed the religion of his oppressors to be the invention of designing men, for the text oftenest quoted in his hearing was, 'Servants, be obedient to your masters.'"[19]

Like Thurman's grandmother, Ball's grandfather understood the dangerous influence of an oppressive religion that utilized traditions to enforce social control. Unlike Thurman's grandmother, Ball's grandfather rejected the religion entirely—not just Paul's admonitions—as an "invention" constructed to encourage the despotic system. His rejection was partly due to the frequent and overbearing preaching on these Pauline texts. Yet Ball was quick to assert that his grandfather remained a theist hanging on to his "native traditions."

More specific accounts of the "master's ministers" and their sermons derive from other formerly enslaved authors: Henry "Box" Brown (1851), Peter Randolph (1855), and Harriet Jacobs (1861).[20] In their accounts, they identify specific ministers, including two particular Baptist ministers and one Episcopalian, who were prominent members of their respective white communities: "The Rev. R. Ryland, who preached for the coloured people, was professor at the Baptist seminary near the city of Richmond, and the coloured people had to pay him a salary of 700 dollars per annum, although they neither chose him nor had the least controul [sic] over him" (from Henry "Box" Brown); "Mr. James L. Goltney was a Baptist preacher, and was employed by Mr.

---

18. Bibb did not specify the references he cited (see Eph. 6:5 and Luke 12:47), nor did he mention the ancient speakers of these words, that is, Paul and Jesus, respectively. The literary, historical context seemed just as irrelevant to Bibb as it probably did to the slaveholding advocates who summoned these passages to support their agenda. The origination of these verses within the Bible itself would be sufficient cause for their authoritative usage in the nineteenth-century setting.

19. Charles Ball, *Fifty Years in Chains, or, The Life of an American Slave* (New York: H. Dayton; Indianapolis, IN: Asher & Co., 1859), 15.

20. Henry Box Brown, *Narrative of the Life of Henry Box Brown, Written by Himself* (Manchester, England: Printed by Lee & Glynn, 1851); Peter Randolph, *Sketches of Slave Life: Or, Illustrations of the "Peculiar Institution"* (Boston: The Author, 1855); Harriet Jacobs, *Incidents in the Life of a Slave Girl. Written by Herself* (Boston: Published for the Author, 1861).

M. B. Harrison to give religious instruction to his slaves" (from Peter Randolph); "When the Rev. Mr. Pike came, there were some twenty persons present. The reverend gentleman knelt in prayer, then seated himself, and requested all present, who could read, to open their books, while he gave out the portions he wished them to repeat or respond to" (from Harriet Jacobs).

Black audiences gathered, occasionally compelled to do so, to hear a white expositor on the Bible. Brown's "Rev. Ryland," Randolph's "Rev. Goltney," and Jacobs's "Rev. Pike" all shared the common passage from Paul, "Servants, obey your masters!" These white biblical interpreters also shared a common agenda, as reported by these black narrators: to utilize a theological interpretation of the authoritative biblical text in order to regulate order within their social institutions. The goal was to maintain the status quo, even if they had to call on the "devil" to do it.

Not only was Rev. Ryland the president of Richmond College (1841–1865); he was a professor at a local seminary and the pastor of the First African Church of Richmond (1841–1865), which numbered between 2,000 and 3,000 members during his pastorate.[21] Yet the racial composition of his congregation did not alter his opinion about the peculiar institution. Rather, as Brown wrote, Ryland "was a zealous supporter of the slave-holders' cause; . . . he was not ashamed to invoke the authority of heaven in support of the slave degrading laws under which masters could with impunity abuse their fellow creatures."[22]

As a kind of mercenary minister, one with less formal ties to a black ecclesial community, Rev. Goltney attempted to convince his hearers that their thoughts of freedom were diabolical: "It is the devil . . . who tells you to try and be free."[23] The devil wanted freedom; God wanted their enslavement. The irony of this theological position was apparently missed or ignored by the clergyman. Though "pious Mr. Pike" was less clear about Satan's purpose in all of this, he too thought that the devil played some role in the thoughts of the enslaved: "Your hearts are filled with all manner of evil. 'Tis the devil who tempts you."[24] What those temptations include may be something other than thoughts of

---

21. The membership numbers come from Albert J. Raboteau, *Slave Religion: The Invisible Institution in the Antebellum South* (New York: Oxford University Press, 1978), 197. According to Raboteau, after emancipation, the Richmond church received its first African American pastor, James Henry Holmes, who had been a deacon in the church for a decade (197). Ryland left these posts at the end of the Civil War. For more information on Rev. Ryland, see Bailey, "Protestantism and Afro-Americans in the Old South."
22. Henry Box Brown, *Narrative*, 32*.
23. Randolph, *Sketches*, 32*.
24. Jacobs, *Incidents*, 106*.

freedom, but Mr. Pike would certainly affirm Rev. Goltney's general conclusions.

To secure these "theological" reflections on the devil, Goltney and Pike had to move outside the literary context surrounding their primary biblical text—"slaves, obey your masters"—within Ephesians and Colossians. Neither "Satan" nor the "devil" occurs in Colossians.[25] In Ephesians, there are two references to the "devil" (Eph. 4:27–28; 6:11), though none to "Satan." In light of Pike's broader sermon, he may have had Ephesians 4:27–28 in mind, though specific references would not be necessary for the general charges he brought against the enslaved.

Punishment—not just that of the eternal kind—for wrongdoing was also always emphasized in these sermons, whether it was Ryland's support of the "degrading laws under which masters could with impunity abuse their fellow creatures" or Goltney's warnings "that it would be his duty to whip them, if they appeared dissatisfied,—all which would be pleasing to God!," or Pike's implied future threat that "God is angry with you, and will surely punish you, if you don't forsake your wicked ways."[26]

Less common was Goltney's threat of excommunication from the local ecclesial community: "If you run away, you will be turned out of God's church, until you repent, return, and ask God and your master's pardon."[27] Here the master's minister was at his best, interweaving God's desires with that of the master's. If the escaped returned and desired forgiveness, this person required not only God's forgiveness but also the exoneration of the earthly master. The spiritual and the physical were intermingling in the lives of black bodies. In his analysis of the themes of black preaching from this period, Eugene Genovese concludes that "Virtually nowhere do we find evidence that they [the enslaved], in any significant numbers, came to regard their enslavement as punishment for their collective sin."[28] Rather, as a form of God's punishment, enslavement was a white Christian message.

A Rev. William Troy, whose father was enslaved, reported an incident of the excommunication of Reuben Smith, who had escaped. Along with other African Americans who had gathered for their monthly meeting at a church in Essex County, Virginia, when the "colored and white meet together," Troy heard an unnamed white minister

---

25. It is possible that the "power of darkness" (Col. 1:8) or the "principalities and powers" (Col. 2:15) are obscure cosmic references to the devil.

26. Henry Box Brown, *Narrative*, 32*; Randolph, *Sketches*, 32*; and Jacobs, *Incidents*, 106*, respectively.

27. Randolph, *Sketches*, 32*.

28. Genovese, "Black Plantation Preachers in the Slave South," in *Louisiana Studies* 11 (1972): 188–214 (213).

preach on Ephesians 6:5 in order to deal with the business of Smith's escape. Black deacons were called on to give their assent:

Deacon R.   Yes, Sir; I know that he ran away from his master, and so far as I know about such conduct, I believe it wrong, and can't be tolerated by us.

Minister.   Will Deacon Edmund—, come forward? State what you know about the case.

Deacon E.   It is true, Sir, that Reuben ran away, and we must exclude him for it.

Minister.   Now, brethren, you hear the statements of your deacons, what will you do with the case?

Deacon R.   I move that we exclude brother Reuben, for running away from master.

Deacon E.   I second that.

Minister.   All that are in favor of that motion will hold up your right hand. It is unanimous. Well, brethren, we have done God's will, let us sing and conclude our meeting. Billy, will you sing?

"Jerusalem, my happy home!
Oh, how I long for thee!
When will my sorrows have an end,
My joys when shall I see?"

The double entendre of Billy's song would not have been overlooked by the black congregants. "Jerusalem" was a future "land" (up North) that Reuben Smith had reached. So to excommunicate him from the local Virginian congregation would have brought a jubilant "unanimous" vote from the remaining sisters and brothers in the pews. As Troy poignantly concluded his written account, "Reuben Smith was a preacher, and an intelligent man: that's the reason he ran away."[29]

The link between the earthly and heavenly masters, from Ephesians 6, was also central to Rev. Pike's theological rhetoric. Harriet Jacobs provided one of the longer summaries of a sermon from the master's

---

29. Rev. William Troy's account was recorded in Benjamin Drew, *A North-Side View of Slavery* (Boston: J. P. Jewett & Co., 1856), 353–57 (357).

minister (i.e., Pike), who preached the following message in the home of a free African American:

> Pious Mr. Pike brushed up his hair till it stood upright, and, in deep, solemn tones, began: "Hearken, ye servants! Give strict heed unto my words. You are rebellious sinners. Your hearts are filled with all manner of evil. 'Tis the devil who tempts you. God is angry with you, and will surely punish you, if you don't forsake your wicked ways. You that live in town are eye-servants behind your master's back. Instead of serving your masters faithfully, which is pleasing in the sight of your heavenly Master, you are idle, and shirk your work. God sees you. You tell lies. God hears you. Instead of being engaged in worshipping him, you are hidden away somewhere, feasting on your master's substance; tossing coffee-grounds with some wicked fortuneteller, or cutting cards with another old hag. Your masters may not find you out, but God sees you, and will punish you. O, the depravity of your hearts! When your master's work is done, are you quietly together, thinking of the goodness of God to such sinful creatures? No; you are quarrelling, and tying up little bags of roots to bury under the door-steps to poison each other with. God sees you. You men steal away to every grog shop to sell your master's corn, that you may buy rum to drink. God sees you. You sneak into the back streets, or among the bushes, to pitch coppers. Although your masters may not find you out, God sees you; and he will punish you. You must forsake your sinful ways, and be faithful servants. Obey your old master and your young master—your old mistress and your young mistress. If you disobey your earthly master, you offend your heavenly Master. You must obey God's commandments. When you go from here, don't stop at the corners of the streets to talk, but go directly home, and let your master and mistress see that you have come."[30]

Pike addressed expressively the theme of idleness, that is, what the enslaved did with his or her time when not in the presence of an earthly master. For the enslaved who did not physically escape, these minor acts of rebellion were subtle forms of resistance to the institution. The slaveholding community desired to monitor even the time outside of slave labor. In this brief summary, Jacob's Pike repeated the phrase "God sees" five times and included one "God hears" for good measure. Pike's God was the all-seeing, ever-present, "heavenly Master" who functioned as the master's overseer, virtually managing the affairs of the

---

30. Jacobs, *Incidents*, 106–7*.

enslaved in the absence of the earthly master. To "disobey" one was to "offend" the other. Pike weaved together a theological conception that moved well beyond the cited text, which was the primary focal point for this sermon (Eph. 6:5).

Less central to the sermon, though no less important, Pike attacked the use of the "little bags of roots," a practice carried over from African indigenous traditions. In addition to controlling the enslaved's time, it was necessary to limit indigenous practices, in order to manage the slavocracy of the day, since, as Albert Raboteau stresses, such practices had the potential "to unify the slaves and thus enable them to resist or rebel."[31] Some of the enslaved, as Lawrence Levine shows, utilized the Bible to "validate" their use of the roots.[32] The Pauline junctions would not be among those passages.

The emphasis in Pike's sermon fell on a simple theological equation: to obey God, one *must* obey the "earthly master." Within the biblical text, however, the emphasis lies elsewhere. On the one hand, these ancient passages support enslavement, encouraging the maintenance of Roman society's economic structural order. On the other hand, the ancient author(s) of these Pauline documents appropriated the image of the heavenly Master as a forewarning *for the earthly master*, not to abuse their earthly servants, since slave masters also had a Master in heaven (Eph. 6:9; Col. 4:1). The delimited duties of masters toward the enslaved would itself create a fundamental challenge to the peculiar nineteenth-century institution. As for Rev. Pike's sermon, the preacher redirected the biblical emphasis, away from the *master's* behavior toward the enslaved, and instead focused on the *enslaved's* behavior toward the master. In revision or subversion of the biblical text, any note of compassion the Paul of Ephesians may have required of the ancient master was completely removed. More seriously, any biblical buffer Paul may have provided against the nineteenth-century masters' physical violence, sexual exploitation, and psychological warfare was obliterated. "Thus Paul became, in the minds of both slave and master," as Allen Callahan recognizes, "the patron saint of the master class in the antebellum United States."[33]

---

31. Raboteau, *Slave Religion*, 4, 80–81. Some of the formerly enslaved questioned the appropriate use of these roots, but this did not hinder others from relaying success stories as well. E.g., Douglass tells a story about the possession of a root in his famous fight with Covey (Douglass, *Narrative*, 70–72*); Bibb has a story about a successful use of the root, despite his general opposition to it (Bibb, *Narrative*, 25–28*).

32. Lawrence Levine, *Black Culture and Black Consciousness* (New York: Oxford University Press, 1977), 57; see Theophus Smith, *Conjuring Culture: Biblical Formations of Black America* (New York: Oxford University Press, 1995). Perhaps they are referring to Gen. 1:29–30, which Rodney Sadler suggested to me.

33. Callahan, *Talking Book*, 30.

Some of the literate enslaved, who had access to a Bible, recognized this omission and distortion of the biblical texts. The Rev. William Troy, whose father was enslaved but whose mother was free, exclaimed, "I used to go to church regularly, but never heard them preach from, 'Masters, render unto your servants that which is just and equal.'"[34] Leonard Black, who escaped enslavement in 1837, recalled the larger literary context of Ephesians 6:5: "Should we not remember them that are in bondage as bound with them? Say not only slaves be obedient to your masters according to the flesh, but also say, masters, render unto your servants that which is right; and if that principle were carried out, slavery would be abolished."[35] Troy, Black, and others recognized that Colossians 4:1 and its parallel provided the potential for fairer treatment, even if it did not abolish the institution itself.

A few white interpreters also recognized this dilemma. Prominent Northern biblical theologian Charles Hodge published a widely popular commentary on Ephesians. In his comments on Ephesians 6:9, he focused his attention on what would be "just" and "equal" (from the parallel in Colossians) for the enslaved: "Justice requires that all their rights, as men, as husbands, and as parents should be regarded."[36] As a gradual emancipationist, the Presbyterian Hodge thought that the Southern practice of enslavement did not follow accurately the biblical admonition.[37] Biblical teachings like these were ignored or, as in the case of Rev. Pike's exegesis above, distorted. Hodge's understanding of "equality" is worth stating in whole:

> Slaves are to be treated by their masters on the principles of equality. Not that they are to be equal with their masters in authority, or station, or circumstances; but they are to be treated as having, as men, as husbands, and as parents equal rights with their masters. It is just as great a sin to deprive a slave of the just recompense for his labour,

34. See Drew, *North-Side View of Slavery*, 355*.

35. Leonard Black, *The Life and Sufferings of Leonard Black, a Fugitive from Slavery. Written by Himself* (New Bedford: Benjamin Lindsey, 1847), 54*.

36. Charles Hodge, *A Commentary on the Epistle to the Ephesians* (Broadway, NY: Robert Carter & Bros., 1856), 368. As Paul Gutjahr writes, "Hodge once again shows how little he appreciated the effects of slavery's more brutal aspects as it was practiced throughout much of the Union. . . . [T]he degradation and cruelty of the institution is lost in the careful semantics of Hodge's prose. . . . Hodge's notion of sanctification through obedience took no notice of the harsh realities of the broken families, back-breaking labor and pitiful living conditions that characterized slavery in America" (Paul Gutjahr, *Charles Hodge: Guardian of American Orthodoxy* [Oxford: Oxford University Press, 2011], 296).

37. For the various groups that comprised the emancipationist wing, see James Stewart, "Abolitionists, the Bible, and the Challenge of Slavery," in *The Bible and Social Reform*, ed. Ernest R. Sandeen (Philadelphia: Fortress Press, 1982), 31–57.

or to keep him in ignorance, or take from him his wife or child, as it is to act thus towards a free man.[38]

Similarly, some Southern whites concerned themselves with these biblical injunctions. In 1849, the Alabama Baptist State Convention held a contest and awarded $200 (a sizable amount in the middle of the nineteenth century) to the top essays on the topic "The Duties of Christian Masters to Their Servants." Ephesians 6:9 and Colossians 4:1 were invoked frequently by the authors of the submissions. Among other points made in the essays, one of the three winners in the contest, the Rev. A. T. Holmes of Georgia, advocated that earthly masters should be a friend, a protector, a guide, and a teacher.[39] On the topic of that teaching, however, Holmes proffered a more oppressive understanding on the meaning of what was "just":

> Teach him how to read and write? Instruct him in those branches of learning taught in our schools and colleges? Make him acquainted with those matters of general interest which agitate and disturb the political world? We answer, no; but teach him that he is a *sinner*, and that the Lord Jesus Christ is the sinner's friend. Teach him the absolute necessity of repentance toward God, and faith in the crucified Redeemer. Teach him that he must deny himself all ungodliness and worldly lusts, and live soberly, and righteously, and godly, in the present world.[40]

Holmes's essay stated more bluntly and harshly what was more latent in Hodge's commentary: sprinkle religious discourse throughout antebellum rhetoric in order to maintain the enslavement system. Granted, both Hodge and Holmes used their respective genres in hopes of mitigating some of the daily abuses within Southern plantation life, but neither advocated for the (immediate) abolition of slavery itself. To be sure, a growing number of white interpreters began to "contend that, when properly interpreted, Scripture did condemn *the kind of*

---

38. Hodge, *Ephesians*, 369. See also Hodge's essay on "Slavery" in which he wrote, "No one denies that the Bible condemns all injustice, cruelty, oppression and violence. . . . But what stronger argument can be present to prove that the sacred writers did not regard slaveholding as in itself sinful, than that while they condemn all unjust or unkind treatment (even threatening) on the part of masters towards their slaves, they did not condemn slavery itself? While they required the master to treat his slave according to the law of love, they did not command him to set him free" (Charles Hodge, *Essays and Reviews: Selected from the Princeton Review* [Broadway, NY: Robert Carter & Bros., 1857], 485); Digital Presentation in the Theological Commons, http://commons.ptsem.edu/.

39. A. T. Holmes, "The Duties of Christian Masters" (1851), reprinted in *Defending Slavery: Proslavery Thought in the Old South: A Brief History with Documents* (Boston/New York: Bedford/St. Martin's, 2003), 96–107.

40. A. T. Holmes, "The Duties of Christian Masters," 106, Holmes's italics.

slavery practiced in the American South."[41] But slavery itself was not a sin that deserved condemnation. Furthermore, Hodge advanced a "moderate" position on the treatment of the enslaved, as he advocated on behalf of literacy training for the enslaved as part of the responsibility of the master class. Yet neither one challenged directly the institution itself, despite Hodge's more moderate leanings and his position in favor of gradual emancipation. Their contemporary views on race (i.e., the superiority of whiteness) continued to exercise a decisive influence on their exegetical decisions, even when interpreting the ancient biblical letters of Paul.[42] From their perspective, the Bible's advocacy of fair treatment—for example, Ephesians 6:9 and Colossians 4:1—could be easily adopted along with the unequal yoke of racial groups living together in the Americas.

"*There Is a Great Difference between Christianity and Religion at the South*"[43]

Many of the white sermons above recorded within the narrative tradition of the formerly enslaved were located within a wider and more general treatment of the nature of religion within Southern communities. A number of authors subtitle these sections within their respective accounts, for example, "Sabbaths and Religious Meetings" (Randolph), "State of the Churches in Slave Countries" (Brown), "The Church and Slavery" (Jacobs). They reported these stories to provide their Northern white audiences glimpses into the impact (or lack thereof) of white biblical interpretations and Christian faith practices on the collective spiritual well-being of the enslaved. The narrative tradition consistently condemned white-sponsored, socially controlled attempts to manage the religious sensibilities of black Christians. Lawrence Levine has suggested that this control was so pervasive that even some black preachers, under the watchful, vengeful eye of their white masters, were inclined

---

41. Mark Noll, *The Civil War as a Theological Crisis* (Chapel Hill: University of North Carolina Press, 2006), 45, Noll's italics.

42. Noll's sensitive description of Hodge runs in this manner: "If Hodge, the most perceptive Old School Presbyterian in the North, could not tell the difference between slavery in general and the enslavement of one race in particular, it is little wonder that the distinction between slavery and the enslavement of African Americans was completely lost on his Southern counterparts" (Mark Noll, *America's God: From Jonathan Edwards to Abraham Lincoln* [New York: Oxford University Press, 2005], 420).

43. Jacobs, *Incidents*, 115*.

to proclaim similar, proslavery messages from these well-worn Pauline texts.[44]

The samples above were, of course, summaries (with specific highlights) of the general tenor of white expressions of Christian faith in the presence of black audiences. In addition to offering a general impression of these white-sponsored sermons, these black authors selected specific details they wanted to share with their audiences. They needed to shape these stories in particular ways in order to have the desired political effect on white abolitionists' ears and to gather empathy for the cause of abolition. But how did the enslaved hear the master's minister?

A few of the formerly enslaved authors suggested that these white-led, highly biased sermons contributed to the immoral condition of the enslaved, rather than having the effect for which the white ministers had hoped. Henry Bibb observed how these sermons failed to allow any sincere outlet for moral education. After hearing such sermons, the enslaved "cannot believe or trust in such a religion," so they find themselves "without friends, without protection, of law or gospel, and the green eyed monster tyranny staring them in the face."[45] Peter Randolph put it this way: "The slaveholders will allow the slaves to dance, but do not want them to pray to God."[46] If they were led to pray, they must pray to their "heavenly Master," who desired only that they faithfully serve their earthly masters. Undoubtedly they would not be encouraged to pray publicly to the God of liberation, who preferred their freedom, as a step toward individual and communal agency and psychological well-being. Douglass agonized in prayer as he watched the boats sail up the Chesapeake Bay: "I am left in the hottest hell of unending slavery. O God, save me! God, deliver me! Let me be free! Is there any God? Why am I a slave? I will run away. . . . It cannot be that I shall live and die a slave."[47] This was the prayer of the enslaved.

These black authors understood that not all white-packaged presentations of Christian faith supported white control of the social structure. They noted that some ministers actually cared about black bodies (and their souls). Henry "Box" Brown referred to two white ministers as points of comparison between liberating and oppressive interpretation of biblical texts.[48] As a point of comparison to Rev. Ryland, Mr.

---

44. Levine, *Black Culture*, 48. See Eugene D. Genovese, "Black Plantation Preachers," 136–62.

45. Bibb, *Narrative*, 24*.

46. Randolph, *Sketches*, 31*.

47. Douglass, *Narrative*, 64–65*.

48. Henry Box Brown, *Narrative*, 31–32*. Brown also compares Ryland to two other ministers in this chapter: (1) John Cave, whose conversion was due to an enslaved person; first, his mind "converted," and he viewed human bondage a sin; but, in the end, he sold off the enslaved to a "good master"; (2) Mr. Jeter, who preferred separate

Knopp, a visiting Northern white minister apparently preached such an arousing message on the passage "O! Jerusalem, Jerusalem which killest the prophets" (Matt. 23:37) that the white locals ran him out of town. On the other hand, Rev. Ryland continued to proclaim the typical tyrannical message that the enslaved should passively submit to their masters.

Peter Randolph compared a certain Rev. Goltney's laborious and negatively oriented sermons to those of Mr. Hanner. The latter reached for liberating biblical texts like Luke 4:18, "The Spirit of the Lord [is] upon me, because he hath anointed me to preach the gospel to the poor." But the white mob also chased him away "for preaching a true Gospel to colored people."[49] Harriet Jacobs preserved more positive recollections of an unnamed Episcopal minister who became much more popular among the enslaved than Mr. Pike. He periodically preached within the community for short periods of time. On one such visit to the black community, he concluded with the following: "Your skin is darker than mine; but God judges men by their hearts, not by the color of their skins."[50] Unsurprisingly, many within the slaveholding community deeply disapproved of him as well.

Finally, other authors of the narratives compared the forceful, unpersuasive sermons on enslavement to the vivacious brush arbor (black only) religious ceremonies.[51] Early in his chapter on "Sabbaths and Religious Meetings," Randolph gave one example: "Not being allowed to hold meetings on the plantation, the slaves assemble in the swamps, out of reach of the patrols. . . . Enlightened people call it excitement; but I wish the same was felt by everybody, so far as they are sincere."[52] Like Randolph, Jacobs surrounded the literary context of Pike's sermon with the wider interest of the enslaved in the comfort of private black religious services.[53]

Both Randolph and Jacobs discussed the role of music in particular, especially the creation of the spirituals, which played a central role

---

worship settings for blacks and whites; so he coaxed blacks into funding their own building project for a separate religious space (Henry Box Brown, *Narrative*, 28–31*).

49. Randolph, *Sketches*, 33*.

50. Jacobs, *Incidents*, 111*. During his longest stay within the community, the minister's wife died an untimely death. Upon her death she liberated the (five?) enslaved persons in their household (107–8*).

51. Cf. Raboteau, *Slave Religion*, 211–88.

52. Randolph, *Sketches*, 30–31*.

53. Jacobs, *Incidents*, 107–9*. Despite her high-church Episcopal preferences, Jacobs still expressed a more complex analysis of the shout. She left the following question unanswered: "If you were to hear them at such times, you might think they were happy. But can that hour of singing and shouting sustain them through the dreary week, toiling without wages, under constant dread of the lash?" (Jacobs, *Incidents*, 109*).

in these meetings.[54] Jacobs included several stanzas from one of the songs. The common theme in this spiritual was the wicked busyness of "Satan,"[55] which may be an indirect response to the "devil's" role in Mr. Pike's sermon.

Jacobs had her own devils to deal with. She closed the chapter on "The Church and Slavery" by telling of a sustained confrontation she had with the slaveholder (Dr. Flint), who had recently joined the local Episcopal church. He solicited sexual favors from her; Jacobs resisted his overtures by responding with the Bible. Flint exploded, "How dare you preach to me about your infernal Bible!"[56] She closed the section with the spiritual she had cited throughout the chapter: "Ole Satan's church is here below; Up to God's free church I hope to go."

Overall, the impression found in the narratives is a dismal view of the white-promulgated version of Christianity that the enslaved were subjected to hear. Peter Randolph negatively described Mr. Goltney's administering of the Lord's Supper to the enslaved community. Goltney, in the pen of this formerly enslaved writer, was no follower of that Lord. The enslaved had their own theological conceptions about who was on the Lord's side. It was said about one particular cruel slaveholder (a Mr. Harrison) who was mysteriously murdered, "so he went to judgment, with all his sins on his head."[57]

Similar judgments would have been thought about many slaveholding ministers. As Frederick Douglass noted in his description of his slaveholder's "conversion": "It neither made him to be humane to his slaves, nor to emancipate them." Instead, "after his conversion, he found religious sanction and support for his slaveholding cruelty."[58] The enslaver—now also a preacher—continued to promote human bondage, but now under the auspices of the gospel. As evidenced by their escaped comrades, the enslaved could distinguish between a proper expression of Christian faith—what they would call the "pure religion of Jesus"[59]—and the false one that was proclaimed by the master's minister.

54. Randolph, *Sketches*, 31–32*; Jacobs, *Incidents*, 107–8*.
55. Jacobs, *Incidents*, 108*.
56. Jacobs, *Incidents*, 115*.
57. Randolph, *Sketches*, 32*.
58. Douglass, *Narrative*, 54*.
59. Henry Box Brown, *Narrative*, 32*.

PHILEMON AS REPRESENTATIVE
OF THE CHRISTIAN SLAVEHOLDER

One part of the New Testament widely discussed in the middle decades of the nineteenth century was Paul's letter to Philemon. Paul's willingness to "return" Onesimus to Philemon (Phlm. 12) was viewed as biblical proof for the politically motivated policies surrounding the Fugitive Slave Law of 1850.[60] According to J. Albert Harrill, proslavery advocates considered Philemon the Pauline mandate for the federal slave law.[61] Slaveholders summoned this letter to convince their contemporaries that the return of escapees had Christian underpinnings. Radical white abolitionists—fox example, William Lloyd Garrison—advocated renouncing any biblical rationale whatsoever in the fight against slavery.[62] For this wing of the abolitionist movement, the Bible was a proslavery book. The absence of Philemon from black-authored narratives did not mean that the formerly enslaved were unaware of this letter's influence.

John Passmore Edwards, a well-known white British philanthropist and abolitionist, in 1852 published *Uncle Tom's Companions: Or, Facts Stranger than Fiction.*[63] His goal was to introduce the British public to real accounts of escapees in order to support the popular but fictional work of Harriet Beecher Stowe. Edwards's list included some of the leading black abolitionists of the 1840s and 1850s, whose own narratives, speeches, and sermons circulated far and wide (e.g., William Wells Brown, Frederick Douglass, Henry Highland Garnet, James Pennington, Moses Roper, and Peter Wheeler). The final story he related in his book was the following account from Frederick Douglass, based on a speech given in Scotland in which Douglass juxtaposed "men-stealers" (1 Tim. 1:10) with Paul's letter to Philemon:

> They have undertaken to show, that neither Christ nor his Apostles, had any objection to slaveholders being admitted to church fellowship. They have undertaken to show, that the Apostle Paul, in sending

---

60. Some contemporary biblical scholars call into question the "fugitive" thesis of the letter, which assumes that Onesimus "escaped" to Paul from Philemon. How Onesimus comes into contact with Paul is unclear. See Allen D. Callahan, *Embassy of Onesimus: The Letter of Paul to Philemon* (Valley Forge, PA: Trinity Press Int., 1997), 5–6; Joseph A. Fitzmyer, *The Letter to Philemon: A New Translation with Introduction and Commentary*, Anchor Bible 34C (New York: Doubleday, 2000), 13–14; Emerson B. Powery, "Philemon," in *The New Interpreter's One-Volume Commentary*, ed. Beverly Roberts Gaventa (Nashville: Abingdon Press, 2010), 877–78.

61. J. Albert Harrill, "Use of the New Testament in the American Slavery Controversy," 151.

62. See Noll, *The Civil War as a Theological Crisis*, 31.

63. Edwards's full title was *Uncle Tom's Companions: Or, Facts Stranger than Fiction. A Supplement to Uncle Tom's Cabin: Being Startling Incidents in the Lives of Celebrated Fugitive Slaves* (London: Edwards and Co., 1852).

Onesimus back to Philemon, sanctioned the relation of master and slave. (Hear, hear.) Their arguments on this question are vain, being quoted in the United States by the slaveholding, pro-slavery papers against the abolitionists, and against those who are separating from the slaveholder. (Hear.) Now I have to bring certain charges against that deputation. I charge them, in the first place, with having struck hands in Christian fellowship with men-stealers.[64]

Douglass's rejoinder was not to tackle the exegetical concerns of the Philemon story directly, but rather to redirect the focus to another Pauline passage. Douglass turned his audience's attention to 1 Timothy 1:9–10 (KJV): "Knowing this, that the law is not made for a righteous man, but for the lawless and disobedient, . . . for whoremongers, for them that defile themselves with mankind, for menstealers, for liars, for perjured persons, and if there be any other thing that is contrary to sound doctrine."

To counter one biblical passage with another was a common exegetical strategy in a biblically literate world of the United Kingdom in the nineteenth century. Among abolitionists, it was common to use First Timothy and its injunction against the slave trade to refute the form of enslavement practiced in the US model. But First Timothy's injunction could be equally appropriated by nineteenth-century slaveholding advocates, who condemned the trading of slaves while still promoting the institution itself.[65] This appeal to some Pauline passages was an attempt to uphold respect for the authority of the Bible, while arguing against the slave mandate of other biblical passages.

Douglass, among others, upheld the Bible's usefulness in the cause of abolition, in a speech given on American soil a few years later.[66] Along with many black abolitionists, Douglass was not willing to hand over the Bible to the proslavery side, despite challenges Scripture itself created.[67] The contemporary concern was more serious than what Paul (or a disciple of Paul) may have written in an ancient context. Douglass was concerned less with figuring out a potential Pauline inconsistency on

64. Edwards, *Uncle Tom's Companions*, 220–21*. The speech was not recorded in either of Douglass's earlier narratives (1845, 1855) "written by himself." The language of "men-stealers," however, did occur in his two accounts: *Narrative* (1845), 119*; *My Bondage and My Freedom* (1855), 409, 438*.

65. The import of slaves was legally abolished in the United States in 1808, even though the domestic slave trade continued. See J. Albert Harrill, *Slaves in the New Testament: Literary, Social, and Moral Dimensions* (Minneapolis: Augsburg Fortress Press, 2006), 119–44.

66. Speech in Boston, Feb. 8, 1855, cited in Harrill, "Use of the New Testament in the American Slave Controversy," 160.

67. In 1855, Douglass explained his break with Garrison as a disagreement over the Constitution—which Douglass interpreted as an antislavery document—and the initiation of *The North Star*, Douglass's antislavery paper (*My Bondage and My Freedom*, 395–96*). He would view the Bible in the same way.

ancient Roman slavery than he was with the global implications of US Southern Christianity and its evil pact with the peculiar institution.[68]

The speech itself (if recorded accurately) concluded with a stunning repeated crescendo of "Send back the money." Douglass wanted the Church of Scotland to return funds they had received from the slaveholding churches in the United States to support their Christian mission. (Great Britain had legally ended the slave trade in 1807.) Apparently the crowd loudly expressed their agreement with their dark-skinned guest speaker. "Send back the money" was the repeated refrain, rather than "Send back the fugitive." This was how John Passmore Edwards ended his entire volume on *Uncle Tom's Companions*.[69]

PAUL, OUR FELLOW SUFFERER

Nineteenth-century black authors who penned the semibiographical and fully political stories of their experiences in the system of enslavement did not know only the master's Paul. They also gained access to New Testament stories about and words from a Paul with whom they could empathize. The Paul of Acts, as Abraham Smith has shown, was available to many people with limited access to the printed text.[70] They even gained insight into the Paul of the letters, absent the "servant" texts to which they were frequently exposed by white interpreters. For those who discovered this other Paul, many of them found a cosufferer who could relate to their present circumstances of abuse, neglect, and impoverishment while they travelled on their own journeys.

Solomon Bayley

In 1825, almost a decade before the establishment of the American Anti-Slavery Society (1833), which made a widespread call for more fugitive narratives to expose the exigencies of Southern enslavement,

---

68. See Douglass's 1846 letter to Garrison regarding his speeches in London on the same issue, though without reference to the Pauline passages (Gilder Lehman Center for the Study of Slavery, Resistance and Abolition; http://www.yale.edu/glc/archive/1098.htm; located on Feb. 20, 2015).

69. Harriet Beecher Stowe's *Uncle Tom's Cabin* was written partially as a response to the passing of the 1850 Fugitive Slave Act by the US Congress. See Nancy Koester, *Harriet Beecher Stowe: A Spiritual Life* (Grand Rapids: Eerdmans, 2014), 105–20.

70. See Abraham Smith, "Paul and African American Biblical Interpretation," in *True to Our Native Land: An African American New Testament Commentary*, ed. Brian K. Blount et al. (Minneapolis: Fortress Press, 2007), 34–37.

Solomon Bayley penned *A Narrative of Some Remarkable Incidents in the Life of Solomon Bayley, Formerly a Slave in the State of Delaware, North America.*[71]

He framed his *Narrative* with Paul's words. On the title page, he cited 2 Corinthians 4:9 (KJV): "Persecuted, but not forsaken; cast down, but not destroyed."[72] Following two short accounts of the deaths of his daughters, Bayley concluded the entire brief (forty-eight-page) narrative with a list of verses that he often recalled for self-encouragement:

> Now, dear friend, in this exercise of mind there were some scriptures came into my mind, to encourage and strengthen me; such as, the II. Corinthians, xii. 9—II. Kings, v. 4—I. Corinthians, i. 21, 27, 28, and chapter xi. 3. also chapter ix. 16, 22—II. Corinthians, xi, 29—Daniel xii. 3—Isaiah vi. 5—Jeremiah i. 6—John i. 15, and chapter iii. 2—Hebrews xi. 34; all these scriptures mightily helped to encourage me to go forward in speaking to a dying people, the words of eternal life.[73]

Paul's letters were prominent in Bayley's list. More than half of these verses (eight out of fifteen) derive from 1 and 2 Corinthians. He was attracted to these two letters primarily because they detail the first-century apostle's own struggles in ministry. Here Bayley discovered other Pauline passages, besides what the master's minister commented on, to instruct the enslaved. In a manner distinctive from other narratives in the genre (which usually began with one's birth place, date, and the naming of one's parents), Bayley's *Narrative* imitated the opening of many of Paul's letters: "SOLOMON BAYLEY, unto all people, and nations, and languages, grace be unto you, and peace from God our Father, and from the Lord Jesus Christ."[74]

Bayley initiated his *Narrative* with his name—which was already listed on the title page—and addressed a universal audience before offering the common biblical greeting of the Pauline letters: "Grace be unto you, and peace." This distinctive opening differentiated it from others within the genre. This formerly enslaved author hoped to

71. Solomon Bayley's title continues: *Written by Himself, and Published for His Benefit; to Which Are Prefixed, a Few Remarks by Robert Hurnard* (London: Harvey & Darton, 1825).

72. Only one other antebellum narrative, *Memoir of Old Elizabeth* (Philadelphia: Collins, 1863), included a Pauline verse (Gal. 3:28) on its title page. This narrative was not written by Elizabeth but was "taken mainly from her lips in her 97th year" (*Memoir*, 3*) by an unknown author. It is difficult to determine if the verse originated with the transcriber or with Elizabeth. Elizabeth heard the Bible read by her father every Sabbath (*Memoir*, 3*) and eventually became an itinerant preacher herself. It is possible that Gal. 3:28 was her suggestion for the title page, but there is no apparent evidence for this conclusion.

73. Bayley, *Narrative*, 47–48*.

74. Bayley, *Narrative*, 1*. Cf. 1 Cor. 1:1–3; 2 Cor. 1:1–2; Gal. 1:3; Eph. 1:1–2; Phil. 1:2.

transport his readers to a different time and place. In his mind, he had a global audience and mission: "all people, and nations, and languages." After all, this formerly enslaved author published this short volume in London, in which there was a growing abolitionist presence,[75] and he eventually traveled to Africa. He was becoming a global citizen in spite of his early history, as one *"Formerly a Slave in the State of Delaware."* Finally, he would echo the great apostle to the Gentiles in order to present his account of the "remarkable incidents" in his life.

Most attractive to Bayley were Paul's sufferings. In addition to the passage on the title page ("Persecuted, but not forsaken"), which overshadowed the entire narrative, Bayley also discovered comfort in 2 Corinthians 12:9 ("And he said unto me, My grace is sufficient for thee: for my strength is made perfect in weakness. Most gladly therefore will I rather glory in my infirmities, that the power of Christ may rest upon me") and 1 Corinthians 9:22 ("To the weak became I as weak, that I might gain the weak: I am made all things to all, that I might by all means save some").

In the New Testament, the emphasis highlights the suffering Paul and God's power to utilize that suffering, weak human individual to carry out a divine mission. William Anderson, Bayley's late contemporary, shared this attraction to Paul (see below). Bayley also found appealing Paul's focus on weakness, as underlined in each of these verses. This theme would underscore Bayley's account of his story, as it did the apostle's own story (see 2 Cor. 11:29,[76] which is also on the list). Among the examples, he discussed the sufferings of his youngest daughter—during a long illness that led to her death—and her willingness to refrain from complaint, since, he claimed, she had in view Christ's sufferings.[77] The location of God's "strength" in human weakness allowed Bayley to connect directly with Paul's words in 1 Corinthians 1:27–28: "But God hath chosen the foolish things of the world to confound the wise; and God hath chosen the weak things of the world to confound the things which are mighty; And base things of the world, and things which are despised, hath God chosen, [yea], and things which are not, to bring to nought things that are."

---

75. The slave *trade* was abolished in Britain in 1807. Slavery was officially abolished in the British Empire in 1833.

76. This Pauline idea follows a long list of verses in which Paul details his own sufferings (see 2 Cor. 11:23–28), an episode that probably effected the details of Bayley's abuses.

77. Bayley, *Narrative*, 46*.

This passage, along with 1 Corinthians 1:21 (also on Bayley's list),[78] encouraged Bayley, despite his unsuccessful efforts to secure ministerial training, which he alluded to only in the brief description of his calling at the end of the *Narrative*. In a self-deprecating manner, he acknowledged that God "knows how to get himself honour and praise by the most feeble."[79]

More troubling, from a contemporary viewpoint, was Bayley's inclusion of 1 Corinthians 11:3 as a passage in which he found inspiration: "But I would have you know, that the head of every man is Christ; and the head of the woman [is] the man; and the head of Christ [is] God." Like many others in nineteenth-century society (both black and white), Bayley was blind to the interconnectedness of racial enslavement and gender inequality in his day. The same cultural hierarchical hegemony determined both. Yolanda Pierce helpfully attempts to explain the complexity of Bayley's choices in this context and how he may have understood his role: "Bayley attempts to reclaim domestic authority for black men by showing that—once allowed the opportunity to *be men* rather than slaves—black men can be both husbands and fathers, can head their households just as Christ heads the church."[80] Yet in trying to redeem Bayley's actions, Pierce expresses her own ambivalence: "To what extent do we applaud his taking proper authority back from the white patriarchy and to what extent does he simply replicate that patriarchy to the dismay of black women and children, who are now subject to husbands and fathers in much the same manner that they were subject to slave masters?"[81]

Our ambivalence need not detract us from acknowledging Bayley's struggles within his context, a context in which he frequently found himself without legal rights over his own personhood or his marriage. Both issues were central to his short narrative.[82] Pierce's explanation that Bayley was simply attempting "to reclaim domestic authority" in a patriarchal context in which white males possessed such authority may be a legitimate way to understand Solomon Bayley's preference for Paul's words. On the other hand, in his own context, Bayley was no Peter Randolph or Frederick Douglass, both of whom partnered with their African American sisters in the claiming of their own rights,

---

78. "For after that in the wisdom of God the world by wisdom knew not God, it pleased God by the foolishness of preaching to save them that believe" (1 Cor. 1:21 KJV).

79. Bayley, *Narrative*, 47*.

80. Yolanda Pierce, *Hell without Fires: Slavery, Christianity, and the Antebellum Spiritual Narrative* (Gainesville: University Press of Florida, 2005), 77; Pierce's italics.

81. Pierce, *Hell without Fires*, 47.

82. Bayley, *Narrative*, 2–3*, 25–28*.

before God and others, even as they advocated for the civil rights of black males.

"If You Love the God of Love, Clear Your Hands from Slaves": Richard Allen's Appreciation for Paul [83]

In 1833, a period shortly before the establishment of the slave narrative as a widely employed political tool, Bishop Richard Allen wrote at the earnest request of friends "to leave a small detail of my life and proceedings."[84] Part of his account included a description of the role religion played in the life of the enslaved. In the widespread debate about the impact religion could have on enslaved laborers, his master believed that religion would promote "better" service, so Allen and his brother desired to prove the correctness of the assertion.[85] In these religious services, Richard Allen developed pious sensibilities and leadership skills.

Allen's willingness to hone his spiritual skills did not mean that he had little awareness of the tragedy of the slave institution, because he could just as easily pen, "[S]lavery is a bitter pill, notwithstanding we had a good master."[86] Furthermore, Allen held a clear theological view of whose side the God of the Bible was on in this great conflict. Near the end of this short narrative, he composed a short "Address to the People of Colour in the United States" on the subject of slavery.[87] He addressed three audiences in this short statement: slaveholders, African Americans, and abolitionists. When addressing the first group, Allen drew on the exodus motif to argue that God is "the protector and avenger of slaves" and that "God himself was the first pleader of the cause of slaves."[88] Yet he bemoaned the bloodshed on both sides, pos-

---

83. *The Life, Experience, and Gospel Labours of the Rt. Rev. Richard Allen* (Philadelphia: Martin & Boden, Printers, 1833), 46*. Some scholars do not formally classify Richard Allen's narrative among the freedom narratives. Marion Wilson Starling's classic study, however, discusses it as part of the narratives prior to 1836, whose storytellers viewed "the world as a stage," and the unfortunate parts they were granted on that stage (Marion Wilson Starling, *The Slave Narrative: Its Place in American History* [Washington, DC: Howard University Press, 1988], 101–5, esp. 105).

84. Allen, *Life*, 3*.

85. Allen, *Life*, 6–7*. Although Allen did not condemn him, this same "good master" sold off the author's mother and sisters because of financial stress (*Life*, 6*). Eventually, he allowed Allen and his brother to work for and purchase their freedom.

86. Allen, *Life*, 7*.

87. Allen, *Life*, 45–49*.

88. Allen, *Life*, 45, 46*. Allen's use of the exodus motif was rare within the freedom-narrative tradition in the antebellum period. Sylvester Johnson suggests that the motif became prominent after the Civil War (*The Myth of Ham in Nineteenth-Century American Christianity: Race, Heathens, and the People of God* [New York: Palgrave MacMillan, 2004], 53).

sibly referring to the 1831 Nat Turner rebellion, which was still fresh on everyone's mind.

When he addressed the "people of colour," he hoped the enslaved would honor God *by* honoring their "masters," which *may*, in turn, lead to their freedom.[89] The emphasis was less on their obedience to their masters than on the potential result of liberation. To the enslaved, he insisted that there were white vocal supporters for the cause of emancipation,[90] an observation he based almost exclusively on personal experience, since his master permitted him to purchase his freedom. He charged the enslaved to remember their obligations to remain diligent in their endeavors, so as to give whites no cause to complain. Apparently he accepted the position that Christian faith in particular could assist in creating more submissive laborers. More importantly, recent insurrections—and the backlash on black bodies—would have been near to everyone's mind. But his advice to the enslaved did not mean that he chose the side of proslavery advocates.

When Allen turned his attention to the abolitionists, he acknowledged their willingness to remember "the most abject of our race brethren,"[91] recalling Acts 17 and the "one blood" doctrine. Allen concluded the entire section with an echo of Psalm 68. The Bible floods this short address, as Bishop Allen reflected on the biblical underpinnings of nineteenth-century antebellum life. Following specific statements on the subject of slavery, Allen provided a kind of sermonic review on biblical love. A definition of "love" begins with Jesus' attention to physical bodies—through his actions and words—and not just their souls. True Christians would follow this Jesus, he argued, and must "love one another."[92] Furthermore, Paul's words share Jesus' admonishment, as Bishop Allen juxtaposed 1 Corinthians 13 with Jesus' actions and words:

> Hearken to St. Paul, speaking of this most excellent way or duty, and then judge ye, my brethren, of the necessity of putting it in practice. Though I speak with the tongue of men and angels, and have not charity, I am become as a sounding brass or a tinkling cymbal. And though I have the gift of prophecy, and understand all mysteries, and all knowledge, and though I have all faith, so that I could remove mountains, and have not charity, I am nothing. And

89. Allen, *Life*, 47*.
90. Allen, *Life*, 48*.
91. Allen, *Life*, 49*.
92. Allen, *Life*, 50–51*.

though I bestow all my goods to feed the poor, and though I give my body to be burned, and have not charity, it profiteth nothing.[93]

Allen concluded this section by outlining proofs of "charity" (KJV), which was, for him, committed love, "which consists in the applying and bestowing some part of our substance, or the produce of our labours, towards the relief and support of the poor and needy."[94] For Allen, love must be seen in action. The only change the bishop made to the Corinthian passage (1 Cor. 13:1–3) was to drop Paul's personal "me." Paul writes, "it profiteth me nothing"; Allen's omission stretched the personal benefit into a broader application: "it profiteth nothing." A lack of "charity" (or active, engaged love) profits no one, not the slaveholder, "people of color" (enslaved or free), or abolitionists. No one would benefit from a failure to put love into meaningful action on behalf of the less fortunate and the marginalized. This is the way of Jesus and the way of Paul.

Thurman's grandmother would also approve, because after "long intervals," she too required her grandson to read Paul's "love" chapter to her. Whatever else Paul may have written about the enslaved, Richard Allen firmly placed Paul on the side of the oppressed. As he wrote to the slaveholders, shortly before his citation of 1 Corinthians, "If you love your children, if you love your country, if you love the God of love, clear your hands from slaves."[95] This is the way of Jesus . . . and the way of Paul.

William Anderson's "Suffering Paul"

A generation after Allen, who founded the African Methodist Episcopal Church, another AME minister published his *Narrative* in the Midwest. William Anderson's tale did not, apparently, find as popular an audience as some of his contemporaries in the late 1840s, even though he developed an interesting view on the biblical origins of whiteness (see chap. 4). Nonetheless, his story supplies another example of the African American attraction to a Christian Paul who suffered as they suffered: "When I thought of my previous life in old Virginia, my mother and friends, my poor heart would sink within me, and I could

---

93. Allen, *Life*, 51*.
94. Allen, *Life*, 51*.
95. Allen, *Life*, 46*.

but exclaim, with Paul, 'O, wretched man that I am; who shall deliver me from this body of death.'"[96]

In Romans 7:21–25, Paul discusses the struggle between his mind and his body over the will to do good ("God's law") versus the desire to do evil ("sin's law"); so he can write, "[W]ith the mind I myself serve the law of God; but with the flesh the law of sin" (Rom. 7:25).

Anderson explored Paul's spiritual struggles for his own immediate context, in particular the challenges of living on a large plantation of a wicked enslaver, "widow Hampton," who whipped the bodies of the enslaved constantly and failed to provide for their physical nourishment. In addition, the mistress widow prohibited any religious instruction or rest on the Sabbath. This context was one in which there were "eight or ten runaways in the woods constantly."[97] In the midst of this crisis, Anderson also contemplated an escape. Removed from his family (who remained in Virginia), he remembered Paul's words and struggles: "O, wretched man that I am; who shall deliver me from this body of death" (Rom. 7:24). Anderson placed the apostle in a long line of biblical sufferers who fought spiritual battles for their respective causes and aligned himself in that tradition in retelling his story: "Therefore I will trust in Him, as did Job, Peter, Paul and all the Apostles of old."[98] This allusion to the "suffering Paul" came alongside the "suffering Job," who was a common reference in other narratives.

Finally, this recollection of a cosuffering Paul—similar to Solomon Bayley's use of Paul—allowed Anderson to reflect also on the greatest cosufferer in the Christian tradition, the suffering Christ: "Every Christian who has passed through affliction, has been inclined, I doubt not, to inquire of his God the reason of all his torments, and I know that some have exclaimed, 'O God, why forsakest thou me?'"[99] Here Anderson indicated that the common dilemma of the sufferer—as Jesus inquired centuries before—was to wonder how a God in control of the universe could allow such violent suffering on the abused and downtrodden.[100] Anderson's query, like that of Frederick Douglass,

---

96. William Anderson, *Life and Narrative of William J. Anderson, Twenty-four Years a Slave; Sold Eight Times! In Jail Sixty Times!! Whipped Three Hundred Times!!! Or The Dark Deeds of American Slavery Revealed. Containing Scriptural Views of the Origin of the Black and of the White Man. Also, A Simple and Easy Plan to Abolish Slavery in the United States, Together with An Account of the Services of Colored Men in the Revolutionary War—Day and Date, and Interesting Facts* (Chicago: Daily Tribune Book and Job Printing Office, 1857), 29*. See Rom. 7:24. Anderson slightly alters the ending, which reads "from the body of this death" (KJV).

97. Anderson, *Narrative*, 29*.

98. Anderson, *Narrative*, 44*.

99. Anderson, *Narrative*, 30*.

100. One other example is worth notice. Anderson used Paul's words in a discussion of the challenges he had received from others who have told white authorities about his acts of assisting fugitives: "If God be for me, who

was the outcry of the enslaved. "Is there any God? Why am I a slave?
. . . It cannot be that I shall live and die a slave."[101]

OTHER MISCELLANEOUS MEMORIES
OF PAULINE INFLUENCE

Of course, the antebellum freedom narratives offer a number of other
allusions to Pauline passages, although many of these examples seem
more symbolic and fail to advance the direction of the author's story.
Aaron (whose last name is unknown) was unable to read, so he dictated his brief account in 1845 and included a passage from "Paul to
the Galatians" (5:19) among his favorite passages.[102] It is not clear if
the passage was his way of recalling only Paul's list of inappropriate
sexual activities, like "lasciviousness," or was a general reminder about
all "works of the flesh." Another reference to Galatians in the antebellum narratives occurred on the title page of *Memoir of Old Elizabeth,
A Coloured Woman* (1863): a citation of Galatians 3:28. We might
expect this verse—"there is neither bond nor free"—to receive prominent attention within the narratives, but it did not.[103] Both of these
accounts were dictated narratives, so they may be complicated by the
rhetorical strategies and religious commitments of their white editors.

THE PAUL OF ACTS 17: "[GOD] HATH MADE
OF ONE BLOOD ALL NATIONS"

Nineteenth-century readers of the Bible would not have differentiated
the Paul of Acts from the Paul of the letters. That distinction was just
coming of age, due to the rise of historical criticism. It would take
decades (and in some circles much longer) before this critical issue in
biblical studies would receive a broader hearing. So it is no surprise that
African Americans would have valued Luke's Paul as much as any other

---

can be against me?" (Rom. 8:31). Feeling under attack from his own (black) community, Anderson personalizes
Paul's plural (and more communal) form.

   101. Douglass, *Narrative*, 64–65*.

   102. Aaron, *Light and Truth of Slavery*, 19–20*.

   103. In the more than sixty narratives searched, it occurred only once. The other surprising absence is the omission of 1 Cor. 7:21. Caroline Shanks mentions the latter as a prominent passage among the abolitionists but does
not cite any specific reference ("The Biblical Antislavery Argument of the Decade, 1830–1840," *Journal of Negro
History* 16 [1931]: 150).

portrayal within the New Testament.[104] In the narrative tradition, there was no more prominent Pauline passage (so to speak) than Acts 17:26, which eventually led to what became known as the "one blood" doctrine. As discussed in chapter 4, several formerly enslaved authors recalled Acts 17 as a direct response to the "curse of Ham" myth.

In the Areopagus speech (in Athens, Greece), placed on Paul's lips by the author of Acts, Paul acknowledges a universally human religious quest for God. In Lukan theology, each person contains an innate capacity to desire after the Divine, since God has created all ("from one ancestor" in the NRSV). Nineteenth-century Americans in touch with their African spiritual roots and the nearness of spirits would be attracted to the oft-cited words surrounding verse 26: "[God] is not far from any one of us. For in him we live, and move, and have our being" (Acts 17:28 KJV). Many would agree with Paul's sentiment. Furthermore, many of the formerly enslaved would know from experience how their newfound freedoms had indeed allowed them to "search for God" (Acts 17:27) in ways that Luke's Paul seemed to imply.[105]

In the freedom-narrative tradition, appeals to the Paul of Acts 17 would complicate the biblical argument of slave obedience. There were many who reclaimed this Paul. In addition to Harriet Jacobs, William Craft, Richard Allen, and J. D. Green (see chap. 4), one final example is in order. Frederick Douglass's 1892 narrative recognized Acts 17 (though absent from the earlier 1845 and 1855 accounts), along with other biblical motifs, as one "document" that supports "equal rights" for all:

> If it [the Civil Rights Bill] is a bill for social equality, so is the Declaration of Independence, which declares that all men have equal rights; so is the Sermon on the Mount; so is the golden rule that commands us to do to others as we would that others should do to us; *so is the teaching of the Apostle that of one blood God has made all nations to dwell on the face of the earth*; so is the Constitution of the United States, and so are the laws and customs of every civilized country in the world; for nowhere, outside of the United States, is any man denied civil rights on account of his color.[106]

---

104. Smith, "Paul and African American Biblical Interpretation," 34–37.

105. Pierce's study suggests that the earliest narrators found *spiritual* freedom first, which aided in the process of securing their *earthly* freedom (*Hell without Fires*, 9).

106. Douglass, *Life and Times of Frederick Douglass, Written by Himself* (Boston: De Wolfe & Fiske Co., 1892), 669*; emphasis added.

As popular as Acts 17 was to support discussions related to the *origins* of human beings, it was more often utilized (in the narrative tradition) as a statement supporting the *equality* of all humans. African Americans discovered a biblical Paul who advocated a conception of God that they shared, and this literary freedom allowed them to claim the sacred texts as their own. As James Curry would claim, "I studied the Scriptures. . . . There I learned that it was contrary to the revealed will of God, that one man should hold another as a slave. . . . But in the Bible, I learned that 'God hath made of one blood all nations of men to dwell on all the face of the earth.'"[107] In black interpretations of the Bible, Acts 17 trumped "slaves, obey your masters"!

CONCLUSION

Howard Thurman's grandmother is a hermeneutical witness of liberation. Her survival technique—promoted by her grandson—was to avoid, understandably, the Paul of slaveholding society. The healthier strategy was to ignore some biblical passages, push back when necessary, and be more selective in her reading of the Christian book.[108] Many followed this same approach to the Bible. Some of her contemporaries rejected the Christian religion altogether, while others found a hermeneutical way of negotiating the interpretations of difficult biblical texts. Talking back to the "talking book" has always been a key component of an African American hermeneutics of survival.

Yet even Nancy Ambrose would occasionally allow the reading of 1 Corinthians 13! The present chapter shows how a powerful story can turn into a tradition that oversees the way people envision the past. Thurman's tale about his grandmother's experience of reading (or not reading) Paul has become one of those influential myths that continues to inform African American ways of reading in the modern world. It is cited frequently in various settings in contemporary life, and it presents an understandable account of a shared history.

The problem, of course, is that it fails to relay the whole story. As the freedom narratives attest, many of Nancy Ambrose's contemporaries found ways around the debilitating religious experiences when the enslaved encountered the master's minister. Deep down within

---

107. James Curry, *Narrative of James Curry: A Fugitive Slave* (*The Liberator*, 1840), n.p.*.

108. As Nancy Ambrose confessed, "[I]f I ever learned to read and if freedom ever came, I would not read that part of the Bible" (Thurman, *Jesus and the Disinherited*, 31).

their spirits, they knew that the Pauline letters had to be read or, more precisely, *could* be read in alternative ways. Paul's "servants, obey your masters" could not and would not be the final biblical word. They knew that "if you love the God of love," then love would have the final word. They knew that the last word—God's word for them—would not be that "it was God's will that we were slaves and how, if we were good and happy slaves, God would bless us."[109] As challenging as the New Testament was for the abolitionist position,[110] these early African American interpreters—with their "backs against the wall"—knew how to develop a survival technique that included reclaiming a cosufferer in Paul, who believed in a God who "hath made of one blood all nations."

---

109. Thurman, *Jesus and the Disinherited*, 31.

110. Caroline Shanks's conclusion: "Even the abolitionists had to admit that the New Testament passages which they quoted as opposing slavery did so only indirectly. The gist of their arguments was that the system of slavery was repugnant to the whole tenor and meaning of the Gospel, which breathed a spirit of kindness and love" ("The Biblical Antislavery Argument," 151).

Excursus

"Jesus Christ Was Sold to the Highest Bidder"

Jesus Christ in the Freedom Narratives

In Albert Raboteau's classic guide to the religious views and practices of the enslaved, he reported the story of one enslaved woman, living in South Carolina, who juxtaposed the significance of her personal religious experience with a faith derived from a book: "Oh! I don't know nothing! I can't read a word. But, oh! I read Jesus in my heart, just as you read him in de book."[1] Raboteau's retelling of this account emphasized the woman's claim to possess Jesus in her soul as a sign of her spirituality, over against a Jesus encased in the white Bibles of the slaveholding community.

Of course, the interpreted book was not always a safe text for the enslaved, who frequently heard white-sponsored lessons that supported the slave institution (see chap. 5).[2] It was not uncommon, for example, to hear slaveholders utilize Luke 12:47, from one of Jesus' parables, to support violent beatings: "And that servant, which knew his lord's will, and prepared not himself, neither did according to his will, shall be beaten with many stripes" (KJV).[3] For many of the enslaved, the starting point was the experiential encounter of "Jesus in my heart," an occasion that usually occurred outside the context of white-sponsored religious services. On the other hand, the enslaved did not always

---

1. Albert J. Raboteau, *Slave Religion: The Invisible Institution in the Antebellum South* (New York: Oxford University Press, 1978), 242.

2. Occasionally, some of the enslaved did not hear about Jesus at all on the plantation (e.g., James Pennington, *The Fugitive Blacksmith* [London: Charles Gilpin, 1849], 43–44*). See Raboteau, *Slave Religion*, 214.

3. See below for a fuller discussion of Luke 12:47 in the freedom narratives.

avoid the Jesus of the biblical text. To put it more precisely, the formerly enslaved never hesitated to take Jesus as a metatext, something beyond—though loosely connected to—the written letters on the page. In Jesus, they discovered a reconciler, a redeemer, a fellow sufferer, a companion, and a confidante who understood their deepest sorrows as they faced extraordinary trials on Southern plantations.

JESUS, CONVERSION STORIES, AND FREEDOM

Many of the enslaved, like Raboteau's unnamed woman, thought Jesus communicated directly and individually with them. Many accounts of conversion to Christianity included visions of Jesus Christ, often with claims that he spoke with them.[4] For example, Sojourner Truth felt separated from God and prayed for a reconciling act to alleviate this distance. She described this subsequent vision to Olive Gilbert, who wrote it out:

> "Who are you?" was the cry of her heart, and her whole soul was in one deep prayer that this heavenly personage might be revealed to her, and remain with her. At length, after bending both soul and body with the intensity of this desire, till breath and strength seemed failing, and she could maintain her position no longer, an answer came to her, saying distinctly, "It is Jesus." "Yes," she responded, "it is Jesus."

On the other hand, some of the enslaved reported less dramatic conversion stories with simplicity. Frederick Douglass, in his 1855 account, provided a description of his spiritual transformation prior to his awareness of the formal antislavery movement.[5] Peter Randolph depicted his conversion account, in 1855, with no spectacular vision either. In fact, Randolph was frustrated that Jesus would not communicate with him, although Jesus personally communed apparently with many of his contemporaries.[6] Nonetheless, Randolph was at peace,

4. Sojourner Truth, *Narrative of Sojourner Truth,* ed. Margaret Washington (New York: Vintage Books, 1993), 67–68*; Noah Davis, *A Narrative of the Life of Rev. Noah Davis, a Colored Man. Written by Himself, at the Age of Fifty-Four* (Baltimore: J. F. Weishampel, Jr., 1859), 24–25*; and Aunt Sally, in Isaac Williams, *Aunt Sally* (Cincinnati: American Reform Tract and Book Society, 1858), 45*.

5. Frederick Douglass, *My Bondage and My Freedom* (New York: Miller, Orton & Mulligan, 1855), 166*. Douglass omitted this story from the 1845 narrative but included it a decade later to emphasize his own bona fide religious experience.

6. Peter Randolph, *Sketches: Or, Illustrations of the "Peculiar Institution"* (Boston: The Author, 1855), 25–26*.

as "[t]he eyes of my mind were open, and I saw things as I never did before."[7]

Like Randolph, James Watkins described his conversion, not with the visions more popular in other accounts, but with a powerful reflection on the transformation of his mind.[8] His encounter with Jesus was more than just a spiritual experience; it enabled him to see the world differently, imagining life with alternative possibilities. He recounted this transformation with words that offer insight into what an encounter with Jesus could mean for enslaved people:

> Gradually as the truths of Christianity broke in upon my mind, I felt a new man, and I yearned for freedom with the most intense anxiety. The truths of the gospel filled my heart with excess of joy; I became conscious of the sins I had been guilty of, and in the joy which overspread my soul I became filled with the love of Jesus. Teach the slave the gospel, and you will make him free. Teach him that there is a God that loves him, that cares for him, that died for him to cleanse him from earthly sin, and all the task masters and slave owners in the Land of Stripes, or in any other part of the world, wherever it may be, cannot retain that infamous power which the present system grants them—property in man. Christianity is life, and light, and freedom, instil this into the slave, and you burst his bonds asunder for ever.[9]

His encounter with Jesus altered his reality, introducing him to a loving God who would act on his behalf. This image of God and Jesus was juxtaposed with "task masters and slave owners in the Land of Stripes" as a substitute source of power. Jesus was more than an allusive abstraction, because to Watkins Jesus meant "freedom" that "burst his bonds asunder for ever." Herein was the danger that many slaveholders hoped to avoid by withholding the gospel from the enslaved or by twisting the gospel into a tool for the perpetuation of the larger social order. This simple life-affirming love offering encounter with Jesus became more than just a religious event on the spiritual plane for this person viewed as chattel. This encounter with Jesus became the basis of his conception of liberation and redefined his humanity and cosmic worth on theological grounds. Jesus meant freedom.

---

7. Randolph, *Sketches*, 26*.

8. For discussion on conversion accounts within some of the earliest narratives, see Yolanda Pierce, *Hell without Fires: Slavery, Christianity, and the Antebellum Spiritual Narrative* (Gainesville: University Press of Florida, 2005).

9. James Watkins, *Struggles for Freedom; or, The Life of James Watkins, Formerly a Slave in Maryland, U.S.* (Manchester, England: Printed for James A. Watkins by A. Heywood, Oldham Street, 1860), 20*.

SUFFERING OF JESUS AS AN EXAMPLE
OF THE SUFFERING OF THE ENSLAVED

Identifying with Jesus was a common experience for the enslaved. Peter Randolph emphasized how Jesus' suffering served as an example of the hardships of enslaved people: "The slaves talk much of the sufferings of Christ; and oftentimes, when they are called to suffer at the hands of their cruel overseers, they think of what he endured, and derive patience and consolation from his example."[10] According to Randolph, this was a conventional way of thinking among the enslaved. Though they drew "patience and consolation" from this Jewish fellow sufferer, they did not discover in these abuses anything beneficial, as if their torment would build human character. Rather, even Jesus' human suffering was detrimental to his development, as some of them considered "Jesus to be inferior to God in size; and that the reason why He is so small is, that He once dwelt in the flesh, and was so badly treated as to hinder his growing large!"[11]

Despite this unusual theological reflection on the physical size of Jesus, Randolph depicted Jesus as the ultimate representative for enslaved humanity. After a brief opening chapter, which did not follow the generic features of the traditional freedom narrative, Randolph movingly described a slave auction.[12] By naming the individuals auctioned off—Emanuel, Lucy, Harry, Mary—Randolph humanized the enslaved and personalized these sketches, challenging the general myth of the inhuman nature of enslaved property. In addition, Randolph appealed to the mothers of the Northern abolitionist community, who have a responsibility to teach their children of the wrongs of slavery in the land. Finally, in his account, he came to Jenny, a Christian who would, according to the auctioneer, "neither lie nor steal: what she says may be believed. Just let her pray, and she will keep right." In the person of Jenny, as representative of every individual ever sold in a human auction, "[h]ere Jesus Christ was sold to the highest bidder." For Randolph and for many of his enslaved contemporaries, the human Jesus was the model for the genuine humanity of the African American mother, father, and child.

10. Randolph, *Sketches*, 34*.
11. Randolph, *Sketches*, 34*.
12. Randolph, *Sketches*, 7–11*.

COMFORT OF JESUS IN THE TRIALS
OF SLAVERY THROUGH PRAYER AND SONG

Furthermore, the enslaved community sought comfort in Jesus as they struggled with the emotional and psychological torments of the peculiar institution, not just the physical challenges of the enslaved condition. Reflecting on the departure of his first wife and children when their slaveholders moved, Thomas Jones contemplated the tremendous turmoil the institution imposed on the community. The lack of any legal rights to challenge the systemic destruction of black families was a common motif throughout these black-authored narratives. Despite the benefits of literacy, the continual practices of slavery and Jones's own personal loss caused a deep psychological and spiritual pain:

> I could read and write, and often enjoyed much happiness in poring over the very few books I could obtain; and especially, at times, I found great peace in reading my old worn Testament. . . . I read and pondered with deep earnestness on the blessed rule of heavenly love which Jesus declared to be the whole of man's duty to his fellow: each to treat his brother as he would be treated. I thought of the command given to the followers of the loving Savior, to teach all nations to obey the blessed precepts of the gospel. I considered that eighteen hundred years had gone by since Jesus plead [sic] for man's redemption and salvation, and, going up to heaven, had left His work of mercy to be finished by His children, and then I thought that I and thousands of my brothers and sisters, loving the Lord and pressing on to a blessed and endless home in His presence, were slaves—branded, whipped, chained; deeply, hopelessly degraded,—thus degraded and outraged, too, in a land of Bibles and Sabbaths and Churches, and by professed followers of the Lord of Love. And often, such thoughts were too much for me. In an agony of despair, I have at times given up prayer and hope together, believing that my master's words were true, that "religion is a cursed mockery, and the Bible a lie." May God forgive me for doubting, at such times, His justice and love. There was but one thing that saved me from going at once and fully into dark infidelity, when such agony assailed my bleeding heart,—the memory of season's of unspeakable joy in prayer, when Love and Faith were strong in my heart. The sweet remembrance of these dear hours would draw me back to Jesus and to peace in his mercy. Oh that all true Christians knew just how the slave feels in view of

the religion of this country, by whose sanction men and women are bound, branded, bought and sold![13]

Questioning God's actions, as Jones epitomized, would have been common fare among his contemporaries. It was a theological conundrum that required an a priori understanding of God and God's justice. For example, James Pennington in his 1849 narrative concluded that God could have Christianized the enslaved by some other means:

> There is not a solitary decree of the immaculate God that has been concerned in the ordination of slavery, nor does any possible development of his holy will sanctify it. He has permitted us to be enslaved according to the invention of wicked men, instigated by the devil, with intention to bring good out of the evil, but He does not, He cannot approve of it. He has no need to approve of it, even on account of the good which He will bring out of it, for He could have brought about that very good in some other way.[14]

Thomas Jones wrestled through his theological convictions and psychological anguish through prayers that "would draw me back to Jesus." Of course, many spirituals function like prayers as well, recalling the role of Jesus in the life of the earthly sufferer.[15] For most of the enslaved, who could not read the Bible, these songs provided access to meaning and spirituality informed by the community. As Raboteau noted, the Bible itself was interpreted "by verses from the spirituals."[16] Harriet Jacobs recalled one of these songs, remembering Jesus' companionship along the way:[17]

> Old Satan is one busy ole man; He rolls dem blocks all in my way;
> But Jesus is my bosom friend; He rolls dem blocks away.

According to this refrain, slaveholders were Satan's tools, setting up obstacles in the way of the enslaved. Recognizing white slave owners as Satan's instruments coincided with what many of the enslaved believed: the sinful act of slavery could be perpetuated only by deep-seated,

13. Thomas H. Jones, *The Experience of Thomas H. Jones, who was a Slave for Forty-Three Years* (Boston: Printed by Bazin & Chandler, 1862), 27–28*.

14. James Pennington, *The Fugitive Blacksmith* (London: Charles Gilpin, 1849), 76–77*.

15. See Luke Powery, *Dem Dry Bones: Preaching, Death, and Hope* (Minneapolis: Fortress Press, 2012); Cheryl Kirk-Duggan, *Exorcizing Evil: A Womanist Perspective on the Spirituals* (Maryknoll, NY: Orbis Books, 1997).

16. Raboteau, *Slave Religion*, 212–13, also 243–66.

17. Harriet Jacobs, *Incidents in the Life of a Slave Girl. Written by Herself* (Boston: Published for the Author, 1861), 108*.

nonbelieving sinners opposed to the justice-working actions of the Christian God.

ONE CANNOT BE A FOLLOWER OF JESUS
AND A SLAVEHOLDER

As William Lloyd Garrison noted in the preface to Frederick Douglass's 1845 biography:

> Reader! are you with the man-stealers in sympathy and purpose, or on the side of their down-trodden victims? If with the former, then are you the foe of God and man. If with the latter, what are you prepared to do and dare in their behalf? Be faithful, be vigilant, be untiring in your efforts to break every yoke, and let the oppressed go free. Come what may—cost what it may—inscribe on the banner which you unfurl to the breeze, as your religious and political motto—"NO COMPROMISE WITH SLAVERY! NO UNION WITH SLAVEHOLDERS!"[18]

The contrast between the two ideological camps of slavers and abolitionists was clearly established in the words of Garrison, and the camps were clearly to be antithetical in all their ways. According to this leading white abolitionist and the many enslaved people whom he represented, there could be no fellowship between slaveholders and abolitionists in this great country. Not only was there an ideological impediment; there was also a religious obstacle to such intermixing. The starkness of the either/or in this regard does not attend just to worldly communion, but even to fellowship with God: "If with the former, then you are the foe of God and man." Thus his opinion and that of so many others was that you could not be a follower of Christ and be a slaveholder, for the Christ whom abolitionists worshiped opposed slavery.[19]

Garrison's sentiment was reflected in the thinking of his good friend and compatriot, Frederick Douglass. Douglass held that "[t]hose ministers who defended slavery from the bible, were of their 'father the

---

18. William Lloyd Garrison, "Preface," in Frederick Douglass, *Narrative of the Life of Frederick Douglass, an American Slave. Written by Himself* (Boston: Anti-Slavery Office, 1845), xii.

19. In contradistinction, see Leonard Black, who believed that persons could be "good christians in other respects" and hold to the "religion of Jesus Christ" while being slaveholders (Leonard Black, *The Life and Sufferings of Leonard Black, a Fugitive from Slavery. Written by Himself* [New Bedford: Benjamin Lindsey, 1847], 53–54*). Even here it seems that Black's assertion of the Christianity of the enslavers is suspect, particularly as his conclusion is qualified with "in other respects," noting the problematic notion of combining slaveholding and Christianity (Black, *Life and Sufferings*, 10*).

devil;' and those churches which fellowshiped slaveholders as Christians, were synagogues of Satan."[20] In this instance the juxtaposition between slaveholders and Christians was clear and stark; for, in his estimation, to welcome slaveholders as Christians was to have allied oneself with the enemy, not just on the physical level, but on the spiritual level. Douglass went even further:

> What I have said respecting and against religion, I mean strictly to apply to the *slaveholding religion* of this land, and with no possible reference to Christianity proper; for, between the Christianity of this land, and the Christianity of Christ, I recognize the widest, possible difference—so wide, that to receive the one as good, pure, and holy, is of necessity to reject the other as bad, corrupt, and wicked. To be the friend of the one, is of necessity to be the enemy of the other. I love the pure, peaceable, and impartial Christianity of Christ: I therefore hate the corrupt, slaveholding, women-whipping, cradle-plundering, partial and hypocritical Christianity of this land.[21]

Douglass used the concept of the "impartial" Christianity of Christ to suggest a purer form of the religion of those who were enslaved than that which was practiced by their enslavers. In the midst of this account, we can also see the way that Christ functioned in this quotation. Christ served as the antislaveholder, the one who presented a religion that was incompatible with the slavocracy and who was inevitably opposed to this evil. Furthermore, Douglass utilized the Christ figure as one who would have been the commonplace paragon of moral goodness and rhetorically made the enslavers the epitome of all things evil to the enslaved person, such as "slaveholding, women-whipping, cradle-plundering, partial and hypocritical Christianity of this land."

A similar tact was taken by Aaron in his dictated book *The Light and Truth of Slavery*.[22] In the following quotation, Aaron meditates on the matter of conversion as the moment of differentiation between the two types of religious beings. For him, a person truly was in Christ when he saw the world from a renewed perspective in Christ:

> Whenever a man is cleansed from his sin and iniquity, he is a new formed creature in Christ Jesus. Christ is in that white friend the hope of glory, and he is in Christ, and so therefore there is no respect to persons. He will treat an African brother as well as a white

---

20. Douglass, *My Bondage and My Freedom*, 355*.
21. Douglass, *Narrative*, 118*.
22. The author is unknown.

brother. He will not oppress him. If he is a wolf clothed in sheep's clothing, he will stand up and say, it is right to enslave the African brother.—But if he is a sincere, godly man, he will not stand up and say it is right.[23]

To be a follower of Christ and a "new formed creature," one must have a theological transformation that inhabited one's very being with the truth that "there is no respect of persons." The incompatibility of slavery with the religion of Christ thus became absolute, and Christ became the inhabiting force that prevented the idea of the legitimacy of slavery from taking root in the human soul.

The overall argument of this antithesis finds even greater expression in the work of James Pennington, who determined that there was no relationship between the gospel and slavery:

> Let me urge upon you the fundamental truths of the Gospel of the Son of God. Let repentance towards God and faith in our Lord Jesus Christ have their perfect work in you, I beseech you. Do not be prejudiced against the gospel because it may be seemingly twisted into a support of slavery. The gospel rightly understood, taught, received, felt and practised, is anti-slavery as it is anti-sin. Just so far and so fast as the true spirit of the gospel obtains in the land, and especially in the lives of the oppressed, will the spirit of slavery sicken and become powerless like the serpent with his head pressed beneath the fresh leaves of the prickly ash of the forest. There is not a solitary decree of the immaculate God that has been concerned in the ordination of slavery, nor does any possible development of his holy will sanctify it.[24]

In Pennington's theology, the faith associated with Jesus in no way concerns itself with "the ordination of slavery." The decree of the "immaculate God" could do so only when it was "seemingly twisted" into a bastardized form. Indeed, the true faith of Jesus as it was "rightly understood" was the remedy for the sin of slavery. It was only in that bastardized form that it could be seen as a supporter of slavery.

It was precisely that distorted form of religion that was evident to so many enslaved people in the American South. It was a religion that spoke with an undeniable certainty of the legitimacy of this institution

---

23. Aaron, *The Light and Truth of Slavery: Aaron's History* (Worcester, MA: The Author, 1845), 4*.
24. Pennington, *Fugitive Blacksmith*, 76*. See Henry Bibb, *Narrative of the Life and Adventures of Henry Bibb, An American Slave, Written by Himself* (New York: Author, 1849), 203*.

and its obligations upon those who found themselves chattel in its system. So Henry "Box" Brown confessed:

> My mother used to instruct me in the principles of morality, according to her own notion of what was good and pure; but I had no means of acquiring proper conception of religion in a state of slavery, where all those who professed to be followers of Jesus Christ evinced more of the disposition of demons than of men; and it is really a matter of wonder to me now, considering the character of my position that I did not imbibe a strong and lasting hatred of everything pertaining to the religion of Christ.[25]

Maternal discernment of the contrast between the "disposition of demons" (the slaveholding faith) and the "good and pure" enabled Brown to develop an ethos that stood against the prevailing perversion of Christianity that was presented to him. Her discernment hints at the level of choice that must have been present in the lives of the enslaved to find and conceive of an understanding of a "pure and good" religion that made life palatable, despite the slaveholders' intent to foster a faith in their own favor. The account of Rev. Ryland, a white preacher employed to pastor the African Americans of Richmond might serve as a fitting example of the challenges that were present:

> The Rev. R. Ryland, who preached for the coloured people, was professor at the Baptist seminary near the city of Richmond, and the coloured people had to pay him a salary of 700 dollars per annum, although they neither chose him nor had the least controul [sic] over him. He did not consider himself bound to preach regularly, but only when he was not otherwise engaged, so he preached about 40 sermons a year and was a zealous supporter of the slave-holders' cause; and, so far as I could judge, he had no notion whatever of the pure religion of Jesus Christ.[26]

Thus the (white?) Christian antithesis can best be described as a religion that fostered and legitimated slavery and furthered the notion that it was a divinely sanctioned institution meant for African peoples. The "pure religion of Jesus Christ" was lost in a web of oppressive ideologies that circumvented the primacy of God and Jesus, replacing the centrality of divinity with the self-serving ambitions and system of the

---

25. Henry Box Brown, *Narrative of the Life of Henry Box Brown, Written by Himself* (Manchester, England: Printed by Lee & Glynn, 1851), 3*.
26. Henry Box Brown, *Narrative*, 31*.

Southern slavocracy. This religious ideological perspective did more than support enslavement; it was a religion based on the superiority of whiteness, which even Northern nonslaveholding communities generally supported.

The description of this appointment of Rev. Ryland also demonstrates the extent of the depravity of a system where the oppressed were forced to facilitate their own oppression by "employing" an emissary of an adversative ideology to instruct them in the mode of religion that served "with impunity" to abuse them. It is no wonder that the enslaved could see no aspect of purity, divinity, morality, goodness, Christianity, or the religion of Jesus/Christ in the pretense of religion thrust upon them by the Southern slavocracy.

But the true religion of Jesus Christ was something more. In the religious perspective of the enslaved, it was permeated with the notion of justice and fairness for all of humanity. It was predicated on what was often mistakenly identified as the prophetic dimensions of the biblical heritage, but more accurately seen as the core theological imperative that persists throughout the extent of the biblical narrative. It is this realization that seems both to define the "religion of Jesus" for the enslaved and to distinguish it from the machinations of the enslavers. Peter Randolph aptly described this dimension:

> The sin of holding slaves is not only against one nation, but against the whole world, because we are here to do one another good, in treating each other well; and this is to be done by having right ideas of God and his religion. . . . The slaveholders say we have not a true knowledge of religion; but the great Teacher said, when he came on his mission, "The spirit of the Lord is upon me, because he hath anointed me to preach the gospel to the poor. He hath sent me to heal the broken-hearted; to preach deliverance to the captive, and recovering of sight to the blind; to set at liberty them that are bruised, and to preach the acceptable year of the Lord." This ought to be the work of the ministers and the churches. Any thing short of this is not the true religion of Jesus.[27]

Peter Randolph gravitated toward the justice dimensions of the Christian faith predicated in the initial proclamation of Jesus to his colleagues in Nazareth. Herein is faith authentic, as it calls its adherents

---

27. Randolph, *Sketches*, 10–11*. Randolph goes even further than questioning their faith by questioning their humanity: "The seller or buyer of a human being, for purposes of slavery, is not human, and has no right to the name" (*Sketches*, 8*).

to "do one another good." This simple message was for him and others of his lot the core ethos that must be not only espoused but incarnate, enfleshed, borne out in bodily actions to make the faith "true." Furthermore, for Randolph, this theological reflection was the lens through which he desired his audience to view his sketch of the common human-slave auctions of his day. It is this aspect of the faith that has continued in the expression of African American religion over the years and formed the foundation upon which movements for liberation, integration, equal rights, and justice have been built since the times of the initial engagements of our African ancestors with these texts.

THE SLAVEHOLDERS' USE OF JESUS' WORDS IN LUKE 12:47

Since many of the enslaved questioned the sincerity of the slaveholders' religious commitments, it was not surprising that they disregarded any biblical teaching that proceeded from people whose ethical practices were considered suspect. One biblical passage frequently on the lips of religious slaveholders was Jesus' teaching in Luke 12. Many of the enslaved reported the use of these words in physically and psychologically abusive settings. Surprisingly, the enslaved rarely if ever provided explicit recognition that these words derived from the lips of Jesus, presumably because Jesus Christ was the one in whom they found comfort, even while they publicly challenged the association of these words with the abuse they received.

Douglass's multiple narratives afford a rare opportunity to observe the development of thought that went into some of these stories. This was the case with this account. In his first narrative in 1845, Douglass explained how Thomas Auld, shortly after finding religion, set out to whip Henny mercilessly while quoting Luke 12:47:

> I have said my master found religious sanction for his cruelty. As an example, I will state one of many facts going to prove the charge. I have seen him tie up a lame young woman, and whip her with a heavy cowskin upon her naked shoulders, causing the warm red blood to drip; and, in justification of the bloody deed, he would quote this passage of Scripture—"He that knoweth his master's will, and doeth it not, shall be beaten with many stripes."[28]

---

28. Douglass, *Narrative*, 55–56*.

Douglass attacked the use of religion as a sanction for the kind of physical abuse the enslaved received. A decade later, in 1855, he relayed the same story but with subtle revisions to express a more implicit critique of the use of this passage as justification for the brutal nature of the slave system. Specifically, in the 1855 narrative Douglass added an indirect yet clearer assessment. In place of the earlier phrase "in justification of the bloody deed," Douglass included that Auld "would quote the passage of Scripture" as a "blood-chilling blasphemy."[29] For Douglass, the violence of the whipping in association with cited words from Luke's Gospel was a bastardized appropriation of the pure religion of Jesus, one which he labeled a blasphemy.

In one of the more detailed accounts of Luke 12, Solomon Northup (1853) provided the following reference to the biblical passage, as he explored, in particular, one overseer's interpretation:

> Like William Ford, his brother-in-law, [Peter] Tanner was in the habit of reading the Bible to his slaves on the Sabbath, but in a somewhat different spirit. He was an impressive commentator on the New Testament. The first Sunday after my coming to the plantation, he called them together, and began to read the twelfth chapter of Luke. When he came to the 47th verse, he looked deliberately around him, and continued—"And that servant which knew his lord's will,"—here he paused, looking around more deliberately than before, and again proceeded—"which knew his lord's will, and prepared not himself"—here was another pause—"prepared not himself, neither did according to his will, shall be beaten with many stripes."
>
> "D'ye hear that?" demanded Peter, emphatically. "Stripes," he repeated, slowly and distinctly, taking off his spectacles, preparatory to making a few remarks.
>
> "That nigger that don't take care—that don't obey his lord—that's his master—d'ye see?—that 'ere nigger shall be beaten with many stripes. Now, 'many' signifies a great many—forty, a hundred, a hundred and fifty lashes. That's Scripter!" and so Peter continued to elucidate the subject for a great length of time, much to the edification of his sable audience.[30]

Northup described Peter Tanner as an "impressive commentator" and attempted to communicate some of the cadence of these comments. The fact that Tanner understood "many" with excessive numerical

29. Douglass, *My Bondage and My Freedom*, 201*.
30. Solomon Northup, *Twelve Years a Slave* (Auburn, NY: Derby & Miller, 1853), 127–28*.

values may not have been good exegesis, but it brought much "edifica-
tion" to his black, enslaved audience. The audience understood that
this was a level of interpretation geared toward the benefit of those in
power, not for the unfortunate. Frequently, as Charles Peyton Lucas
would learn from experience, on another plantation, the slaveholding
Baptist minister would follow up a public reading of Luke 12 by taking
Lucas and others "to the barn-yard and give me a practical explanation
with raw hides."[31]

Lucas's experience in Loudon County, Virginia, was shared every-
where among the enslaved, as Douglass (in Maryland) and Northup
(in Louisiana) attested. William Wells Brown described the situation in
St. Louis, Missouri, with attention to the broader proslavery religious
ideology's attachment to the peculiar institution:

> It was not uncommon in St. Louis to pass by an auction-stand, and
> behold a woman upon the auction-block, and hear the seller crying
> out, "How much is offered for this woman? She is a good cook,
> good washer, a good obedient servant. She has got religion!" Why
> should this man tell the purchasers that she has religion? I answer,
> because in Missouri, and as far as I have any knowledge of slavery
> in the other States, the religious teaching consists in teaching the
> slave that he must never strike a white man; that God made him
> for a slave; and that, when whipped, he must not find fault,—for
> the Bible says, "He that knoweth his master's will, and doeth it not,
> shall be beaten with many stripes!" And slaveholders find such reli-
> gion very profitable to them.[32]

Whites in support of the Southern plantation system had developed
a religious argument for their dehumanizing practices. This white-
sponsored religion hoped to evoke belief in a god who had created
enslaved people, who in turn must succumb to physical violence when
necessary and never forcibly strike back. According to the freedom narratives, enslaved blacks were not convinced by the religious argument
of Luke 12, even while they understood the central contemporary role
the Bible was playing in the ideological debate of the day.

It was no different in Kentucky, as Henry Bibb attested. Bibb supported Northup's understanding that the black audience fully disbe-
lieved in the linkage between their experiences of brutality and the

31. Charles Peyton Lucas told this story to Benjamin Drew, in *A North-Side View of Slavery* (Boston: J. P. Jewett
& Co., 1856), 105*.
32. William Wells Brown, *Narrative*, 83–84*.

Luke 12 passage. He wrote that the enslaved "have no confidence at all in their preaching because they preach a pro-slavery doctrine" before citing the Pauline passages about obedient slaves and Luke 12. As a Christian minister, following his escape from enslavement, Bibb expressed concern that "[t]his kind of preaching has driven thousands into infidelity," but he fully understood that it was impossible to "trust in such a religion" as depicted in this slaveholding instruction.[33] In order to survive, the enslaved needed to rely on what was "pure and good."

Along with Raboteau's unnamed woman from South Carolina (see above), many of the enslaved trusted the Jesus in their hearts much more than any Jesus associated with references in the Bible, especially when interpreted through the proslavery hermeneutic. Their own hermeneutic of suspicion raised doubts about this alternative hermeneutical approach. For them, Jesus was on the side of the oppressed and downtrodden and was "light and life and freedom." The authenticating justice core of the African American Christian hermeneutic was evident in this aspect of the "religion of Jesus" and in the Christ upon whom this interpretive stance was predicated. The lingering fingerprints of this interpretive tradition persist in subsequent African American readings of the text in both obvious and subtle ways and continue to offer a critique of mainstream interpretive traditions void of such a core.

33. Bibb, *Narrative*, 24*.

Chapter 6
Summary and Hermeneutical Implications

If one primary question could be identified as providing the main catalyst and goal of this project, it might be, how do these examples—in *The Genesis of Liberation*—inform an early history of African American biblical hermeneutics? What might it mean to claim that black biblical hermeneutics began with these formerly enslaved individuals, who interpreted the Bible as an important religious document and a means of survival rather than as an oppressive and proslavery support text of the white establishment? Other related questions loom as well: What was the modus operandi of the formerly enslaved in reading the sacred text? Where did their engagement with the "talking book" lead with respect to their collective identity and an understanding of their placement within the developing US society?

Contemporary African American biblical hermeneutics may take various forms, but critical approaches often engage the following issues: the interpretation of the black presence within the biblical text/world; cultural interpretation of the Bible from the perspective of contemporary black readers; detection of ideological assumptions of biblical writers/texts.[1] Occasionally, interpreters may perform more than one of these hermeneutical tasks at a time, but more often than not,

---

1. See Emerson B. Powery, "African American Criticism," in *Hearing the New Testament: Strategies for Interpretation*, ed. Joel B. Green, 2nd ed. (Grand Rapids: Eerdmans, 2010), 326–49. Powery borrowed the taxonomy from Randall Bailey, who includes an additional category, responses to racist interpretations of the text ("Academic Biblical Interpretation among African Americans in the United States," in *African Americans and the Bible: Sacred Texts and Social Textures*, ed. Vincent Wimbush [New York: Continuum, 2000], 696).

contemporary exegetes undertake one of these approaches with the intention of challenging prevailing racialized or racist interpretation that persists in the "official" academic guild of the present day. Do these hermeneutical approaches have interpretive forebears in the cultural history of this country? Do precedents exist for today's hermeneutical strategies? Were the readings of the past unique creative elucidations reflecting readings of the Bible that can still inform, even challenge, current African American hermeneutics?

From the beginning, our assumptions have been that current exegetical approaches existed in African American cultural history and have been passed on, mostly indirectly, through various ecclesial and para-ecclesial venues. This project is an attempt to explore one dimension of this cultural hermeneutical history by tracing nineteenth-century examples among the formerly enslaved, a group significantly marginalized by history, economics, political will, and, of course, dehumanizing racism. In the next few pages, we want to explore the specific connections (and differences?) between what we have identified in the nineteenth-century freedom narratives and the way black biblical hermeneutics has been practiced in recent history.

In Allen Callahan's extensive treatment of the cultural relationship between the Bible and the African American community, he has drawn the following incisive conclusion:

> For African Americans, the Bible has not been a book that answered questions. Indeed, it was precisely biblical answers that the first African-American readers called into question. Their encounter with the Bible provoked the development of a critical sensibility, a penchant for interrogating themselves and others. The Bible has been their license for calling things into question.[2]

The development and interrogation of a critical identity over against others and in relationship to surrounding myths, religious or otherwise, has been a central concern of black hermeneutics since the initial contact of Africa's children with America's Bible. The initial contact (through the interpretation of the majority race) suggested that the Bible was opposed to their existence as equals within the human race. But this conclusion did not completely hinder their efforts to struggle with the biblical text on their own and to determine that they could

---

2. Allen Callahan, *The Talking Book: African Americans and the Bible* (New Haven, CT: Yale University Press, 2006), 242.

construe the Bible in a manner that would come to the aid of their cause.

In the nineteenth century, interpreting the Bible was both an act of identity formation and a feat of the imagination. These interpretive activities were multilayered engagements with self, community, tradition, and world. For those enslaved, without the benefits of legal, political, or (frequently) ecclesial support structures, these textual encounters were acts of survival, life or death. From this vantage (or *dis*advantaged) point, a hermeneutical approach from the underside required creative and critical tools, learned frequently through the harshness of enslaved experience and participation in the secretive brush-arbor community.

Slavery itself was also a stern tutor, which allowed them to develop a critical sensibility about human nature, communal structures, and religious myths. Engaging the Bible through the lens of slavery made them judicious interpreters of their surroundings and themselves. As Callahan recognizes, the Bible became "their license for calling things into question." It was never as simple as exegeting the meaning of particular passages in the Bible for the sake of doctrinal disputes. Rather, slavery, black identity, and the Bible merged to determine their critical sensibilities. What E. Brooks Holifield observed about the crucial implications of slavery for nineteenth-century white Christians could be applied to African Americans as well: "Long before biblical criticism made significant inroads into the consciousness of most Christian thinkers, the debate over slavery would introduce American readers to critical questions."[3]

Holifield's words express clearly what we have attempted to claim in our analysis with respect to a critical, black hermeneutic. The difference between white and black readers was the decisive effect an interpretation would have directly on black bodies. For African American interpreters, the meaning of slavery, fused with the worth of dark-skinned Christian identity, demanded a critical, black hermeneutic. These early black interpreters developed crucial hermeneutical skills that allowed them to understand both their Bible and their world. There are no simple explanations for the complex, dynamic "relationship" between formerly enslaved African Americans and the Bible. A few closing observations can be made about this contact between a people and an ancient iconic book.

---

3. E. Brooks Holifield, *Theology in America: Christian Thought from the Age of the Puritans to the Civil War* (New Haven, CT: Yale University Press, 2005), 494–95, 504.

SPACE MATTERS

From the religion of their oppressors, African Americans inherited a belief in the Sabbath that encompassed rest from labor and a gathering for spiritual renewal. For those granted these opportunities for religious nourishment, it was a relief from the turmoil of daily, relentless labor. Some of the enslaved, however, also viewed this day as an occasion for more subversive activity, a time for intellectual nurture and an opportunity for escape. Much of the discussion in the narratives of the formerly enslaved emphasized how slave laws obstructed the religious observance of the Sabbath (see chap. 3). Many freedom narratives interrogate generally the "expected" periods of rest obligated in this cultural practice.

In the narrative tradition, the discussions of the Sabbath day focus on two major motifs. First, if local communities established Sabbath-day schools, the meetings were ridiculed by some of its citizens and therefore frequently temporary affairs. Few lasted long enough to develop the kind of morally supportive community necessary for enhancing human well-being. As discussed in chapter 3, Frederick Douglass, who participated in one provisionally successful Sabbath group, described the participants as people who "would have died for each other."[4] His fortunate contact with a few of these individuals later in life would have been the exception among his peer groups. But the existence of this type of network, even if impermanent, would have held inexplicable benefits for the persons living in bondage.

This formative network created a kinship among the enslaved that allowed for encouragement in many areas of life for those struggling to survive in a system opposed to their basic humanity. Even as it encouraged survival skills, it was also a space that stimulated the ultimate act of survival: a literal, physical escape. A number of narratives explain how often the Sabbath day was the day when the enslaved would risk their lives to venture into the unknown frontier of freedom. This "holy day" frequently provided enough "free" time for escapees to distance themselves from the slaveholder. As Leonard Black would explicitly recall, his brothers advised him to escape on some opportune Sabbath.[5] Those who remained behind at those Sabbath meetings would

---

4. Frederick Douglass, *Narrative of the Life of Frederick Douglass, an American Slave. Written by Himself* (Boston: Anti-Slavery Office, 1845), 83*.

5. Leonard Black, *The Life and Sufferings of Leonard Black, a Fugitive from Slavery. Written by Himself* (New Bedford: Benjamin Lindsey, 1847), 17*.

then have additional reasons to pray for the safety of their friends and family members.

Both motifs—the development of community for purposes of literacy and information and a day to plan an escape—exemplify the activities associated with freedom, be it understood spiritually, emotionally, intellectually, or literally. Rhetorically, African Americans utilized these stories to persuade their white abolitionist audiences that even this biblical commandment was consistently constrained by slave society. When it was practiced, however, it provided an opportunity frequently for African American community and a time for liberation. Desires to acquire a black Sabbath were attempts to secure a space for their own conversations and hermeneutical engagements with the biblical tradition, in its written and oral forms, away from the white gaze. Without these communal spaces, the production of and learning of the hermeneutical investigations of the Scriptures would have been difficult to secure. Even within the confinement of slavery, these occasional, loosely organized groups among the enslaved were significant steps toward the establishment of black leaders and the emergence of critical biblical hermeneuts. *Space matters.*

RACE/IDENTITY MATTERS

The text the interpreter chooses matters. Even with the dominant cultural texts of the day, racialized interpretation was key for maintaining the ideology of black enslavement. As a number of African American interpreters would recognize about Noah's curse, the Canaanites were not the ones *presently* enslaved in the Americas. With respect to the significance of a hermeneutics of identity (that connected to contemporary politics), African Americans did not simply and automatically qualify as descendants of the ancient mythic Ham.

The Bible was filled with identity texts, especially if one was engaged in the nineteenth-century fascination with discovering the biblical origins for the various racial groups coming to reside in the United States. Nevertheless, people were more prone to uncover biblical support for the slavocracy of the day than they were willing to discuss the various passages for a "biblical" analysis of "race." On the latter issue, interpreters were much more selective. This was true for African American interpreters as well, as William Anderson's choice of 2 Kings 5 attests (see chap. 4).

At the forefront of these hermeneutical discussions was the identity of the interpreter. For most whites, even those advocating the eventual gradual end of American slavery, read the Bible with a basic assumption of the superiority of the white race. As historian Eric Foner has convincingly argued, President Lincoln advocated the colonization of blacks as a form of abolition partly because he could not imagine blacks and whites living together in this country on equal terms.[6] In an earlier essay, George Fredrickson would concur: "Lincoln could reject the most blatant forms of racist ideology without escaping an underlying emotional commitment to whiteness and white supremacy."[7] What was true of the Great Emancipator—as Lincoln was frequently called in African American circles—was no less true of some of the leading biblical scholars of the day.

Black interpreters struggled with the biblical witness in order to provide alternative ways to understand difficult biblical texts but also engage larger cultural assumptions, even among many of those presumably on the side of emancipation. William Anderson offered one excellent example of how African Americans would occasionally locate black counter-myths by overturning the cultural assumption of white superiority. From an imaginatively creative reading of 2 Kings 5, Anderson argued that *whiteness* was the curse, not blackness! This was not Anderson's attempt to promote a new racial hierarchy but was a sophisticated exegetical act of "reading darkly,"[8] to level the playing field and encourage the humanity of the nonwhite race. Selecting the appropriate text matters.

Both his status as one formerly enslaved *and* his identity as a black reader of the Bible allowed Anderson to interpret texts in ways that evaded many other interpreters. To Anderson's credit, he apparently expressed his opinion in numerous settings in front of various audiences. More significantly, for our purposes, he wrote the *Life and Narrative of William J. Anderson*, a story in which he explored this biblical passage (2 Kgs. 5). His selection of and interpretation of this text was situated within a wider cultural fixation on other biblical stories that

---

6. Eric Foner, "Abraham Lincoln," in *Slavery's Ghost: The Problem of Freedom in the Age of Emancipation* (Baltimore: Johns Hopkins Press, 2011), 31–49. Lincoln's Emancipation Proclamation was a turning point in Lincoln's thinking about race, slavery, and society (Foner, "Abraham Lincoln," 45). See John Hope Franklin, *The Emancipation Proclamation* (Garden City, NY: Doubleday & Co., 1963).

7. George Fredrickson, "A Man but Not a Brother: Abraham Lincoln and Racial Equality," *The Journal of Southern History* 41/1 (Feb. 1975), 47. See Frances Smith Foster, *Witnessing Slavery: The Development of Antebellum Slave Narratives* (Westport, CT: Greenwood Press, 1979), 59.

8. See Vincent Wimbush, "Reading Darkness, Reading Scriptures," in *African Americans and the Bible: Sacred Texts and Social Textures*, ed. Vincent Wimbush (New York: Continuum, 2000), 3–43.

were at the forefront of conversations on the biblical origins of the races in that period.

Anderson's choice matters because it enlarges our historical horizons, allowing us to witness alternative ways of construing the biblical origins of racial identities in nineteenth-century society. Marginalized stories must also be told (and heard), because they complicate the historical record by providing alternative (and sometimes unconventional) explanations that challenge the majority account. Anderson's experience of enslavement mattered for his interpretation, as one who lived through the ramifications of misplaced ideological commitments enforced by religious practices. The impact of white supremacy—encouraged by a particular understanding of the sacred texts of the day—had real implications for Anderson and his fellow African Americans.

What Vincent Wimbush concludes about Equiano's creative work to make the Bible perform in a particular kind of way could be generally concluded about Equiano's hermeneutical sons and daughters: "The *white* scriptures are taken up, in this case by a *black* stranger, and interpreted to mean that God is on the side of the oppressed *blacks*."[9] It was a black engagement of the Scriptures that led to the discovery of 2 Kings 5, which resulted in the creation of a countertext to, and reading against, the dominant cultural selection of Genesis.[10] Anderson's distinctive hermeneutical decision for exploring racial origins and the interpretation that ensued were missed or ignored by many proslavery advocates, who intensified their gaze upon Genesis 9 as the dominant text of choice instead of 2 Kings 5. A more diverse and complicated hermeneutical decision may have allowed proponents of the slavocracy to question their own assumptions about Scripture's bases for racial divisions. *Identity matters.*

IDEOLOGY MATTERS

A number of scholars—for example, Shanks, Harrill, and Noll—have argued how proslavery advocates, generally speaking, held the more defensible position with respect to the Bible's authority in convincing the white majority of the validity of their interpretations. Since

9. Vincent Wimbush, *White Men's Magic: Scripturalization as Slavery* (New York: Oxford University Press, 2012), 187 (Wimbush's italics).

10. Interpretation of ancient texts often (always?) includes the privileging of certain people groups. Careful attention should be paid to the interconnectedness of identity politics and hermeneutics.

proslavery proponents more accurately appealed to and adhered to the *historical* contexts of biblical passages, they could claim a historical foundation for their view of biblical authority that was absent from the abolitionists' position.

If Paul organized a community in which masters and slaves could share Christian faith and life, then why should contemporary American citizens not continue this practice within their own society and time? Was this not the true meaning of biblical authority and its appropriation? American Christians could apply Paul's words more directly if their society shared the social context of enslavement. The practice of slavery during the span of centuries between the apostle's ancient context and the nineteenth century also underscored the rightfulness of one human being holding another human being in bondage.

So why should the Christian community alter this (biblical?) history? To do so would be to challenge explicitly the direct authority of the Bible. This hermeneutical approach to the biblical text and method of interpretation was, of course, deeply entrenched within the preferences, people groups, and politics of the dominant white establishment. This methodological decision privileged some people in contemporary society, while disenfranchising and scorning others, far removed from the contexts and conflicts of the ancient Mediterranean world.

For many African Americans slaveholding ideology could not be detached from Christianity. The only option was to reject and turn away from this oppressive religion. But those who chose to accept and develop a Christian faith cultivated a hermeneutical strategy that allowed them to manage the biblical stories, interpret them, and integrate them in meaningful ways that contributed value to their identity. They sought spaces in which they could engage conversations with like-minded people, who shared their experiences of blackness in a white-constructed world.

The letters of Paul were a primary contested site that black interpreters needed to occupy. While the Paul of the Bible could say, "Slaves, obey your masters"—the most prominently cited text among proponents of the slavocracy—it was pointed out that he could also write, "[B]ut if thou mayest be made free, use it rather" (1 Cor. 7:21 KJV). Some African American interpreters understandably ignored the Pauline documents altogether. They performed their hermeneutical right to select those passages useful for a life-affirming ethic and brand of wisdom. Others decided to tackle these passages directly. For them (and for some white abolitionists), not only was the authority of the

Bible promoted by resituating biblical passages and settings within a new, contemporary context; the authority of an ancient text could also be based on other grounds.

Within the freedom-narrative tradition, we discover many formerly enslaved writers who chose this latter option. In story form, these authors relayed the experience of hearing sermon after sermon in which white-sponsored ministers used a Pauline text as a focal point, to proclaim a "gospel" message to the African American community. Not one of these black-narrated accounts expressed agreement with the minister's sermon. Not one of these stories considered the message to be a divinely sanctioned word. Not one of these narratives decided that the spoken word was biblical in any way. Their collective hermeneutical assessment, in narrative form, was to recognize that the preacher imposed his own ideological slant onto the biblical passage.

A communal hermeneutics of suspicion stood at the forefront of these experiences, and this strategy allowed them to remain Christian, to believe in the overarching freedom message of their Bible, and to attempt to locate alternative ways to interpret the sacred texts of their faith. For formerly enslaved African Americans, the starting hermeneutical assumption was a God of freedom, and not even direct language about slavery within Scripture could convince them that such a practice was the same as the one that presently surrounded them. Their theological presuppositions about God mattered; their hermeneutical approach to the Bible followed suit.

Many of the enslaved knew that the Pauline letters could be read in other ways than the ones provided by their white oppressors. Derived from a theological assumption that a divinely ordered universe stood on the side of all humanity, their hermeneutical strategy encouraged them to talk back to the "talking book." These formerly enslaved thinkers would have agreed with the ancient wisdom of the Wisdom of Solomon, that "the universe itself comes to the defense of those who do what is right"(Wis. 16:17 CEB).[11] The command "Servants, obey your masters" could not be the final biblical word. Rather, they believed that love would have the final word. These early African American biblical interpreters applied a hermeneutics of survival that found the dominant Pauline word in a non-Pauline affiliated book,

---

11. The NRSV is more ambiguous, but note also the translation of this verse in the most recent translation project on the Septuagint: "for the world fights on behalf of the righteous" (*The New English Translation of the Septuagint*, http://ccat.sas.upenn.edu/nets/edition/29-wissal-nets.pdf).

in which the character Paul proclaimed that God "hath made of one blood all nations" (Acts 17:26). *Ideology matters.*

Callahan's conclusion—on the freedom the Bible gave African Americans to call "things into question"—corresponds well with our own reading of the narratives of the formerly enslaved. For them the Bible—at least, the first half of the biblical story—promoted a Sabbath day, a day on which rest was the primary purpose, which in itself could lead to useful humanizing activities like leisure and literacy. Many of these early African Americans demanded, with limited means for persuasion, opportunities to secure space for this Sabbath-type activity. In addition, they called into question the use of the Bible to support the division of the races, especially as it pertained to arguments defending the superiority of one race over another. Many of them found biblical support in order to challenge cultural perceptions prevailing in the South and North, clearly evident in policies put forth even by their Northern "friends" advocating colonization plans, whether in US lands or elsewhere outside of the country.

Finally, African Americans reacted to the prevailing words of the apostle Paul on the obedience of the enslaved. Something had to be said about Paul! They recorded various accounts of settings in which this proslavery sermon was the dominant gospel message in many Southern communities. They responded in a variety of ways, both exegetical and otherwise. But they reacted partly because they, as critical readers, discovered in Paul a fellow sufferer with whom they could attempt to find a common humanity. The common experience of suffering was something they knew all too well. Their marginalized societal location coupled with their minoritized hermeneutical lens strongly encouraged a different kind of reading of the sacred texts of the Christian faith. So they placed that identity at the forefront of their approach to life, attached to a hermeneutics of survival that encouraged them to tell their own stories even as they were developing a unique, critical perspective on American life.

The key to this story is not the centrality of the biblical text but the negotiation black readers navigated with the sacred writings. As the early black writers within the narrative tradition attest, the "talking book" had a profound impact on the manner in which they came to understand how knowledge, power, and identity were constructed in this new land. Now they were giving voice to those concerns as they nurtured a deeper understanding of the sources (e.g., the Bible, the Constitution) that allowed their opponents to convince others, rhetorically and politically, to maintain the system of bondage. These formerly enslaved individuals found ways to gain access—to literacy, to community, to God—that encouraged their own gifts of articulating, through voice and pen, an abolitionist agenda that went against the majority structures that undergirded the slavocracy system.

One dominant way to describe the variety of uses of Scripture within African American communities is to oppose a nonrational (i.e., African American) approach to the so-called (white) "rational" approach of proslavery.[12] This description fails to appreciate the irrational nature of all hermeneutical enterprises, which attempt to appropriate ancient stories and passages onto the contemporary situation in specific ways.[13] Application of the past onto the present involves frequently illogical processes for any contemporary employment of ancient ideas, since cultural boundaries must be crossed—and many ignored. Cultural assumptions about race repeatedly determined the meaning or outcome of a given biblical passage.[14] The field of hermeneutics has more recently begun to appreciate the incisive role readers play in the interpretive process.

To put it more explicitly, the Bible chooses no sides! The talking book does not speak on its own. In the great debate between Douglass and Garnet (see chap. 2), Douglass understood this more clearly. The Bible's opposition to New World slavery must be demonstrated. Scripture requires interpretation or, more precisely, an interpreter who can assist in the transfer of ancient ideas into contemporary analogous words, ideas, and actions. The preference of one biblical text over another one—or even the so-called divide between the letter and the spirit of a text—equalizes the alleged authoritative weight the Bible may lend to anyone's cause.[15] More importantly than the choice of a text, then, was how readers engaged that biblical passage. Was a type of biblicism to hold sway? For some white radical abolitionists (e.g.,

12. See Caroline Shanks, "The Biblical Anti-slavery Argument of the Decade 1830–1840," *Journal of Negro History* 16 (1931): 151; Mark Noll, *America's God: From Jonathan Edwards to Abraham Lincoln* (New York: Oxford University Press, 2005), 405–6. By 1861, according to Noll, proslavery advocates had won "the battle for the Bible" (*America's God*, 393), even though (as Noll also discusses) they had *no* hermeneutical support outside the United States.

13. "Contrary to some fears, the Bible's significance, relevance, and vitality do not cease if it is read from a stance other than the traditional one" (Cheryl Anderson, *Ancient Laws as Contemporary Controversies: The Need for Inclusive Biblical Interpretation* [Oxford: Oxford University Press, 2009], 136).

14. As E. Brooks Holifield recognizes, "More than most other theological debates of the period, moreover, the slavery controversy displayed the extent to which cultural assumptions governed biblical interpretation. Especially visible was the intrusion into theology of assumptions about race" (*Theology in America*, 502).

15. As Stephen Haynes recognizes, the South's apparent "literal" approach to the biblical text blinded them from observing that the curse was upon *Canaan* and not Ham (*Noah's Curse: The Biblical Justification of American Slavery* [New York: Oxford University Press, 2002], 77).

Garrison), the opponents' commitment to a fairly strict literalistic approach to ancient texts forced them to conclude that the Bible was no longer useful in the larger social crisis of the day.[16]

This theological decision troubled many of Garrison's ideological companions (for example, Douglass, Garnet, and Harriet Beecher Stowe). Many African Americans in the nineteenth century anticipate what many interpreters in the modern pluralistic society assume: people cannot determine how to live and act ethically only by reading the Bible. Along with her contemporaries many decades ago, Nancy Ambrose, Howard Thurman's grandmother, wisely recognized that some biblical texts are better left alone! Perhaps that is one of the enduring gifts of African American biblical hermeneutics: the necessity to critique the mainstream Christian community when it has forgotten how to interpret the Bible in light of Jesus Christ's core commitments to a justice orientation and to denounce it when it exists comfortably with injustice, inequality, and other forms of dehumanization.

---

16. William Lloyd Garrison practiced what Harrill called an extreme form of a "hermeneutics of moral intuition" (J. Albert Harrill, "The Use of the New Testament in the American Slave Controversy: A Case History in the Hermeneutical Tension between Biblical Criticism and Christian Moral Debate," *Religion and American Culture* 10 [2000]: 157–59). James Stewart assessed the abolitionist hermeneutic as one that "in short, left behind no enduring tradition that clearly linked Protestant evangelicalism and Scripture to the ideal of racial justice" ("Abolitionists, the Bible, and the Challenge of Slavery," in *The Bible and Social Reform*, ed. Ernest R. Sandeen [Philadelphia: Fortress Press, 1982], 52). Also, Haynes, *Noah's Curse*, 183.

Index of Scripture

Index of Subjects and Names

CPSIA information can be obtained at www.ICGtesting.com
Printed in the USA
LVOW08s0007040516

486371LV00001B/1/P